Days with Bernard Shaw

DAYS WITH BERNARD SHAW

BY STEPHEN WINSTEN

The Vanguard Press, Inc., New York

THEY SAID. . . .

THEY SAID:
> that it is most unwise to take him seriously or to contradict him
> *that he wants to be taken seriously and enjoys a good argument*

THEY SAID:
> that he is arrogant and conceited
> *that he is modest and gentle*

THEY SAID:
> that he is obsessed with money and cares only for the rich
> *that he is a saint and has the same regard for all people*

THEY SAID:
> that he is surrounded by parasites and flatterers
> *that he numbers the wisest among his friends*

THEY SAID:
> that he regards artists as rogues and vagabonds
> *that he thinks of God as an artist*

THEY SAID:
> that he will say and write anything to irritate and amuse
> *that he uses the platform and theater to express his convictions*

THEY SAID:
> that he is an atheist
> *that he is a mystic and is profoundly religious*

THEY SAID:
> that he is extremely unconventional and anarchic
> *that he is a very respectable citizen*

THEY SAID:
> that he is ungenerous and miserly
> *that he gives without stint*

THEY SAID:
> that he is completely uneducated
> *that he knows everything*

THEY SAID:
> that he is unprincipled
> *that he has remained amazingly consistent in his principles*

THEY SAID:
> that he has never known what it is to be young
> *that he is young at ninety*

THEY SAID:
> that he doesn't count
> *that he is the most influential person alive*

THEY SAID:
> that to know him is to be disillusioned
> *that to know him is to be inspired*

THEY SAID:
> that when he dies he will soon be forgotten
> *that he is immortal*

ILLUSTRATIONS

ACKNOWLEDGMENTS

Frontispiece and photographs facing pages 131 (bottom), 170, 250, 251, and 258 are printed by courtesy of Studio Lisa, Welwyn Garden City, England; those facing pages 130, 131 (top), 163, 194, and 290, courtesy of Reece Winstone, Bristol, England; those facing pages 99 and 291, courtesy of Keystone Pictures, Inc., New York; the one facing page 234, courtesy of The Associated Press, Ltd., London, England. All other photographs are used by courtesy of the author.

Days with Bernard Shaw

1

We lived in Ayot for months before he called on us. I knew him sauntering along the lane in that queer Norfolk suit of his, tweed cap well over his forehead, tipped rakishly to display one eyebrow, swinging his stick round and round in the air, not bad for a man in his eighties. I had seen him on a stile with a chorus of birds overhead, squirrels running up the tree behind him, and I passed softly by, glad that he was at home in this world; and I had seen him merging into the haze of the lime grove, his old green Irish cape slung over that long frame of his in the manner of Tolstoy; and I had seen him standing in the snow in a long white raincoat, eagerly taking snaps of the demolished abbey, and I thought he has been here thirty years and he still finds everything exciting and new. I knew the tip-tapping of his stick against the gravel path as well as I knew the laugh of the green woodpecker. All this time I knew him as I wanted to know him.

One day he came walking up the path.

"Anyone in?" he shouted.

He left his embroidered gloves, his wide-awake hat, and his stick at the entrance and settled himself comfortably and bolt upright in the settee, arms folded and long legs crossed, and started his conversation as if we had been conversing for years. Perhaps we had. My wife smiled as he became more and more at home, swinging one foot, stressing his speech with forefinger, telling us the things we knew, the whole world knew about him, for had he not built up for the last fifty years a very clear picture of himself? Everybody knows everything about George Bernard Shaw: what he wears, what he eats, what he thinks, and what he looks like. Never has there been a man more publicized in this era of easy publicity. I caught Clare's smile and understood. Twenty years back she had asked him to sit for her for a portrait and his answer was in the strain of Eliza Doolittle. She had said then, "One day he will come to me!"

"Have you noticed," he asked us, "that there is an aura about Ayot Saint Lawrence, a certain stillness, a silence about the place?" That is just the thing that attracted us toward it, we told him. The village seemed to have stood still for the last five hundred years. He brushed this idea aside and said:

"My house is not very old, a commonplace Victorian rectory, redeemed by plenty of window space. They were only too glad to give it over to a heretic like myself. I had a garage built, of course, to house my cars, and for that I got Barry Parker, the Letchworth architect, to design a thoroughly modern and up-to-date place, functional, in fact."

Yes, I knew that garage. It certainly was functional and seemed a thing apart in that narrow winding lane with a neighbor of a wooden farmhouse, with cows and horses and pigs.

"You see," he went on, "I have a Rolls-Royce and another car, and they must have proper housing. Have you noticed that it has been the way for the last twenty years to build garages instead of nurseries?"

We offered him some apple juice, but he refused. He explained that he ate and drank nothing between lunch at 1:15 and the evening meal at 7:30.

"Besides," he said, "I find that a meal gets in the way of sociability. One can't talk when one eats." Then he recalled his Italian travel and burst into song, head thrown back and beating time dramatically with one hand. At precisely ten minutes to six he took out his large gold watch, begged forgiveness, explaining that he must return to his wife.

"I daren't be late. We always listen to the six o'clock news together." He said this almost humbly, and his voice softened. He collected his gloves and hat from my hands, carefully dressed, and strode away with head in the air, turning neither to right nor left. He left us with the impression of an extremely happy and self-satisfied man, virile and proud, carrying the heavy years very lightly indeed.

We were very busy folk with a thousand interests. England was fighting at the moment with everything against her except the knowledge that she would come through. The future was living and dying from minute to minute. But in Ayot Saint Lawrence it was peace, an island of quiet; the nearest useful railway station was six miles away, there were no buses, and

petrol restrictions made a car immobile. Only a fool like myself could think of living here when it was imperative that I
should be in London, in the very center of things, at an early
hour. It meant a long walk in the darkness of winter mornings
and evenings, often in snow and rain, but it also meant meeting
the sunrise and the early dawn choir. I had the winding lanes
to myself, and by the time I reached tired London I felt I had
lived a whole lifetime. Then the journey home, hidden behind
a newspaper, each passenger behind the ghastly headlines,
and not a word between us.

Back into this island of quiet. Which was the real life, I
often asked myself? Was Ayot Saint Lawrence but a dream?

The rector was a thin man with drawn, ascetic face. It was
a warm spring day, but he had a huge muffler round his neck
in the manner of the undergraduate and a balaclava round his
head. He came to talk about the church but found himself talking about everything else; the ornate building with its Doric
columns and green copper roof, transplanted, as it were, from
a provincial town into a corner of the park, was as remote from
our conversation as it was from the village. He talked to us
about his wife, who had recently passed away. She was a sweet
woman of French origin and a great lover of flowers and children. He and she had come from a slum parish and regarded
this living as a reward and a consummation. But peace did not
come to them in their old age. The war brought many evacu-
ated children into their home, and the work naturally fell on
the willing hand. She tended the children, and she tended the
flowers, until she herself needed tending. Such was the story

he told us, lovingly and without regret. The world was at war, and he was glad that they, even in their old age, could offer their lives. To him practice and precept were one.

The bells in those days could not call the people to church, for they were now meant to sound only as a warning of imminent invasion. He was always the first to walk along the long gravel path leading to the church, hands behind his back and head bowed, to be followed by two or three who made up the congregation. After the service he generally called in and talked over a cup of coffee.

It was quite a long time before the name of Bernard Shaw was even mentioned, and we put it down to the fact that he must have considered his oldest parishioner an atheist.

"I always enjoy a chat with the old man," he said one day. "You see, he's met so many interesting people. You know he's met Bradlaugh, and I had the greatest respect for that doughty fighter."

"Even though he was an atheist?" I asked with a smile.

"It's always good to have a strong opposition. God strengthened His cause by creating a strong opposition. When you think of it, it is the atheists who feel passionately about religion, and therefore you can argue with them."

"So the devil was really God's device for propaganda purposes?"

"Have you noticed that all people who do God's work are called servants of the devil some time or other? Look at Shelley and Shaw. The whole history of the human race is made up of passionate hatred and persecution of its prophets. I was reading only the other day that Shelley was called the darkest of fiends clothed with a human body to enable him to gratify his enmity against the human race! I, of course, personally regard him as one of our great religious teachers and would read his poetry in church along with the poetry of the Bible. . . ."

"What would you do if you turned up and found Shaw sitting in the church? The only worshipper perhaps?" I asked.

"I would go on as usual with the beautiful service. In the eyes of the Lord he is as all others. God does not know people by their reputation or wealth."

"So what would you say He makes of the crowd at Westminster?"

He laughed for the first time. Then he answered:

"I know you don't mean the politicians. I think He has a special regard for the Poets' Corner. I am Victorian enough to read a little poetry every day, the more familiar the better. But to get back to Bernard Shaw, I find him quite a gentleman, and deeply interested in theology. Now I am not in the least interested in theology, you know."

"When I was a child I was taken to hear Bernard Shaw preach at the City Temple," I recalled.

"Oh, it must have been very impressive, that tall bearded figure."

"Yes, it was in the days of R. J. Campbell."

"I knew Campbell very well," the rector mused. "Though he was Congregational he was my ideal of a clergyman. In a way he inspired me, he and Lansbury. I shall never forget a meeting I attended where both W. B. Yeats and R. J. Campbell were on the platform. Yeats read his poetry, and Campbell presided. I thought I lived in the Greek days as I saw them side by side. They were the handsomest men I had ever known. You see, what was so pleasant about them was that they wore no beards."

"I thought you said that a beard made a person impressive?"

The rector nodded. "Impressive, yes. But it's a personal prejudice of mine; I can never get myself to fully trust bearded people even though I was brought up among bearded folk, and the intellectuals of my time cultivated attractive beards—Browning, Tennyson, Carlyle, Watts, William Morris."

"Surely you have no doubts about William Morris?" I asked, and added, "Can you imagine any of them without a beard? Of course, Shaw was born with a white beard."

He laughed. "I suppose that's how most people know him. I knew him as a dark infuriating figure . . . talking to crowds at Tower Hill. Most people have forgotten *that* Shaw and now only know him as the gentlemanly white-bearded philosopher. He has age on his side. While most people lose in some way or other by getting old, he has turned it to his advantage, as he turns everything to his advantage."

"But you have never succeeded in getting him to come to church?" I insisted.

"Once he took the Sunday school. I shall never forget the way he spoke above the heads of the poor village children, getting involved in economics and biology and pushing the life force. The children listened very politely, as only children can."

"I suppose they were thrilled, knowing who he was?"

"They knew nothing about him except that he was a rich man with a car. Considering that he could fill the Albert Hall it was good of him to talk to half a dozen children and tell them that the world was larger than this village—and that if they wanted to know more they should read books like *Pilgrim's Progress*. He read a page to them and made them laugh, of course, for he's a born actor, you know."

Now I look back I remember that he asked me nothing about myself and that he took me for granted, as one does a brother.

Next time he came with a barrowful of rare plants. He said that his wife would have brought them herself if she were alive. Every day he would walk to his wife's grave with a handful of simple flowers and come away refreshed. He begged me to come with him collecting kindling in the park and in the wood behind the church.

It was a long time before Bernard Shaw called again. This time he assumed the avuncular role. He wanted to know what we all did, called us by our Christian names, and even by our nicknames. He told us that he disliked the name George, and it was obvious we were not to use that appellation for him.

"The name George has a bad sound," he said, "I don't like it. I tried to discard it long ago. I've taken the liberty even of putting it in brackets in *Who's Who.* You see, I am known everywhere as George Bernard Shaw, and I can't leave it out because people might not know the significance of the initials G.B.S. And then I do not wish to be confused with the women novelists who disguise their femininity by assuming what they think is the most masculine Christian name: George Eliot and George Sand. H. G. Wells was never known as George."

"I don't think Christian names matter in the least. Look at Shelley's Christian names. And wasn't Meredith a George?"

"Oh, people survive in spite of their names, you know. Sam Johnson is hardly a name for a great writer." It took me some time to realize that he was not alluding to a boxer but to the revered Doctor Samuel Johnson.

We ourselves began to address him as G.B.S., and that seemed acceptable.

Though we had made up our minds not to get involved in parochial affairs we could not help noticing that the young children had no play center. Of course, they had the whole countryside to roam in, but that exactly was the difficulty. They hung about the lanes, staring or kicking anything kickable, and they considered their greatest achievement taking off the iron gate from Shaw's entrance and depositing it in a distant ditch.

It was only too obvious that the education at school gave them no way of spending their leisure hours satisfactorily. Since we found haven in this village, we felt that we must contribute something to the children's welfare. We felt, however, that we should ask one or two other people to share in this and approached George Bernard Shaw. We told him that we were willing to take upon ourselves the major portion of the expense and trouble but would be happy if he also contributed something. This brought him immediately to our doorstep.

"This little bit of England, like everything beautiful, is made up of every conceivable vice. Rape, murder, treachery, are just commonplace occurrences." Changing his voice from anger to encouragement, he added, "However, it is not for me to discourage civic enterprise, but you mustn't expect a penny from me. You see, I have been reduced to penury by the heavy taxation, and if it were not for the insurance gained through the bombing of my books I would never have been able to pay my supertax."

He elaborated this theme with fact and figure and more or less proved that he was paying for the war. He said:

"I make a fortune from running down the policy of the Government and then hand it over, but for a few pence for current expenses, to the Government to keep it going."

Then he dropped the subject by asking me what I thought of Ayot. I told him that I found the place always beautiful and gave him a description of my early-morning walks and the return in the evening sunsets. He listened attentively and again referred to the aura of the place.

"When Charlotte and I came to this village from over the hill we rented this house from the previous rector because it was too large and expensive for him and his wife to run. She was a poetess, and the housework ran away with her inspiration. We stayed a short while, and so many of our things accumulated here that to avoid a removal we found it cheaper to buy the house. Mind you, we went into it pretty fully before we took the plunge. Charlotte and I found that so many people lived to a ripe old age here that eighty was considered young, which is, of course, the sensible attitude to life."

"In spite of the rape, murder, and what not?" I teased.

"As we were very rich, the wife of the lord of the manor

tried hard to lure us into the hectic social life here. I explained that I did not hunt, I did not shoot, I did not play cards, I did not play golf, and I did not drink; in fact, that I was a barbarian and futile. 'Then what on earth do you do with yourself?' she asked me. I told her that I had to fill up my time somehow and so I write plays. 'That's your work,' she explained, 'but how do you amuse yourself?' I had to explain that I never amuse myself. I have to amuse others, and that wants some doing. She had to accept me as hopelessly useless to society, and I must say she left us both to ourselves."

He thought it necessary to explain that they lived in the village because *he* liked it and that Charlotte preferred Whitehall Court.

"You see, Charlotte has always objected to the village and only lived here for my sake. She married me because she thought me a genius. When all that money was left to her she looked round for a useful object. Beatrice Webb intended her to marry Graham Wallas, but I got in first. By the time I married her I had already made two thousand pounds, so was economically independent. Now I am as wealthy as she is. By the way, you mustn't think I don't do anything for the village. When we first came here the squire's wife induced me to give something at Christmas time. Charlotte and I decided that every Christmas the children should have a shilling with which to buy sweets for themselves. To make sure that their mothers didn't get hold of the money we arranged for the children to call personally at the house for their shilling apiece. And sometimes as many as ten come to the back door."

"So you do celebrate Christmas," I said.

The plea of penury was not very convincing, and he made a point of coming again soon after because he was obviously worried. The last thing in the world that we wanted to do was to worry him. In the most friendly manner he wished to know our views on the way children should be brought up because he liked the way we all lived together.

"I notice," he said, "that your children call you by your Christian names. This is the first time I have come across this. My visit to George Meredith was spoiled by the presence of his children. I went to his house full of respect and left full of pity. I myself called my father papa. I couldn't think of calling my mother Lucinda Elizabeth, which was her name. I was called Sonny until I was a young man, and then I had to rebel, but like all rebellions it proved a turn for the worse, because they called me George after that! Not that they cared very much as to what I felt or what happened to me. I was allowed to roam about, and instead of hanging about the streets I was led, a solitary wanderer, into enchanting scenery, to the magic of which I was very susceptible. What saved me was my passion for the arts. Ten years ago I visited a Russian penal settlement and was asked to talk to a crowd of boy thieves, and I had to tell them that though I now looked as if I had never been young I really had been a child once and would have been in a similar institution if I had been found out. I asked them if their notion of play was to throw stones at elderly gentlemen with beards. I had once found myself a target of a barrage of stones, heavy and sharp enough to injure me seriously if they had found their mark."

"But you have not had such an experience here, have you?"

"I rarely see a child here. They must get out of the way when they see me coming. I get on very well with babies. I let them tweak my nose. One must keep perfectly still with children, as with animals, and let them examine one to their complete satisfaction."

"Yes," I agreed, "when my daughter Theodora was a babe two or three years old, Lucien Pissarro was very fond of her. He made her sit on his lap and beamed as she studied him and stroked his voluminous dark beard."

"The nicest beard I have ever seen and one which I myself would have liked to touch was that of Rabindranath Tagore. It was blue and of the softest silky texture."

"Yes," my wife agreed.

"Did you know him?"

"Among other artists I was invited to meet him when he came over and gave a reading of his poetry. I was only a young girl, but I always was amused by ceremony and ostentation. I missed a great deal of the poetry through the posing."

"My dear Clare, one has to pose! I dislike it as much as you do, but one has to dramatize oneself or else remain completely insignificant. I shall never forget walking in London one night and suddenly, in the light thrown by a shop window, appeared the most handsome couple I have ever seen: William Butler Yeats and Maud Gonne. But for the dramatic effect created by the light and the unexpected place I would never have realized how magnificent they were."

"You are a romantic, G.B.S.," Clare remarked.

"It is a fact of human nature, romantic or not romantic," G.B.S. snapped out. He added, "I wish I could have made

Sidney Webb dramatize himself a little—instead of always remaining in the background. [A reputation must be fostered.] By the way, I had a letter the other day from a schoolmaster. He wants my permission to abridge my play *Saint Joan* for school purposes. I answered that I was not aware that there was a word too much in any of my plays! If the children were to enjoy my books when they grew up my work must be kept out of the schools. Shakespeare, I told him, was completely spoiled for everybody by being turned into a school subject. The world can't afford to wreck its geniuses. A genius is not created every other day. What it takes three hundred years to produce (and that is what it took for me to come after Shakespeare) the schoolmaster can destroy within a day."

I had to contradict him here. "I personally feel," I said, "that Shakespeare survived because he was fostered at school."

"He survived because I attacked him," G.B.S. maintained.

"Well, they are now setting *your* plays for examinations."

"I don't mind in the least, as long as the schoolmasters don't edit my plays with notes and commentaries! I myself have never been able to pass examinations and would certainly fail in an examination on my own works. What kind of questions are asked?"

I suggested: "Was it Webb or Wells who wrote the Shaw plays?"

G.B.S. laughed. "As a matter of fact, Webb might have written them, because he had a sense of fun. Webb wrote the plays and Wells wrote the prefaces. How could a completely uneducated person like Shaw write anything?"

"I wonder what Beatrice would have said if Webb had taken to writing plays instead of tracts."

"I don't see the difference. They both had a clear idea as to what they intended to do and set themselves to do it. I shouldn't at all be surprised that theirs will be the only literature that will survive. You know, they lacked the aesthetic sense completely, like most Fabians."

I disagreed entirely with this statement. Beatrice Webb, when asked why she prayed, answered that it was through prayer that she discovered the goal of human endeavor and that is why prayer has always been associated with the arts and the great emotional mysteries of nature.

G.B.S. almost shook with dissension. "What absolute nonsense! Who on earth can know the goal of human endeavor, prayer or no prayer? We can only see a bit ahead at a time. It is the artist-philosopher who sees that little bit. There was always a queer streak in Beatrice. The Webbs used to take furnished houses for the summer, and I always went with them, so I had an opportunity of knowing her very well. Having been brought up in a *ménage à trois,* I fitted in perfectly. At one of these places we found in an outhouse a penny-farthing and, being of a mechanical turn of mind, I at once started practicing on it. Of course, I always fell, much to Beatrice's amusement. She told me she had never laughed so much in her life. Sidney, hearing this laughter, came out to join in whatever fun was going. He wanted to try this penny-farthing himself, of course, but Beatrice rushed up to him, flinging her arms round him, and held on, imploring him not to endanger his life. It didn't matter to her what happened to me, you see."

My response led G.B.S. to tell another cycling story.

"So you like cycling stories? Well, here is another. One afternoon I was flying down a steep hill with my feet up on the rests, going at a speed that took the machine miles beyond my control. Bertrand Russell was in front of me and Webb was behind me. Seeing the road clear before us, I gave myself up to the enjoyment of a headlong tearing toboggan down the hill. Imagine my feelings when I saw Russell jump off and turn his machine right across my path to read the signpost! I rang my bell, shouted my loudest, and swerved desperately to the right. He looked round and backed with his machine to the right, my right, also. Never was a mathematician so exact in his calculation. Smash! Never losing my presence of mind, I managed to make a twist to the left which prevented my going into him absolutely at right angles and thereby destroying the future of mathematics and drama. Webb went on, convinced that we were both killed. I don't think Beatrice ever forgave me for giving her husband such a shock."

"How is it the Webbs had no children?" I asked when his laughter subsided.

"I rather think that Beatrice would have liked just one child to experiment on but Sidney knew better, it seems." There was a twinkle of mischief in the Shavian eye. He added, "It probably would have been a misfit, as so many children of geniuses are." This brought us back to the children of the village. He wanted to know where the children were being taught, because the old schoolhouse was used as a home by the rector. I explained that the Ayot children were collected every day and taken by taxi to their school three miles away. This seemed to amuse him. In the good old days children had to walk miles and miles in snow and rain, often underfed and ill-clad, to the so-called place of instruction. "Do they learn anything, however?" he asked.

"They still stare at you if you ask them a question," I answered.

"It is they who should be asking the questions," he said. "Fortunately for me I have no children, or my ignorance would have been exposed to the whole world. I never argued with my father nor asked him why? why? why? As a child I asked him what? what? what? as all children do. Under this pressure he told me many things I did not know, improvising his answers on the spur of the moment, as I found out later, quite correctly. Like all improvisations they were more interesting and nearer the truth than mere fact. Would you say you learned anything at school?" he asked me.

"I don't think so, except that one teacher read poetry so beautifully, especially Shakespeare, that my highest ambition was to be a poet."

"Poor chap. Who has ever made a living as a poet? Was I ever mentioned at your school?"

"Yes—as an example of a man without poetry."

"My plays are essentially poetic dramas and should be sung. The teachers have always been the greatest enemies of culture, don't you agree?"

"No more than the rest of humanity," I answered. "I have never found the world eager to proclaim the prophet."

He smiled. "I haven't done so badly, but I had to do all the teaching, and even now I daren't let go. I mustn't turn my back for a minute. Where is the man to take my place?"

I suggested we were not in need of leaders.

"Yes," he retorted, "but we are in need of intelligence."

"The Germans are a highly intelligent people, and they are leading us to disaster."

"True enough. They were the first to recognize me. They have since had their intelligence knocked out of them. They thought they would frighten us out of our wits, but instead they frightened us into our wits. The war has turned into a struggle between Shakespeare and Shaw. Shall the stage be strewn with corpses, or can we get the characters to sit down and talk things over in the true Shavian manner? You see, Hitler pretends to be a man of action, but he mistakes acting for action, in fact, he's the ham actor!"

"We're a bit tired of leaders and supermen and super-races."

"And yet," he answered very sweetly, "if all people were overmodest like myself we'd never get anywhere. My bane has always been modesty. Like Hamlet I lacked ambition. I was disabled for many years by imagining that everybody knew as much if not more than I knew . . . and could do everything rather better."

Surprised that I did not show astonishment, he at once changed the slide in this mental lantern lecture and showed me Sidney Webb again.

"Sidney Webb refused to become a living lie. He was the only man I knew who refused to do it."

"The world is full of anonymous people who have lived

and now live a life of integrity and service: in this war there must be thousands and thousands of them. But for them, the great ones would have been Hamlets still talking to themselves."

He brushed this aside. No doubt it sounded to him a platitude.

"Perhaps," he added, as if to himself, "I should have included William Morris."

"You were fortunate in your friends."

"Oh, well," he drooped his head smiling, then added, "I do not know what they found in me, because I was just an odious, argumentative young man who made himself thoroughly unpleasant by contradicting everybody. A habit I developed when young and have never been able to throw off."

"The pleasure must have been on both sides."

"Do you think so? Anyhow, it gave me a chance to sharpen my wits." He took out of his pocket the watch and held it aloft. "It is ten to six. I must go. This is a present from my uncle. It cost me fifty pounds to redeem it from the pawn-broker." As he stood up to go, we heard the singing of children. A man was leading them.

"You know," he said, "this man is a bit of a composer. Have you met him? He comes from local stock."

"He is certainly not the kind of man born to blush unseen. . . ."

He came wanting to walk, swinging his stick and humming. There is a cart track behind the house, and we had to cut the path clear of nettles and briar. I held up overhanging branches to let him pass, dreading the thought of a scratch on this agile figure. He brought out a pair of old secateurs, which, he told me, he always carried with him.

"I cut this path years ago, and I haven't been here for a long time."

As we stopped to admire the scene of distant wood and fields, we were greeted by the rector, who looked very tired and crestfallen.

"This war is taking too long. It should have been over." The rector was holding a bundle of wood. At that moment G.B.S. looked younger than his much younger friend. He pulled his tweed cap to one side and beat the nettles with his stick.

"I noticed," G.B.S. said, looking the rector in the eye, "that the demolished abbey is smothered with weeds. It's a grand place for weeds, this. You should see my garden."

"*Il faut cultiver notre jardin.*" The rector's French was perfect.

"I didn't know that you practiced what Voltaire preached," G.B.S. teased.

The rector smiled. "I occasionally even practice what you preach. And I still have hopes that you may even practice what I preach."

We walked back, in single file, of course. Noticing a book sticking out of the rector's pocket, I asked him what it was he was reading. His hands were folded as always behind his back and he turned to us and recited:

"And this
Is certain: never be afraid!
I love what I have made,
I know this is not wit,
This is not to be clever,
Or anything whatever.
You see, I am a servant, that is it:
You've hit
The mark . . . a servant; for the other word. . . .
Why, you are Lord, if anyone is Lord."

G.B.S. walked on and it appeared that he was not listening. There he was, spine erect, swinging his stick at any obtrusive branch. Suddenly he exclaimed: "God is not a servant. He's an artist. God made the world as an artist and that is why the world must learn from its artists."

The rector would not agree. "No, artists must go to nature for their inspiration. I'm all for Matthew Arnold."

"The dandy Isaiah!" Shaw snorted.

The rector was shocked. "One must allow for change of fashion," he pleaded.

"The worst-dressed person I ever knew," Shaw said, "was William Morris. He looked like a sailor in old clothes. You should read *News from Nowhere*."

"I read it as a young man, of course, and was greatly impressed. A very charming picture, like your *Candida*, very romantic and sentimental."

"Well . . . it served its purpose. . . ."

The heavy droning of ponderous planes drowned his voice.

They flew so low that the old beech quivered and shook.

"Evil things," muttered the rector.

We walked silently toward Shaw's Corner, as he has called his house. The rector walked on, a forlorn figure, his head well in advance of his unwilling legs. I caught up with him and we walked right through the village, the six o'clock news booming out from the Tudor cottage, then from the room above the post office, and next from the inn.

"Mr. Shaw takes himself too seriously," the rector said as we turned the corner toward his home on the periphery. "I've been reading his *Blanco Posnet* again. He'll end up like Thomas Hardy and the others, in the Church yet."

A little girl rushed out of his gate to meet him affectionately.

2

In spite of the war and the enemy at our very gates, Shaw settled down to a new book. Even if he had not told me, I would have guessed by the kind of questions he asked. One of his main concerns was education, and we played with this subject inside and out. Whenever I attacked he was quick to defend, and whenever I defended he was quick to attack. The only example I had from him of his actual experience, apart, of course, from his schooling seventy years back, was a visit with Wells to Oundle. Here was a headmaster, Mr. Sanderson, making a great effort to put the new goddess Science on the same pedestal as Classics. The engineer took the place of the poet; and Wells, the prophet of Science, became the disciple. Shaw, however, was left unmoved. From much firsthand experience I could not assure him that schools had radically changed, in spite of the word "new" or "creative" prefixed to everything associated with education.

He declared: "A complete public-school and university training may leave its graduates so barbarously ignorant that when war comes they are found in all directions trying to close public art galleries and museums."

"As a matter of fact," I informed him, "things have gone in the opposite direction in this war. Never has there been such an interest in the arts. Though the paintings of the National Gallery had to be placed in security elsewhere, the Gallery at once sprang into being as a national community center where thousands flocked to listen to the best music and keep in touch with whatever paintings were shown there."

"A reaction to our vile schooling," he answered. "Children have a way of acting in the opposite direction intended. I am always being invited to schools to give out the prizes to the successful ones. It amuses me because I myself would give a prize to the most mischievous lad. What have I to do with a good boy that fits in perfectly with a bad system? I myself have no competitive instinct, nor do I crave for prizes or distinctions; consequently I have no interest in competitive examinations. If I won, the disappointment of my competitors would distress me instead of gratifying me. If I lost, my precious self-esteem would suffer. As few win and the majority lose, the competitive system presses hard on most children. I am invited to these places because I am a magnificently successful person. They do not see that as I am a totally uneducated and self-made man it is a reflection on their education."

"Yet you have always preferred the Fabians, a highly educated lot, to the Social Democratic Federation proletarians!"

"Then," he answered quickly, "you haven't heard what

Lee surrounded by his disciples
  Mother (Mrs. Shaw) on extreme left. Father on extreme right

Away from London

*Meets
his future wife
at the Webbs*

Wells called the Fabians: liars, tricksters, blackguards! I maintain that the only permanently valuable education is the aesthetic education."

"And that can't be taught," I maintained.

"I know. I wanted to be an artist, nothing less than a Michelangelo, but after a little discouragement at the art school I gave it up. I am very easily discouraged. What I can't do well straight away, I give up."

"How fortunate that you had not become an artist. You might have been a poor man and certainly not have been invited to distribute prizes to successful little boys and girls."

"I don't know . . . I would have made art pay. . . ."

"By flattering your sitters?" I suggested.

"I was born without a bump of reverence. But I would have got round that somehow."

"I have been reading George Moore again. . . ."

"Never listen to an Irishman," he warned me. I smiled and reached out for the book from the side table by the window. Shaw swung his foot mischievously as I read to him a passage:

" 'Hail, therefore to the thrice glorious virtue injustice! What care I that some millions of wretched Israelites died under Pharaoh's lash or Egypt's sun? It was well that they died that I might have pyramids to look on, or to fill a musing hour with wonderment. Is there one amongst us who would exchange them for the lives of the ignominious slaves who died? What care I that the virtue of some sixteen-year-old maiden was the price paid for Ingre's "La Source." That the model died of drink and disease in the hospital is nothing compared with the essential that I should have "La Source," that exquisite dream of innocence to think of till my good soul is sick with delight of the painter's holy vision.' "

G.B.S. threw back his head and laughed.

"When art and science," he said, "are opened up to persons not qualified by philosophic moral training, they are plunged into an abyss of stupidity and cruelty from which nothing but outraged humanity can rescue them."

I pointed out that the particular works which so delighted George Moore were of no consequence and certainly did not deserve the sacrifice of a single human being. Truly great work is done at the sacrifice of the artist himself.

"Leave the sacrifice out of it! I thoroughly enjoy my work and if I miss it for a day I am out of sorts. That is why I go down every morning to my hut. I know I can't be disturbed there. Can you tell me why children can't walk into a school, read the books that interest them, make the things they want to make, and leave when they want to leave? Have people there to assist them whenever they so require it, certainly, as in the library, but abolish the schoolmaster. Education will never get anywhere while the schoolmaster is there."

I reminded him that such schools had existed both in America and here in England and that Aldous Huxley described a visit to one, the best example, situated in a slum. There were no timetables but subject rooms, where the boys went at will and chose their books and read freely with a specialist master in the background, who only functioned when a boy came to him for advice. The Huxleys were deeply impressed by the responsible, free, and at the same time co-operative, spirit of the boys. For instead of competing, the advanced boys helped those who were backward.

He showed great surprise and paused longer than usual for his reply: "Aldous was a bookworm, and so this kind of education fitted nicely into the good old world, in the same way as the British Museum served the purpose of Carlyle, Karl Marx, and myself. But is the bookworm the best type of citizen? I always generalize from my own personal experience. While good boys were learning their lessons out of textbooks and receiving prizes for regular attendance and good conduct, I was acquiring through my own efforts an equipment in art, in music, and in literature, building up a spiritual capital which has yielded good interest for the rest of my life. I learned to recognize the works of the old masters at sight, I learned French history from the novels of Dumas and English history from Shakespeare and Walter Scott, and I could sing and whistle from end to end works by Handel, Haydn, Mozart, Beethoven, and Verdi. I was saturated with the works of Bunyan, Shelley, and Dickens. I soon learned that to know a little was to know much more than the specialists who get their knowledge at a university. Instead of answering questions out of their own wisdom they rely on material centuries out of date because that was the stuff which gave them their diplomas."

"I find that the majority leave their education when they leave college. In fact, they have a definite distaste for whatever they have acquired there."

"I myself," he went on, "have never stopped learning, and so I find my greatest enemies are those who have been declared masters of art and of science. William Morris once told me that the money he paid for his master of arts—I believe it was twenty pounds—was sheer economic waste. He could have bought himself a book for that money. Of course, if these diplomas had been decorated by him they would have been priceless . . . and I would have been sorry then that I was not a master of arts."

"Instead, your diplomas are in the shape of your plays. . . ." A smile showed for a moment but immediately disappeared.

"I am really a teacher, and my plays are my method of instructing the 'educated.' The ignorant, I find, don't need me. They are the self-helpers like myself, in the vanguard of all the movements which are slowly transforming the world."

"But not many people are fortunate enough to have a home life where such ignorance is fostered," I could not help saying.

"Fostered! Every conceivable difficulty was put in my way. I never saw my father with a book in his hand, and my mother ignored my existence completely."

"But your mother, I remember, was a very hard worker. When she taught me singing," Clare said, "I did not know how old she must have been, but now I realize that she was almost as old as you are now, and how she worked!"

"My mother and I lived together, but there was hardly a word between us. She was a disillusioned woman. She was most fond of my sisters, especially Agnes, who had pale red hair, really Scotch, not like mine which was quite auburn. Unfortunately she became ill; we called it going into a decline then, but now it is known as tuberculosis, and my mother spent all her time trying to get her well. However, she died in the

Isle of Wight. So, with her favorite daughter dead, my father a drunkard, and her only son a drag on her, what she had done for love of music she had to slave at in her later years for a bare existence. However, when my wife and I married I saw to it that a good settlement was made in her favor."

Prunus and apple blossom, tulip and daffodil had come again and gone. Everybody, from the oldest to the child who could hold a tool, worked at growing food. It seemed wrong to spend the time talking when there was so much to do.

G.B.S. made for his usual seat in the sitting room, facing the fireplace, and when there was no fire in the grate because we wanted to save coal, he looked toward the electric fire, and we would at once put it fully on and as near to him as possible. He loved great heat, and his legs and hands would bask and bake.

"Cold agrees with me best of all," he said, "and I am glad this hot summer is over. How do you enjoy being buried alive in Ayot? I myself like being left to myself. I inherited this from my mother, who was forced to enjoy her own society because society disowned her when my father proved a drunkard. It suits me well. Charlotte, on the other hand, likes to have a lot of young men around her and would have liked to travel. If she weren't ill and confined to the curtilage, she would still have kept me on the move. For her, happiness is always round the corner."

"It's so much of a dream living here, a dream realized, of course, that I have to switch on the news to get back to life, now that I am on vacation."

"Forget the blasted war. It will pass like a thief in the night. And that reminds me, did you hear the planes last night circling round my house?"

"I thought they were circling round mine."

"Undoubtedly looking out for me. They've already burned my books, now they want to spoil my looks. Shaw without a beard would be a monstrosity. But this is the safest place because the I.C.I. is here. The chiefs must be kept alive at all costs, and they must have chosen well."

"They probably chose it because you are here, G.B.S."

"I hear that they are doing my plays even now in Germany. They regard me as Irish and therefore a neutral. I have a great deal of money frozen in that country, and all the heat of the war will not turn the Germans against me. I told them twenty or so years ago an artist is a supernational and is a member of the great republic of art. I was thinking of the old Museum days, when we sat, refugee philosophers from all over the world, and yet not one spoke to the other as far as I know. I never met Karl Marx personally, but the people who have never read him now think him obsolete in order to justify their lack of knowledge. If it weren't for Karl Marx I might still have been writing unreadable novels and like Savage Landor would have boasted of not a single copy sold.

"You know, of course, it was top-hatted Hyndman who introduced Marx to the English proletarian. The strange thing was when Hyndman wrote his historic book on economics he did not mention Marx, and I asked Mrs. Hyndman what had happened. Had her husband gone over to the enemy? Matilda looked at me knowingly and explained that her husband had dinner with Karl and in a fit of high spirits had put on Karl's hat and *found it fitted*. Karl had never forgiven him for this insult. It meant that Hyndman's high hat would have rested comfortably on the uncrowned king of the proletarians. After this meeting with Marx, Hyndman could face anybody, even William Morris and me."

"In the same way," I suggested, "as Bertrand Russell could face the world after dining with Gladstone."

"With Gladstone!"

"Yes, Bertrand Russell was only a child when his parents invited the G.O.M. He was left alone with the frightening old fellow and heard these momentous words: 'The port was good but should not have been served in claret glasses.' "

"I always wondered," G.B.S. mused, "what Gladstone said in eighteen hundred and———"

G.B.S. picked out a sweet from the dish we had learned to place beside him, and this he enjoyed with obvious relish.

"Do you think," he asked, "an audience takes the least notice of what a speaker says? In my play *The Shewing-Up of Blanco Posnet*, Waggoner Jo is supposed to say, 'I came on her on the track round by Red Mountain. She was setting on the ground with the dead baby on her lap, stupid-like. The horse was grazing on the other side of the road.' Instead the actor said, 'She was setting on the ground with the dead horse on her lap, stupid-like. The child was grazing on the other side of the road' and nobody noticed the difference."

He dipped into the dish for a chocolate. "Where do you get these?"

"We bought these in London," we told him. . . . And we

were glad that he liked them. These delicacies were difficult to obtain, and we kept them for him alone. He was always eager to see what we were reading and was surprised to find on the table by the couch a book of Browning's poems.

I referred to a rhyme scheme I had come across:

> "The wolf, fox, bear and monkey
> By piping advice in one key—
> That his pipe should play a prelude
> To something heaven tinged not hell hued,
> Something not harsh but docile,
> Man-liquid not man-fossil."

"Leonardo da Vinci ruled his notebooks in columns headed fox, wolf, bear, and monkey and made notes of human faces by ticking them off in these columns," he reminded me.

"I don't think I ever met the Brownings," he said. "The reason I did not write verse was that instead of saying what I wanted to say in it I had to say something that would rhyme and to find the rhyme I had to go right through the alphabet —a most wearying experience; though I must say I often helped William Morris with the right word when he was stuck. I only like to do things that I find easy, like writing plays. William Morris was like that. He found he couldn't paint so he gave it up. He said: 'Never do a thing that you find difficult, because another person who finds it easy will beat you at the game.'"

"Now, my impression is," I said, "that the person who persists and surmounts every difficulty, like yourself, for example, reaches a higher level than the easygoing person."

In Fitzroy Square

1906. The year he moved to Ayot Saint Lawrence

"Stuff and nonsense! The only difficulty I had to surmount was poverty. It was only when I married wealth that I was able to settle down and write unactable plays like *Back to Methuselah*. The aim of every artist is to reach the unattainable, and that can only be reached when you don't have to cut the path with your own hands."

"Yet the path has to be cut."

"There are always people willing to hurt themselves for you. Those never succeed themselves. The self-sacrificer is always a drag, a responsibility, and a reproach which nobody likes to admit. The result is that the self-sacrificer finds consolation in his failure while the self-helper goes marching on."

"Karl Marx led you to hate material exploitation, but you still seem to justify Samuel Smiles."

He stiffened and spoke slowly and decisively. "I am only stating a fact! We must get the facts of human nature correct before we start tackling its problems. It is no good; you'll never get anywhere until you set to work to find out what the world is really like. What you suppose is the real world does not exist, and men and women are made by their own fancies and live in their own imagination. The disillusion which would make you tragic makes me only derisive. I inherited a comedic love of anticlimax from my father. With me life is too horrible to weep bitter tears; I must retreat to my shelter and indulge in a laugh all to myself over it."

3

It was pouring with rain, and Ayot Saint Lawrence seemed more cut off than ever. I had walked through lanes which had turned into streams, and my clothes were drenched; a few cars passed, and I had to get close to the dripping hedge to avoid the fierce splashing. This was in the days before there was an appeal to motorists to help pedestrians whenever possible. The lights of the cars were so dimmed that the winding lanes with their high hedges might have been narrow paths along a precipice. It was necessary to carry some article in white to warn the oncoming motorist. Bernard Shaw, ever vigilant, had provided himself with a long white mackintosh and white cap. That, with his white beard and pale face, made him look ghostlike. On this day he also carried a huge umbrella, and so the elements had not an earthly chance against him. He laughed on seeing my state when I arrived home, and I ran up to the bathroom to get myself dry.

44

"I haven't long to stay," he warned me, "because I hate going home in the dark, and it gets dark so early these days."

I was not a minute away, and when I came down the fire was indeed a welcome sight and Shaw was spreading out his hands over it and sitting almost on top of it. I could not help wondering how a man who was so very much at home in the cold air and hated hot summer days yet enjoyed scorching by the fire.

"There is a heavy drizzly fog in London," I said.

"It's been quite nice here. I have been very busy in my shelter with this book of mine. I don't know why I am doing it. It is only a resumé and may interest a new generation that always wants everything served up new. I have been told by people that the reading of a single book of mine has changed their whole lives. This puts a heavy, a very heavy, responsibility on these aged shoulders. Older readers have grown familiar with my style and do not take me so seriously, but the new print addicts may find me too grim for their liking."
I do not know how he obtained his knowledge of young people, as he had not met any for years. He continued: "Karl Marx ruined himself by simply telling the purse-proud nineteenth century its own villainous history and so changed the mind of the world. William Morris died a comparatively young man because he insisted on giving time which he might have devoted to his art to propaganda among the masses. Ibsen, once the greatest writer in the world, wore himself away and at seventy-six became a child again trying to begin once more at pothooks and hangers. I am the first to guard my health as well as my genius. The danger is that I shall outlive my welcome."

"That will never be. Why, there is a whole generation growing up ready to read and understand you."

"Do you think so?" he asked, pleased, and then added, "Young people do not like the old."

"And do the old like the young?"

"I should say we accept them as an unavoidable necessity."

"That may be because you have had no children of your own."

"Children are the last people to understand their parents, and parents are the last people to understand their children; in fact, until I came to this house I had never seen parents and children quietly discussing things or listening to one another as you and your family do. What is the secret of your upbringing?" He waited intently for an answer.

"From the first we discussed everything together. We have never said 'don't,' and perhaps we explained everything in a way which caused them to think. But our life is in no way exceptional. . . ."

"It is! You are all individuals with no ready-made morality."

"Nonsense, we are just conventional people like yourself."

"One has to live a conventional life," he said. "Ninety per cent of my life is like everybody else's. The rest is my work." He took out the gold watch as always and, yes, it was the exact time for him to depart. Ten minutes to six.

"I must run," he said, and we helped him on with his long white mackintosh, his cap, and gloves. There was no need for the umbrella, so he used it as a stick, and we saw him walk away, upright and brisk, with his torch flashing a path for him along the gleaming wet lane.

"Have you ever met William Morris?" Shaw began one day.

"I was very much of a child then, but I was taken to hear him speak. He looked more proletarian than the workers who came to hear him. And I seem to think that he affected a cockney accent."

"Because he was ashamed of the class he belonged to. Though he was really a worker if ever there was one. He was always working, and his tastes were really very simple. He told me that he could have lived on plain bread and cheese and onions if he could have had some wine with these things. It was nothing for him, however, to spend hundreds of pounds on a beautiful book. He never challenged the price if he liked a thing."

"Whenever you mention William Morris," I said, "I think of Rossetti's bull. Did you know that he bought a white bull because it had eyes like Mrs. William Morris?"

"Janie?"

"Yes. He tethered it on the lawn of his home in Chelsea. Soon there was no lawn left, only the bull."

"I should have thought a peacock was more in his line."

"He did buy a peacock. A white peacock which disappeared under the sofa and died there. It must have died of terrible loneliness, don't you think?"

"Drink, more likely." G.B.S. had a way of stressing his point with a deliberate wink which ended in a roguish smile. He went on: "You see, some of these Bohemians think that

any old life is all right. I get on very well with animals except-
ing the little dog in my home. It yaps every time it sees me; it
is almost human in its dislike of me."

"Reggie is a very conceited little dog," I said. "He most
likely doesn't think you good enough."

"Does he bark at you? It's my housekeeper's, you know,
and she is the master and no other."

"Yes, we noticed that. I believe your housekeeper is too
class-conscious . . . ."

"Charlotte is very fond of animals. We were cycling once
and we came across a rabbit completely stunned by the approach of a stoat. Charlotte picked it up and carried it four
miles away, but even then it hadn't recovered its playfulness."

He bent down to stroke our cat lying there sprawling at his
feet, daring his big brown shoe to use her as a footrest. "And
what do you think, Fuzzy, about things?" he asked lovingly
of the cat.

"Do you play games?"

I was startled by the sudden question. I feared invitations
to croquet on the lawn, or was the long winter evening straining
his endurance and was I to be invited to a game of bridge? I
was relieved to find that he had no such intentions. He had no
need of these pleasant ways of killing time. Time was very
sweet to him, then why kill it?

"I dislike anything competitive," he asserted again, "besides, too much of my time is wasted on trifles like feeding
and washing and dressing. Your sportsman will countenance,
connive at, and grovel his way through all sorts of meanness,
servility, and cruel indifference to suffering in order to enjoy

a miserable pound's worth of social position, piety, and comfort. However, I miss more than anything else my daily swim at the Automobile Club."

I remembered that he had said somewhere that effectiveness of assertion was the alpha and omega of style. There was no mincing of words here. He did not think that the teamwork developed, say, in football or cricket, that the quick decision and immediate action which is appreciated and demanded in games would show in other fields of activity. That, indeed, is a fallacy of much of our educational system: we are always developing this or that faculty—the reasoning faculty by a miserable emphasis on abstruse problems in arithmetic; the memory by learning long pieces of incomprehensible verse; the aesthetic by painting photographically; and the result is that the young regard these subjects with disgust. When I reminded him of this he was even more sweeping than ever.

"The whole educational system is a fraud. At the end of the ten years of their schooling they are unable to speak even their native language. They may acquire some sort of physical courage through their games, but all moral courage has certainly gone from them. I can remember a relative who insisted that I should ride a horse, though I was unused to them and very much afraid, and she was enormously amused at my terrors and did not seem moved in any way by the possibility that I might break my legs. But when she discovered that I had found a copy of the *Arabian Nights* and was reading it with great delight, she was horror-stricken and hid the book from me. That was reflected in the sportsman's attitude to Ibsen: these people who talked in their clubs of broken collarbones and broken necks whined in terror when faced with spiritual adventure of the highest order. My own moral faculty was only developed after I had dropped the pious habit of saying prayers. Up to that time I had not experienced the slightest remorse in telling the most incredible lies, but with the coming of the urge for telling the truth for its own sake I found my true vocation. It is the birth of moral passion that turns the child into a man."

"Then what on earth made you ask me about games?" I asked.

"I just wanted to place you, that's all," he answered.

I could not help smiling as I remembered his story of Beatrice Webb and how unhappy she was because she could not label him. "When she could label me 'Sprite' she could stand my presence after that."

"I had a neat little label stuck on me today," I said. "I was talking to the road sweeper and congratulated him on the tidiness of our lane. I told him that he worked like two men. He was quick off the mark, like an athlete. 'Sir,' he said, 'you are a very discerning man. You would think that by the way Mr. Shaw treats me—he passes me by, jest like that—' making a sweeping movement with his hand, 'that I'm dirt; but you, sir, are a gentleman!' "

Shaw laughed. "A gentleman indeed!" he taunted me. "Doesn't he know that you work? What spoiled it for me in the village was that when a villager called, my maid told him that I mustn't be disturbed because I was at work. It soon went round that I was no better than themselves. Now, if the maid had told the fellow that I was out shooting I should have been held up as a model gentleman. As to discernment, to an alien like myself all Englishmen are alike, as to an English-man all Chinamen are alike. And yet there must be something of the gentleman in me because Collier painted me looking like a stockbroker, so like me that Charlotte walked straight up to it when she came to Collier's studio and took it for the living article. John painted me looking like a gamekeeper, and Lavery saw me as an angler. The only artist who saw the barbarian in me was Epstein. Nobody looking at his bust of me would suspect me of gambling, shooting, or angling. Ep-stein forgot to brush my hair, and the result was that Charlotte refused to have it in the house. In fact, I had to choose between her and the bust, and I don't know where the bust is at this moment. You see, Charlotte married a genius and saw to it that my hair was brushed."

"And yet Browning disappointed everybody with his care-fully brushed hair, smart coat, and fine manners!"

"Yes, I can't be a real Socialist because I wear a hat, another concession to bourgeois convention. The fact is I don't stop for the road sweeper because, as you know, I can't bear people who talk. Talking about artists: Collier would say to me while he was painting, 'I may not be much of an artist but I could throw off a painting like John's without effort. It's child's play.' When Lavery was doing my portrait I asked him what he thought of John. 'Well,' he answered, 'I'm not too bad as an artist but I would give anything to paint like John.' You will agree that Lavery was infinitely superior to Collier."

"Coming back to your remarks about the pious habit of saying prayers, a friend told me an interesting story the other day. Two men visited Tolstoy, and a room was provided for them where they had to do their own catering, cleaning, and cooking. One of them preferred to stay in bed late in the mornings, and the other found all the work forced on him. The latter prayed and prayed that his lazy friend should see the light and co-operate, but the more he prayed the angrier he became. At last he rose from his knees, pulled the bedclothes off the lie-a-bed, and shrieked, 'You miserable, skulking swine, get up and work!'

"The birth of moral passion!"

Transport was not the only difficulty; that could easily be surmounted, but no domestic servant could be lured into this wilderness without even the oasis of a shop or cinema. The few gardeners already here were too fully occupied to give occasional help. We found ourselves overwhelmed with the housework and gardening as well as our own work. This made it difficult for us to have open house, as we were accustomed to do, and converted many a pleasure into a heavy task.

G.B.S. was not entirely absolved from this anxiety. One of his young gardeners had been called up for service, and it was even likely that one of the younger maids would have to go. This problem worried him more than the world situation, and he spent many a visit thinking out the solution to this insurmountable (so it seemed to him) difficulty. He said:

"I used to pretend that I was the reasonable one with all my wit and omniscience, but now I realize that I am a monstrous falsehood. Who keeps the house clean? Who looks after my clothes? Who prepares my meals? Who looks after the garden?"

His housekeeper and her husband who acted as valet and gardener were loyal to the breaking point and had been with the two old people for thirty years. Their work was pleasant enough in the days before the war when the Shaws came down for a week end or so, but now Mrs. Shaw was practically helpless, and they were in full residence. I occasionally met the old man in the train: he was having osteopathic treatment for his spine, which, as he put it, "was only held together by a thread." He was a tall, thin man dressed in black, starch collar, and bowler hat when he went up to town. The only remark he permitted himself about his master was: "You would not think that quiet man could say boo to a goose and yet I hear he not half gives it to them."

Who the "them" were he didn't quite know.

To cap this trouble, Shaw was actually asked by the local council to take in a few evacuees. It was true that he had a few rooms vacant, but the very thought of children and strangers drove him to distraction. His answer was typical:

"The house contained two octogenarians, two septuagenarians, and who among these could entertain a soul?"

So the Shaw household was left to itself while minute cottages with grandparents, parents, and children found shelter for evacuees.

"You see," he explained, "I run a big business with thousands of pounds involved, and the Government would lose more than it would gain by interfering with my work. I have enough money lost in America . . . of course, I have no doubt I'll get it ultimately when I don't need it. And there is Russia, Germany, China, all holding on to my cash. I mustn't grumble because I can put myself down in the millionaire class. There is one thing I have never ceased from teaching and that is the value of money: money is indeed the most important thing in life, and if you deny it you are an enemy of life."

"I certainly deny it."

How well I knew his argument that a sufficient income is indispensable to the practice of virtue, that living in a world of poor and unhappy people is like living in hell. He had drummed it so long into the minds of labor leader, artist, and writer that he had changed the direction of their thought.

"If this country goes under, it will be mainly, if not entirely, through financial incompetence. It's of no use thinking that all you have to do is to beat the others at the polls and then convert the Sermon of the Mount into legislation," he argued. And he told me, in his inimitable style, of a poet who had to decide between ten per cent and a penny on the shilling and he could not think which was the larger percentage: "Now, if he had come to me for advice, I would have told him to go for the penny on the shilling."

He saw the look in my face and got entangled in arithmetical calculations.

"The fact is, percentages are out of my depth, but a penny is good solid cash. At the vestry we argued for hours whether we should spend twopence or a penny threefarthings on something but passed over sums like a hundred thousand pounds without comment," he explained. "I don't suppose they have changed."

I was glad we avoided a collision on the question of money. If I had maintained that money was the most important thing in life he would have put the case against much better than I ever could. He would have reminded me of those hectic and satisfying days when he wrote for the *Star* and read at the Museum, when money made no appeal to him, when he was arguing Marx with Hyndman and Morris and religion with Bradlaugh and Annie Besant, when he proved at some out-of-the-way debating society that art was exhausted and heard from theater managers that plays without action were unplayable and was advised to stop teaching and get down to murder. It was a poor livelihood but a rich and happy life.

4

There are two things G.B.S. has never regretted: his birthplace and his marriage. In spite of all the patriotic talk which seems to convey that we poor humans have a say in the choice of our birthplace and the color of our hair and skin, Shaw will admit that he did not choose to be an Irishman. But he did choose very deliberately his Irish wife. It needed a very brave woman to marry a man of his temperament. He was a horse for single harness, if he could be harnessed at all. He could not brook interference with his personal habits, and her great achievement was to turn him into the tidy, obedient, and punctual person he soon became. His advice to women was the conventional one: "Get married, but never to a man who is at home all day." He explained: "I go to my hut every morning as a man goes to his office because women like men out of the house, especially men like myself who only sit and think. I was rebuked by Charlotte the other day when I pointed out a thing

56

I had discovered for the first time: 'It's been hanging on the wall for the last thirty years,' she said. And yet I'm much more of a domesticated person than she. I never wanted to travel, and I have always been interested in diet. But for her I would probably still have been living in Fitzroy Square, unless I were crowded out by the stuff accumulating in my room. In my shelter I can be as untidy as I like and so I can always lay my hands on a thing when I want it."

"You give the impression in your plays that it is the woman who has to go running after man, but man is such a static creature that not much running is needed. The running starts after marriage, when they have to run a house, run a family. . . ."

"You know what a French journalist said when he saw my home? 'I thought I was to meet England's most advanced thinker, and what do I find? A bourgeois interior and Madame who has all the appearance of being your wife!' "

"He must have been very disappointed. What could he have expected of the author of *The Quintessence of Ibsenism?* I had a similar experience when I was invited to the home of an extreme modernist and found him living in a pretty thatched cottage. Did he expect to find you in peasant smock and sandals?"

"I tried sandals, but they didn't work. Edward Carpenter made them. He thought he'd make an honest living by the use of his hands. If he had used his brains he would have seen that the living gained by manual work would never have supplied him with books and music and the leisure and freedom necessary for the writing of *Towards Democracy*. He was one of the early people who idealized the manual worker. A great mistake. William Morris made the same mistake, but if all workers lived like William Morris I would have had to change my tune. Anyhow, these people never knew how to speak to workers. I did. Have you ever met W. H. Davies?"

"The supertramp?"

"There is only one Davies, as there is only one Smith, Adam Smith, and only one Morris, William Morris. Give these people different Christian names and they lose identity: George Davies or George Smith or George Morris! It must have been my father's comedic sense of anticlimax that caused me to be called George."

"I knew Davies very well," I said. "The person who helped him greatly was Edward Thomas, who placed a cottage in the country at his disposal to give him an opportunity to write."

"What on earth made him do that? The best nature poetry has always been written in towns."

"Edward Thomas was himself a considerable poet. He told me of a certain literary giant, whom he approached as a young man, who kept him following at his heels for half an hour while he was doing other business. When the famous person looked into the poet's face and saw its weariness and disgust, he said: 'You must follow me if you want a bone to pick.' "

"I always kept off literary giants," G.B.S. said. "It was from men of established reputation that we learned that William Blake was mad."

"W. H. Davies put down his simple speech, the joy of his poetry, to the fact that he kept away from men of sharp wit."

"Yes," G.B.S. agreed, "that is why modest and unassuming

Dinner

Sitting to Troubetzkoy

Sitting to Laura Knight and Stroble

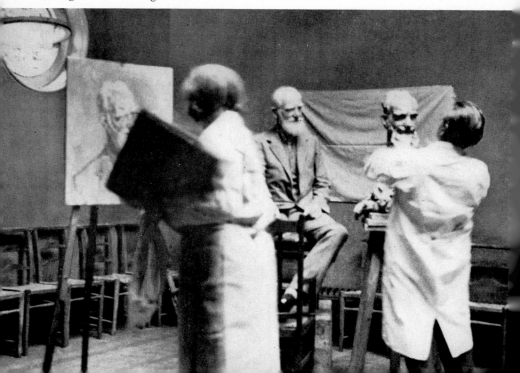

fellows like myself have to develop horns to keep off men of sharp wit. Davies wrote simply and joyously because he was a poet and not a cultured literary gent."

"If another person wrote:

> 'Say what you like
> All things love me!
> Horse, Cow and Mouse,
> Bird, Moth and Bee.'

we'd consider it an affectation."

"This came from The Farm House, Kennington! Now, I could have said the very same thing and quite truthfully, but it would not have been poetry. I was spoiled by my wide reading. He obviously had read nothing but what is written in the leaves of the trees and in the clouds of the skies."

Of course I had to ask if he had written poetry.

"Have you ever seen the poem I wrote to Ellen?" G.B.S. asked. He recited it as though accustomed to say it often:

> "The scene which would a stone unharden
> Is but a view from Bernard's garden.
> Here, standing sideways to the dawn
> And looking northwards up the lawn,
> You see the house that Bernard weeps in
> Because his Ellen never peeps in."

His reading could make the tritest stuff sound great. I said: "I don't know how people have got the impression that you meant to batter your way into fame and that you didn't mind whom you hurt and what pain you gave as long as it served your purpose."

"As a picture of my state of mind when I crossed the Channel, nothing could be falser. As far as I had any resolutions or intentions at all, I left Ireland because I realized there was no future for me there. London was the center of literature, art, and music for me; for in the interval between Lee's emigration and the literary and dramatic revival led by Yeats and Gregory, Dublin was a desert; and as to conquering London, I no more dreamed of such a possibility than the poorest Irish peasant or a tramp living in a Kennington doss house of conquering the United States. I went into England as England went into this war—completely unprepared. My shyness and sense of inferiority were a hindrance, and I managed by sheer perseverance to overcome my natural disinclination to make a laughingstock of myself. I knew that a man never tells you anything until you contradict him, especially in this country where everything was so false that to contradict was to be true. By contradicting everybody and everything, I found people were actually prepared to listen to me. I developed my mental muscles at their expense. Luckily, as a realist I had my world of fantasy to fall back upon, but I knew which was which."

The evening grew chilly, a thrush sang in the apple tree, and we became aware that the plough had stopped in the adjacent field.

"I've been trying to get some decent bread since I've been in England," Shaw complained. "What do you do about bread?"

"We manage to get quite decent bread."

I suppose we would never have worried about his domestic habits unless he had called our attention to them. We took for granted that he could have anything he wanted. He had the means and, besides, the whole world worried about him. He had an overflow of the things all needed desperately and could not get.

"I'm afraid," he said, "I have to eat the things that are put before me as long as they are vegetarian. My meals are dreadfully monotonous." He tasted our bread and liked it.

"That's more like the bread of my childhood," he exclaimed.

We were practically a besieged country, and everything imported had to go through fire and water.

"We are feeling that we have no right to beauty nowadays," I said.

"Stuff and nonsense! You and I have not made this war. Besides, you mustn't fall into the same error as I did in thinking that your feeling for beauty is universal. It's a precious gift. When I look back I realize that it was the beauty of Ireland that has made me what I am."

He searched his pockets, and while searching he told us that he objects to lining for his clothes. At last he brought out the photograph of Torca Cottage on Dalkey Hill which Lee gave over to the Shaw family.

"The view from this hill is not surpassed anywhere I have ever been. It was the happiest moment in my life when my mother told me we were going to live there."

We looked at this photograph for some time, trying to bring

back the people and their life in the home between Dublin Bay and Killiney Bay, where the mother sang and where Lee, the all-pervading Lee, the crank who was to play such an important part in molding the defiant G.B.S., lived as one of them. The mother worshipped Lee, and G.B.S. met a man who defied superstition by sleeping with his window open and challenging the night air to do its worst, and even ate brown bread and survived. The lean boy was bewitched by the beauty, the rocks to be surmounted, the wildness to be inhaled, and the sense of unique possession.

"Lee, George John Vandaleur Lee, was a professional music master, and my mother went to him to have her voice trained. He converted her to his method of voice production, a method based on facts and not assumptions. He had black side whiskers, a chin, and was lame, and his personality was mesmeric. He regarded my mother as a discovery and from the day of his arrival nothing counted with her save music."

It was obvious we were going to hear much of this man. G.B.S. carefully placed this photograph in his pocket and drank the orange juice near him.

"To get back to art: the question is how are we going to make the world safe for artists?"

"No political party would ever sweep the polls on that cry," I suggested.

"I don't know so much. Anyhow, leave the war and politics out of it. You are always dragging in irrelevant side issues. The point is, there are not going to be any more private patrons of the old style. Prices must come down within the means of the people. My chauffeur and my gardener, if they wanted something pretty for their walls to cover up a soiled patch, might then be able to buy a painting. This idea of selling a painting by the foot or inch, if you like miniatures, appeals to me. Madox Brown was paid by the foot for his great Manchester paintings."

"Napoleon, believing that artists, like soldiers, marched on their stomachs, also had the same idea."

"We have many ideas in common. It is fatal to neglect the stomach. It is of no use declaring: 'I am what I am, take me or leave me.' I did it, it's true, but then I was always indifferent to my welfare. I didn't want much. I had so many unremunerative things to do, like writing novels and addressing meetings when I wasn't electioneering that I couldn't be bothered with increasing my income. But then I was a fool. I had a letter recently from a successful artist, Sir William Rothenstein, and he says that, as neither the state nor the church offers work to the artists, they are of necessity parasites on a public who look to them for eventual profit or for social flattery. They become dependent on dealers. So long as the painter and sculptor are not servants of the state, they have to be adventurers. I don't want artists to be adventurers but good practical businessmen."

"There must be adventure, the constant rediscovery of the familiar world. That is why the young rush to art nowadays as the Elizabethans used to rush to sea."

"Culture and life have grown so far apart," G.B.S. explained, "that one goes into culture to avoid life, then into the war to avoid culture. Personally, I condemn the substitution of sensuous ecstasy for intellectual activity, this overindulgence in the nude."

We heard tip-tap, tip-tap, hard against the brick. A thrush was banging a snail on our terrace.

"There," said Shaw, "we have a consummate artist making a wretched living, not only driving a snail out of its home, like a slum landlord, but consuming it."

"In other words, he has got down to business."

He pondered and said, "I realized the full significance of the singular fate which has led me to play with all the serious things of life and to deal seriously with all its plays."

5

"What is the name of that flower?" G.B.S. asked as we stood in the garden by the herbaceous border, a mass of gold and purple. Surely he knew, for had he not lived in the country so many years? But he insisted, pointing to a clump of goldenrod.

"This goldenrod?"

"Goldenrod, yes, goldenrod. I have no memory for names of flowers and country things generally. I'm not a W. H. Hudson. I like flowers about me, of course, and the wilder the better. I don't like cut flowers, though. The rector is the one for flowers; he knows them all by name, like a shepherd his sheep. Have you seen him lately? He looks well on the way to Golders Green."

No, I had not seen him for a long time.

"He was talking about you the other day," G.B.S. continued, "and I asked him why the best people don't go to church. His reply was quite good for a clergyman. 'For the

65

same reason as healthy people don't go to a doctor.' I pointed
out that healthy people should go to a doctor because it is the
doctor's duty to prevent illness. . . . I had a thorough medical examination today and was passed as fit but I shall probably die like Beethoven, shaking my fists at a thunderstorm.
I know a person who has made an art of being bedridden, but
I don't think I like it. I can only rest by doing a hard spell of
work. I look forward to the time when all people will at least
do three or four hours' work a day to keep healthy, and the
rest of the time they can have to themselves."

I do not know why he mentioned death or being bedridden,
because he himself looked extraordinarily well. In fact, when
we talked and walked we forgot difference in age except, of
course, when he became reminiscent, and then we realized
that the people who had become historic figures to us he had
known personally. He went on: "A person should put an end
to himself when he finds he is giving pain and anxiety to his
friends. It isn't his own pain which matters so much. That's
always exaggerated by the other person; one can get used to
almost anything. When I was staying with William Morris, his
favorite daughter had one of her fits, a terrifying experience,
but Morris told me of it in a matter-of-fact way, as if he was
announcing breakfast. He really loved Jenny and told her
everything; his letters to her revealed the man as nothing else
did; a mix up of art, rowdy meetings, translations of Homer,
fights for free speech, attacks on the upper class, and at the
same time designing wallpaper and tapestry for them. It was
the power of the strong man anxious to accomplish something
before his death. I myself have always behaved as a child with

The suit which he has worn for over forty years

At Glyndebourne

"On the rocks"

long years of growth before me. He simply couldn't understand why people quarreled when they had a glorious end in view, forgetting that people can never be friends unless they can quarrel. If they can quarrel without malice, like myself, all the better, but not many have made a fine art of quarreling. When, in the good old comradely days, each was calling the other a liar, a rogue, and a bourgeois, it was meant to hurt: fellowship was life, and what a life!"

"Tolstoy, like Morris, disliked being argued with," I said. "He would go out of the room in a rage and bang the door behind him and then return immediately. 'Forgive me,' he would say, 'all my life my temper has been the worst thing I have had to contend with. When I think I have gained the victory then I am overpowered.' "

"He was a simple man if ever there was one. People talk about Saint Joan as being a simple peasant girl; peasants are never simple, it's the great who are simple. A great man is only a half per cent different from the ordinary person, but that little means very much indeed: they can go with the great man so far and then have to stop because they can't see any farther, while he can. That is why the great man must learn to abide his time, but unfortunately even the great man is impatient; instead of being as a child he grows into an uneasy adolescent."

For the first time he came in the morning. Luckily we were at home. He simply couldn't settle down to his writing that day.

"Did the wretched planes keep you up?" he asked.

"No. We were firewatching on a London roof, and neither

the searchlights nor the noise of the planes awakened us when it was our turn to go off duty."

"We humans can get used to anything vile. It's only beauty we can't stand, and truth, of course. As a fatherlandless person I'm right out of the war, but all the same the war may be a good thing if it brings the nations together. Even quarreling is better than living apart, as every married couple will tell you."

Why had he broken the even course of his routine this morning? I knew he would come to it, but he was moving in a mysterious way. He continued: "If I had died at the age of Shelley and Keats, I would have left behind nothing but a few rejected manuscripts, very neatly written in longhand. I was too lazy and timid by nature to lay hold of half the opportunities or a tenth of the money that a conventionally ambitious man would have grasped. Like an ass it was my lot to be modest, to have developed a good ear, to work hard, and to be content with plain fare, and naturally to be underestimated by the human being. Now, why am I telling you all this? I always put down my strength to my power of forgetting things not immediately useful to me, but I seem now to be remembering trifles and forgetting urgencies. Now . . ."

An Admiral butterfly, a beautiful eager thing, had perched on a mushy decaying potato that had yielded a fine crop of potatoes and even in this state attracted beauty to itself.

"Is that a flower?" he asked.

"No, a butterfly."

"Some of these things go traveling right across the seas. I'm more like a rooted tree."

A tree that stood tall and erect, with his roots exposed to the world. He continued:

"I haven't done too badly. When you consider who we were who set out to reverse the basis of society: a few refugees working in the British Museum, a few spouters, a few saints, and one or two cracked writers and artists who spoiled their limited chances of ever making a livelihood, and now capitalism is reeling and rocking. I know too much about boxing to take for granted that capitalism is going to be counted out. What seems a deadly blow often makes no impression. It's had to take some hard knocks: The *Fabian Essays*, my *Intelligent Woman's Guide*, and soon my new book, *A Gentle Swing to the Left.*"

He left behind some galley proofs for me to read.

We awoke very early to find the house captured. Soldiers in full battle dress stood idling outside, and armored cars and deadly tanks lined the lanes past Shaw's Corner and through the village. The village had been taken by the "Germans," who had a pleasant Northern dialect and a thirst for good strong tea. I had to show my identity card even when I brought out the drink and a packet of cigarettes. They informed me that they had got the English just where they wanted them; they were caught in a trap and would be smoked out. And they wouldn't go before they had got Shaw's autograph.

I had to leave the poor helpless village to the mercy of these intruders. On my way to the station I was asked fifteen times to show my identity card, and though I was carrying a very large suitcase which might have been filled with dangerous matter, I was never asked to show the contents. When I returned they were still there.

Shaw came round as excited as a schoolboy. He wanted to know whether they were interfering with us. He said:

"One managed to get hold of me and demand an autograph. He looked a harmless sort of fellow, bushy eyebrows, terrific chin, and great heavy shoulders, the kind of chap who wouldn't hurt a Shaw. I let him have it but told him not on any account to show it to anybody else. I noticed a terrific crowd round him looking and examining my writing. I find myself with the same tendency to judge people by their writing. When Davies sent his poems out of the blue, I guessed the character of the man before I had read a word. His handwriting was remarkably delicate and individual, the sort of handwriting one might expect from Shelley. In the same way as an artist can tell a Derby winner by the look of the horse, so I wept when I discovered that here was a real poet. Morris estimated his income from poetry as a hundred a year, and Browning threatened to leave the country when the surveyor of taxes assessed him for an imaginary figure derived from his poems. If I, a successful dramatist, received a manuscript from a person with my handwriting, I would know at once that he was cut out for a successful novelist, or, failing that, a successful actor, or, failing that, a successful jurist, or, failing that, a bishop, arch most certainly. I said I left them examining my writing and deciding on my fate. Saudek, the handwriting expert, found a certain resemblance between my handwriting and Napoleon's: a pronounced final emphasis of pressure. Very acute. Napoleon could develop new techniques to meet new situations, but we go the dear old way though everything has changed. We still are presenting arms and forming fours. . . . I suppose it will come out all right in the end; with a fool everything comes out well in the end. The German machines, the very latest, will be obsolete by the time we catch up, and then we'll have the latest devices and the Germans will fall to pieces. It's a diabolical business, and I'm done with the devil."

He certainly looked more like Santa Claus than the devil at that moment. He continued:

"I must put up a notice, something more original than 'Trespassers Will Be Prosecuted.' What about: 'Original Thinker, Beware!' ? That will keep them away."

When the invaders left, everything seemed different. We had grown to like the presence of these jolly youngsters, and now the lanes looked deserted. One soldier only, a lance corporal, was left behind to see that all was left as it should be, and while he was having tea with us G.B.S. came in.

The soldier was saying: "I've got a few Gilbert Murrays in my kit bag which I read on an evening." He told us that he hoped to get back to Oxford if he was young enough when the war ended.

"Your vowels are not Oxford," Shaw said, "they are not bad enough for that. . . . They're Yorkshire."

"I thought I successfully disguised the fact," the soldier replied. He left us to go on with his military duties, clearing tins and broken glass out of the way.

"I must get my alphabet going again. This war is a nuisance. Do you know if they have a choir in the local church?

If so, I can quite understand why the rector is hanging on to life. The prospect of having to listen to cherubim for all eternity is enough to deter anybody from the practice of virtue."

"Your heaven is here," I suggested.

He challenged this statement.

"Heaven indeed! I've had to go through a treadmill of an office, my home in Dublin was a torture, and my school was a prison. I had to go without decent clothes and food in London for years. I've had to undergo all kinds of indignities. When I worked at the office, the firm extracted from me an assurance that I would not discuss religion or politics because I made no secret of my opinions. I agreed, and my conscience has not been easy to this day on account of this promise."

After seeing him off to his gate, I walked through the park and toward the church. I heard singing and went in. I found a dozen youngsters yelling at the top of their voices. They were not of the village but had made themselves at home in God's house. "Roll out the Barrel" was followed by "If you were the only Girl," and then a tune with which I was not yet familiar, but it seemed to amuse them a good deal. Suddenly they became aware of my presence and fled in all directions.

I do not know why I felt these tunes out-of-place, considering they kept up the spirit of our soldiers and of the folk at home, the front line of air resistance. I was sorry they departed in that fashion.

The rector looked ill and depressed. He sat staring at us.

"I've had a good life," he mumbled in a thin and tired

voice. "I'd like to come back to see all the changes that are certain to take place. I've seen many changes already. There were times when I was in the slums I could not walk through my parish without being called after, but now, though religion is declining, the behavior of the people has improved beyond recognition. I feel the people are eager to live cleanly and to give their children more than they had. And I'd like to fill up some of the gaps in my own life. It's silly leaving it unfinished."

G.B.S. came in and at once started bantering.

"There's nothing worse than a lingering illness," he said.

"I'll miss your fun, Mr. Shaw, even more than my garden. Many people can say that you sent them to the grave laughing, because the war has made you more popular than ever."

"I was never so serious in my life." Shaw folded his arms, threw back his head and declared: "You treat death as normal and respectable and do nothing about it except to bless it. I treat it as a ghastly and avoidable nuisance and demand a remedy. You do not treat poverty in the same way. They did until I came along. In my cycle of five plays, *Back to Methuselah*, I demand a lifetime of three hundred years for maturity and condemn the present system of governing as mischievously adolescent."

"Why only three hundred years?" the rector asked teasingly. "Don't you think that in three hundred years you will probably want another hundred years for your complete fruition? The heart never grows better by age; I fear rather worse, always harder. In my youth I was an evangelist, my heart was on fire, and I thought I could never rest until the evils I saw were remedied, but now I almost seem to acquiesce."

"I said once," G.B.S. retorted, "that every man over forty who acquiesces is a scoundrel."

The rector shook his head gently. "In that case," he said, "this is a regular thieves' kitchen. I agree with Somerset Maugham, a Christian if ever there was one. He says: 'In my twenties the critics said I was brutal, in my thirties they said I was flippant, in my forties they said I was cynical, in my fifties they said I was competent, and now in my sixties they say I am superficial.'"

Shaw turned this to his advantage. "When we cease being brutally frank we cease being sincere. You clergymen have never faced up to things because you took your philosophy ready-made."

"Well," said the rector, undisturbed, "it was, and is, a jolly sound philosophy. We have certainly not gone further than the Sermon on the Mount. It is still the way of life. You should read it." He got up to go, extending a hand of long sensitive fingers, and with a charming smile quoted his favorite author: "There is something to be said for old age. Old age brings along with its ugliness the comfort that you will soon be out of it. To be out of the war, out of debt, out of the blues, out of the dentist's hands, out of second thoughts, mortifications, remorses that inflict such twinges and shooting pains, out of the next winter and the high prices. . . ."

G.B.S. roared with laughter. "He consciously watches his descent like an airman who leaves his burning plane. There's more method in my frivolity than you think."

6

Getting about in the blackout in town was a deadly experience even to me, who was accustomed to groping my way in the pitch dark. I had grown to accept darkness when walking, but sitting in a bus with blinds down and blocking out streets while a raid was in progress was a fantastic experience. It certainly had not the sense of security given by a ship of light traveling in a sea of darkness. The girl conductor, doing her utmost to be extra cheerful, suddenly announced:

"Anyone wants John Lewis? You can't have it if you do. It's gone, it's vanished. I know it's a shame, because they had the very things you need fer yer next birthday!"

What trust we put in the driver! With a minimum of light to guide him, he had to change his routes to circumvent the newly damaged roads. However much we prided ourselves on our independence, we realized, as we had never realized before, how mutually dependent we were; we lived on trust.

When I ultimately reached King's Cross it was out of action, and I had to travel hopefully to Finsbury Park. To get to the nearest station to my home, I went a dreary slow route to Hertford and by another train to within eight miles of my home, and then there was nothing left but to walk.

What does one think about in a long journey among silent, brooding passengers with a light much too dim for reading? Strange memories came trickling into consciousness, distant, forgotten incidents and faces. I thought of Gilbert Cannan and our walk across the common, years and years back, the wind-mill in which he lived. . . . He was the coming novelist then, and I read his works with the greatest eagerness, and now where was he? Where were his books? The last time I had met him was with Lytton Strachey: both were to appear before a tribunal and they were not at all sure of their answers to the questions usually put by the military representatives. What would you do if a German attacked your grandmother? "Get in between," suggested Lytton Strachey, but Gilbert Cannan would have argued with him!

What would I have done if that murderous-looking man in the corner took a strong dislike to me and attacked? A stupid question; we were both actually dozing helplessly in our corners.

I had an appointment that evening with G.B.S., and it did not matter very much because he kept late hours, rarely retiring before midnight. Not only did he manage to live much longer than most people, but his day was also longer. When I told him why I was so late he said that the one thing Mussolini had done for Italy was to get the trains to run on time. In

England, he thought, we were getting worse than the Russians in that respect.

"I had taken it for granted you were killed," he said unemotionally.

"I have no doubt you will outlive me," I assured him.

"Well, you never know. I have outlived all my friends."

I wondered here if he knew what had happened to Gilbert Cannan.

"Gilbert Cannan! Isn't he the fellow who said that the doing of something awful was a necessary preliminary to finding oneself? There must be many finding themselves nowadays. The most awful thing that one can do is to tell the truth. It's all right in my case because I am not taken seriously. Samuel Butler got away with his life because they didn't know when he was jesting and when he was serious. I must have been the only man of consequence who took him seriously. I said at the dinner in his honor if I were the only sensible man left in the world I would still maintain that Butler was right in his main contentions: he laid stress on the importance of money, and he also laid stress on the importance of luck—to be unlucky is a crime. The real reason why Butler was unknown during his lifetime was that he was always showing wherein accepted people were wrong, so that they were afraid of openly approving him lest he should turn and rend them. I turned on him once: I said that I regarded his chapter on the 'Rights of Vegetables' as a direct attack on myself, and attacking me has always been the special prerogative of H. G. Wells!"

"Wells has surely exhausted his vocabulary by now."

"Oh, dear, no. He now regards me as a typical Englishman, and if the world were destroyed there would still be left a sufficient number of photographs of myself to help the Almighty to reconstruct Man. Otherwise why was it that wherever he went he was always coming up against photographs of myself!"

He showed me half a dozen recent photographs of himself and gave me a critical analysis of each of them. He not only knew his features but knew the significance of every line and bump. It is a pity that he was never able enough as an artist to give us a self-portrait.

His voice assumed a tragic air. "You know, the rabbits have got into my garden. I found an opening made in the hedge. I don't want the gardeners to set traps. Not that it matters if the rabbits eat up all the vegetables, because I don't each much. This morning I had to release a rabbit from a trap, a ghastly experience."

His blue eyes were watery and dim and his face looked more wrinkled than I had ever seen it. In a twinkling his face resumed its smiling mask. He switched on the wireless and a crooner informed us in the saddest tones how happy, happy, happy he was. He switched off immediately with the remark that it wasn't religion but the wireless which was the opium of the people.

I told him of a visit to an author one afternoon whom I found fast asleep with the wireless full on and I had had to switch it off to wake this good man. As soon as I switched it off, this author woke with a start and cried, "Who switched off the wireless?" He couldn't stand silence.

"I'm all right in that respect. I'm the only one who can stand my continuous presence and I don't mind silence."

"The perfect prisoner?"

"No, the free person."

I stood up to go. He also stood up and said:

"I daren't see you out. I'm completely blind in the dark."

"Don't you come, I'll let myself out," I said.

He opened the door for me and quickly closed it again because no light dare go out into the night. Before I got accustomed to the darkness I tripped over some loose bricks which at once made me realize that I was on the wrong path. So dark was it and so well was the house blacked out that I could not find my bearings. I thought I knew his garden but in the blackness it lost shape and distance. It must have been like this before light was given to the world. Under such circumstances it is possible to go round and round the same center of darkness without ever finding the gate. Suddenly there was a flash of lightning, I got up and walked straight to the gate and down the lane. Before I reached my home the rain came down in torrents.

I was mowing the lawn when the small side-gate opened and G.B.S. almost bounded up the steps. He stood awhile on the terrace looking at the garden and I walked up toward him. The sunset was sweeping across the lawn and the fields beyond leaving trees and bushes afloat in a sea of unearthly beauty.

He said: "You are no doubt thinking of the light playing on tree and lawn. Have you noticed that the beauty of the old Dame was only discovered after man was divorced from her?

When coal created the miserable slums we call towns, then Wordsworth and Coleridge and Keats came along with their nature worship. It was left to Karl Marx to lift the lid and show us what things were really like. He was a great historian if not much of a theorist and I owe a great deal to him. Like all debtors I paid him back by disowning him. He was a wise man but his disciples were utter fools. They insisted on swallowing him neat and excommunicating all those who really understood him, like me. It was not until the Fabians came along that England became ripe for socialism."

As we went into the house he said: "I have been thinking, if the Germans win they may confiscate all I have. Luckily I need very little for I can manage quite well with my house here which is bought and paid for, my flat in town and a couple of cars and the half dozen servants."

"What fun you would have starting all over again," I said. "Your new book will bring you a new fortune."

"Yes, everything I do turns to gold," and he settled himself among the cushions prepared for him.

"I shall never forget Max Nordau coming to see us after the last war and telling us how the French Government had almost reduced him to beggary," I said.

"No, that was my achievement," G.B.S. said. "I knocked him out completely. I was the only man in the country who could take him out of his depth and leave him to drown. I went straight to the top and he went straight to the bottom."

He was referring to that brilliant article he wrote for Benjamin Tucker, *The Sanity of Art*. It was the proudest moment of his life because William Morris, who had never discussed art with him before and had only treated him as an uncouth political agitator, now took him into the fold and even listened.

I pointed out that Tolstoy had treated Nordau's master in the same way. Lombroso, full of the sense of his importance, went down to see Tolstoy, boasting to the great man of the March of Science and the Age of Reason. Tolstoy listened and then led him quietly to a lake and asked him if he could swim. Of course there was nothing Lombroso could not do. Tolstoy dived in; Lombroso followed, went down helpless and came up shrieking for help. Tolstoy brought him out of the water, a wet but chastened man. The lesson was brought home. "Even a man who can explain everything sometimes finds himself helpless."

Shaw laughed and said mischievously: "I would have let him drown. I'm certain the moral was wasted on him. You know, Tolstoy, like myself, wasn't taken in by superstitions like science and medicine."

"And yet I feel that you must have your pet superstitions."

"Yes, a man who sees far ahead must talk in parables and be guided by signs which only he can see or hear."

"Only he?"

"A man at such times differs as much from himself as he does from other people."

"Like yourself I prefer the parables of John Bunyan to the jargon of the materialist. Look at this: 'Beyond the epistemological scholasticism of the empirio-criticism it is impossible not to discern clearly the partisan struggle in philosophy. . . .'"

He interrupted me: "Who on earth said that?"

"Lenin."

He was not surprised. He answered: "The reasons by which men arrive at their conclusions are of little importance. What is of importance is the fact that they reach certain results."

"Did you know that Lenin when in London had little contact with the British Socialist movements? He made a point, however, of visiting the Socialist churches. That proves that Lenin had something of the 'superstitious' in him, considering that the services there were carried on on similar lines to the orthodox churches. You drive out one set of superstitions to call into being another set. I am surprised that there has not come into being, in a world full of cults, a Life Force liturgy."

He shook his shoulders, saying: "The Life Force permits of infinite change and progressive variation, but, once things are permitted to settle into a definite system, then they cease to be open to the inspiration of the Life Force. However, there's nothing absurd that hasn't a religion to back it. What is there more ridiculous than the religion of *tout le monde*"?

There was no indignation in this attitude to *tout le monde*. With Swift, indignation sprang from his intuitive sympathy and affectionate good will toward the people, but with Shaw the democratic machine was grossly inefficient and could therefore be laughed at as the old-fashioned cars that used to make much noise and gave up at the first hill. He heartily despised the animal called Man and said that it was time that it ceased to fill the world.

"With Man I have to hide my good qualities, otherwise I

would never get on. I mustn't even praise these qualities lest he rend me to bits. My only policy is to profess evil and do good."

"That smacks of moral cowardice," I suggested.

"We're all moral cowards. There's not a soul who does not know that war is wrong, but what do we do to those who say so? Ask C. H. Norman what was done to him because he said war was wrong. The defense of the moral coward is the old one, what can one do against so many? If I feed one person, that won't do away with poverty; if I go to the scaffold for my principles, that won't bring the millennium; if I give up all my wealth and live like a Gandhi, that won't do away with evil. We extol democracy and know all the time that the minority is right. It is a simple matter to tolerate evil, but virtue is intolerable. Most people find no difficulty in doing wrong and retaining their faith. In fact it is the only way of retaining one's faith nowadays."

This interested me, because I have watched right through my adult life how people reconcile their actions and their principles. There's only one thing wrong with the monotheists —they aren't. They have their gods for each sphere of life, and the compartments are extremely watertight. Shaw accepted this conclusion as a matter of course.

"Conscience," he said, "is all very well, but it is not universally applied; one can have a conscience about one activity and be hopelessly immoral about everything else. Take Dubedat in *The Doctor's Dilemma*. He's a saint when it comes to art but in matters of money and women and almost everything else he's a scoundrel. The person upon whom I based this character would think nothing of borrowing money because his wife's allowance was due to come in a few weeks and even then forget to return the money, and as to women . . . he was a rogue!"

"Was he an artist?"

"No. He was a scientist."

"Then why did you portray him in your play as an artist? William Morris wasn't like that, nor was Burne-Jones. . . ."

He dismissed this rather petulantly.

"Anyhow, I gave them good value for their money."

I walked up to my bookcase and produced a very old copy of *The Doctor's Dilemma*, published in the sixpenny novel series with pages and pages of patent-medicine advertisements.

"Well, it paid for the publication!"

He was anxious to get away because Charlotte was expecting him. On the way to the gate I expressed anxiety about our position in the war at the time. He turned to me, put his hand on my shoulder, and said:

"Don't worry. If the British can survive their meals, they can survive anything."

7

G.B.S. came in and found to his dismay three little boys stretched on the floor, painting. They had discovered the joy of color and were indulging their imaginations. Nothing was too difficult for them: sky and hill, cow and airplane, all came sweeping on to the large sheets of paper. Their eyes glistened with pleasure as they saw their work taking shape, and they took no heed of our visitor, who seemed to resent the presence of these, the poorest children in the village.

He said to Clare: "Why do you waste your time with these?"

"Wasn't it you," I answered, "who said, 'Fine art is the only teacher except torture'?"

He shook his shoulders in irritation.

"Nonsense! A child must learn the multiplication table before it is offered Michelangelo's Sistine frescoes or Beethoven's Ninth. Without language and at least elementary mathematics a child would grow up virtually deaf and dumb."

"And yet, if you had had the right kind of art teaching, it might have changed the course of your life."

"Yes, we all wanted to be artists in those days. Oscar Wilde and Chesterton actually studied at the Slade School and became quite good writers. It is a peculiar thing but it is necessary to fail in art to become a very witty and successful writer. But what these poor children should learn is the difference between the traveler and the highwayman. They must be made to learn that they must become serviceable and productive members of the community or they will come down with a tumble!"

"Then," I asked, "you would have these children educated differently from the rich?"

"Of course. We must have special schools to train the administrators, the people who will get the four-figure jobs. And by training, I mean training."

This statement was so contrary to all the things he had written about education that I had to say: "How can we prevent the organization of child life becoming the sport of doctrinaires like ourselves?"

He answered: "We can't prevent any human activity being dominated by doctrinaires. Wrong doctrine will finally discredit itself by its failure and sound doctrine will establish itself by its success."

"If you had a child what kind of schooling would you arrange for him or her?"

His head drooped a little, then he said:

"If I had a child I should have to take what our social organization offered. Many who were schooled at Eton, Harrow,

Winchester, or Rugby, and graduated at Oxford or Cambridge have criticized and denounced these schools fiercely, but they have had to send their sons to them all the same, *faute de mieux.* Proletarian parents are equally bound to the nearest elementary school."

"But if a child complained about having to go to school at all?"

"I would explain as best I could, and it is extremely difficult for a parent to explain anything to a child, that it must, if it was to be allowed to go without a nurse and have money in its pockets to spend as it likes."

"In other words," I said, "a child without any form of education would grow up a defective?"

"Would grow up intolerable as a wildcat. I must make it clear, however, that mere knowledge of facts and inferred reasoning will not by themselves produce culture; they may lead to disaster without comprehension of the function of aesthetics in biology and of metaphysics in morality."

We both said nothing for a while, and I could not help seeing a tall, thin boy going off to Eton, very precisely dressed and crammed with all the dos and don'ts of behavior. Would he have been prepared in the right politics and the right religion so that his life there at Eton should be comfortable? I was even following him to Cambridge, the holder of a mathematical scholarship, when G.B.S. himself said:

"It is perhaps as well that I haven't a child. A genius never produces satisfactory progeny."

"Like everything about you, this child might have been the exception," I suggested.

He would not be flattered. "Have you noticed that children invariably take after their grandparents?"

So, while I had endowed his son with a genius for mathematics, G.B.S. saw him secretly drinking and laughing at failure.

If all life were like *The Idiot* and everybody went about turning out their inmost hearts; if, like William Morris, he had a touch of epilepsy in his composition, then I would have learned much at that moment. Instead he asked for the wireless and we were regaled with a jolly tune from Gilbert and Sullivan's *Iolanthe*.

"Ibsen could do that kind of thing much better. Do you remember the chorus in *Love's Comedy*?" I said, and read it:

"Welcome, welcome, new plighted pair
To the merry ranks of the plighted!
Now you may revel as free as air,
Caress without stint and kiss without care,
No longer of footfall affrighted.

Now you are licensed, wherever you go,
To the rapture of cooing and billing;
Now you have leisure love's seed to sow,
Water, and tend it, and make it grow;
Let us see you've a talent for tilling!"

"As I said," G.B.S. laughed, "marriage is popular because it combines the maximum of temptation with the maximum of opportunity."

I found G.B.S. standing beneath a clump of pines staring in the direction of the park. The sun was going down, and a gray mist was creeping over the church.

"Those bushes must be cut away; they hide the church," he complained.

"Elected churchwarden?" I asked.

He took me seriously. "No, certainly not."

He was in a grim mood. Two or three women passed us to put flowers on the graves, forget-me-nots and marigolds, and they did not notice us. He said:

"I must have been an insufferable child, all children are. I forget the things that happened yesterday and remember the things that happened eighty years back as if they were yesterday. I indulged in cruelties that didn't turn a hair of my head. No child should be unaware that if it provokes its elders beyond endurance, it will get its head clouted without regard to the possible consequences. Corporal punishment is not effective unless it is really cruel, which it seldom is. I was never punished at home, and at school the teachers were too indifferent to work up the cruelty necessary to get me to do my lessons. Without Lee I would have remained a barbarian. It was he who proved to me that the world could be safely defied. I've never turned back. I've always slept with an open window, eaten brown bread. When I stayed with William Morris at Kelmscott and slept in midwinter with windows wide open, my jug was frozen deeper than anyone else's."

"Morris was not a vegetarian."

"Mrs. William Morris had to have her meat. She regarded my diet as a suicidal fad. There are people today who regard it so in spite of the fact that I'm on the way to ninety. They still look upon a meatless day as a penance, as they look upon all pleasures. It probably is. A man who dropped his aitches was preferable to a man who dropped his meat. She did not conceal her contempt for my folly. When I dined with them my appetite returned, as it always does at the sight of a particularly nice pudding. Mrs. Morris pressed a second helping on me which I consumed to the entire satisfaction of the family. Then she said: 'That'll do you good, there is suet in it!' That was the only remark she ever allowed herself to make to me. When I die, if ever I will, it will be put down to my diet. I'm always going across the course of nature: I deliberately chose the path of most resistance and rose by the force of gravity."

He put in a word for his youthful rival who was very much in the news. "Winston Churchill smokes, drinks, and eats meat and has managed to survive. Of course, if we stop killing animals and insects, they'd kill us. It's a matter of who is to survive, after all. Rabbits, tigers, and fleas must be slain, and so should incorrigible criminals, dangerous lunatics, and idiots. Of course," he added generously, "the operation should not be cruel."

I suggested that under certain circumstances he himself might have been considered incorrigible and dangerous. "You may remember," I said, "when Tolstoy was excommunicated from the church by the Holy Synod of Russia he was derided and pointed at: 'Look! There goes the devil in human form!' If you had your way Tolstoy would have gone the way of rabbits, tigers, and fleas; so, I have no doubt, would Samuel Butler, for not accepting in full Darwin's theories."

"I was considered as monstrous as Tolstoy after the publication of my *Commonsense of the War*. As a matter of fact, I was excommunicated from every tennis club, every golf club, and even from the Butchers' Guild; in short, from every religious order. I had to stop doing all the things I never wanted to do and never did." He paused a while and then continued: "For myself I am well satisfied. Success comes streaming in on me from every side."

The immediate problem for us was how to get the cows away from the gate, which led out of the park and into the lane. The cows had settled comfortably and obstinately on the high grass, and nothing would move them.

"Anyhow," G.B.S. said, "they fit more happily into the landscape than humans. We'll have to wait."

We stood beneath the old sycamore and admired the peaceful scene.

"It's all extremely artificial, this natural scene. Keir Hardie must have had such a scene in mind when he called the Members of Parliament well-fed beasts."

"Comfort and security seem to destroy the power of action," I said.

"Call no man comfortable or secure while I am still alive. Nobody can yet be sure of what I shall be up to next or whether I shall die in my bed or be hanged. Remember it was Swift who was the inventor of the phrase 'sweetness and light'—and he is now reputed to be the most embittered misanthrope in history. The man who dares to suggest that comfort, security, and happiness are the objects of life deserves the fate destined for these beasts."

Suddenly, as if a cow had stood on its hindlegs and found speech, we heard: "What luck! Here is the greatest man on earth. I've always wanted to meet you."

G.B.S. turned and looked her up and down with a smile. He placed her by her speech, by her clothes and her well-groomed appearance. I saw him make up his mind as to which Shaw to enact. In his gentlest voice he said:

"These cows won't hurt you."

"I'd brave a wild bull to meet you," she answered.

"I'm the only wild bull in Ayot," Shaw assured her.

"If all bulls were like you, as gentle and as approachable," she said in the sweetest of tones. "I simply had to snatch a day from the horrors of London."

"Don't let the war get hold of you," he advised.

"How true. I shall always remember your words and especially the voice in which you uttered them. I can understand how well you understood Saint Joan. It's just what I myself think. I love reading your plays; they take me out of myself into a kind of dream world where all people are charming and witty and there's never an emotional upheaval, as in all these modern works. Whenever I'm in the middle of some awful raid, I say to myself: 'I'm the master of my fate, the captain of my soul.' "

"Henley had no sense of fun. When I contributed to the *Scots Observer*, my claim to writing for a Scots paper being that I'm a direct descendant of Macduff. . . ."

"How wonderful! And to think that Shakespeare put an ancestor of yours into a play."

He ignored her ecstatic remark and continued:

"I did some criticism for Henley, but we couldn't agree. You see, I discovered Wagner, and Henley hated his music, so I stopped writing for his paper, and naturally people stopped buying it. I was easily the most original writer of the day. Frank Harris had an eye for the best people. The silly man says he picked me out of the gutter. . . ."

She was quick off the mark: "What he really meant was that he picked you out in a junk shop, a precious jewel. I know because I've come back with wonderful things from those horrid-looking shops. You were a Socialist in those days, weren't you? And they were in a way junk. You are a *phenomenon*. I shall never forget this day as long as I live. If I had been killed yesterday, I should have died without your blessing. Do you think there is an afterlife?"

G.B.S. was beginning to feel ashamed of this contact. He blurted out:

"I don't know. It's bad enough to have one life."

"I know we'll meet again," was her parting remark.

As we walked down the lane, he said:

"These people who haven't a thought in their heads are always the first to give you a bit of their mind. They will always say sincerely and frankly just what they think. They are the people in control. The greater the mess they get us into, the greater the opportunity for their finer qualities."

It was quite chilly, but he insisted on being outside and again assured me he was happiest in the cold weather. He told me, as if it were a huge joke, that a precious jar had been broken.

I said, "Is there nothing we can do about it? They're fear-fully clever at putting bits and pieces together nowadays."

"You're not going to tell me that these things have an after-life. It's only the things without a soul that survive, not works of art. I think it was William Archer who told the story of a lady who found a vase broken and couldn't be consoled. 'When a friend dies, there is religious consolation,' she complained, 'but with a work of art there is no such consolation.' I have not this sense of property. Ultimately all property is theft."

"But all art is love," I suggested.

"Don't use the word 'love'; it means nothing. The worst things have been done in the name of love."

"Wasn't it Galsworthy who said somewhere: 'I've got a friend on the press who's very keen on Christ and kindness; and wants to strangle the last king with the hamstrings of the last priest?' "

"Epstein told me that he remembers visiting the Leicester Galleries when the Christ was on exhibition and noticed a man just emerging from the room with clenched fist and furious face. It was John Galsworthy. Have you noticed how men often typify the very things they attack?"

"Only too often," I answered, smiling.

"I am amused to think that Christ has found his resting place at last in a fine old Adam house. Our neighbor, Cherry-Garrard, has it. It has a nicely lit alcove all to itself. You must go and see it."

"What would the Germans do if they got hold of it?" I asked.

"Once you're dead, another crucifixion doesn't make much difference. . . ."

I remembered that Epstein wanted to make it a hundred feet high, set it up on a high place where all could see it, to warn people that peace must be the way of life, and here it was hidden away in a country house and the world was at war.

G.B.S. continued: "You should also go down to Tunbridge Wells and see the fine Morris window in which Burne-Jones made the figure on the Cross a glorious Greek god. I personally have a soft spot for Von Uhde's Christ where He is depicted as a poor man conversing with men in tall hats, just people like ourselves. It must have been a pleasant change for these people to come in contact with an original mind. I shouldn't think they found much calm and sweetness in him. . . . What about walking that way?"

We walked across a field and along a grove.

"There is another thing I learned from Lee. Nearly all his best singers were Roman Catholics, and acquaintance with them rooted out of my mind the notion that Catholics were inferior people not to be associated with and predestined to eternal damnation. I soon came to like them. I learned there is only one religion, though there are a hundred versions of it. The really religious people are not empty. They have dignity, conviction, sobriety, and force. However impossibly narrow and stupid the mere articles of their creed may be, it is obvious that they are respectable, efficient, and able to do without happiness. And they can do extraordinary things, from early churchgoing to martyrdom. Presently the race develops a degree of intelligence to which their reverence for the miraculous, their belief in it because it is miraculous, is impossible. You then get two sorts of people, irreligious people, whom no amount of culture can make otherwise than worthless, and artists, who find in their art an irresistible motive. But the artists, having to make extraordinary exertions, cannot do it without extraordinary resources. They must either have re-creation, in the literal sense of that profoundly significant word, or else stimulation. Now, recreation is the secret of the religious life. You meditate and are profoundly rested and recreated. You die at a stupendous age, unexhausted in spirit.

"My most religious experience was aesthetic, when I touched with my own hand Michelangelo's Sibyl in the Sistine Chapel. There is always religion if you can reach it, the religion of Beethoven's Ninth Symphony, the religion which rediscovers God in man and the Virgin Mother in every carpenter's wife, which sweeps away miracle and reveals the old dogmas as the depths of which everyday facts are only the surface, which sanctifies all life and substitutes a profound dignity and self-respect for the old materialistic self. This is the most recreative of all religions; with it you can live on half a bean a day, if that is all that your bodily well-being requires."

8

In certain parts of the South Seas the *ménage à trois* is the accepted thing. A child grows up to find a man, his uncle, before whom the mother almost trembles, whose word is really law to her and her children. The child soon learns that this third person is not only to teach him the arts of life but the rules of conduct. Of course, the father is always there as well and is merely the man who lives with the mother and is never to be appealed to in serious matters.

G.B.S. explained in greater detail how the *ménage à trois* came about in his case:

"Lee was a mesmeric conductor and had collected an amateur orchestra, eked out occasionally by a soloist from a military band. It was Lee who trained my mother to sing; when his brother died he was left alone with an old housekeeper, reputedly a terror. She was got rid of somehow, and our household took her place. If Lee had not come into the family and I left with my mother, who was a thoroughly disgusted and disillusioned woman suffering from a hopelessly disappointing husband, what would have become of me, I daren't think."

"You would have remained a mute inglorious Milton," I suggested.

"I suppose something else would have turned up. My grandfather's uncle, I am always proud to relate, was hanged as a rebel. I know this: if I had remained in the office I would have ended up by murdering somebody and would have been hanged before I was born. I would have got into the papers somehow!"

"It is interesting that the two writers who count most," I said—

G.B.S. interrupted me.

"Who is the second?" he asked.

"Wells, of course."

"There are a lot of horses following well behind and it's difficult to make out which is which. Wells's father was a cricketer, a professional and therefore not a gentleman, and his mother a housekeeper in a large country house. My mother knew nothing of housekeeping, nor of money, nor of hygiene. His father had to keep fit, but my father was a lonely drinker at the grocer-publican's. Then Wells had a flair for examinations, for the storing of a lot of facts, but I was at a disadvantage in that respect; I could never pass examinations: the only things that stuck were the things that interested me. And then I had a nasty unscientific way of rushing to conclusions, leaving it to men like Wells to supply the evidence. So you see he

Art critic

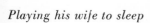

Playing his wife to sleep

The portrait of his wife by Sartorius

had everything in his favor. All the same, he hasn't done too badly. In spite of Barrie's advice that editors always reject views on politics and reflections on art and theories of life, we both managed to make money out of these unimportant subjects. We both thought ourselves original and profound, and in a way we were. The main difference was that I looked it and he didn't; I sounded it and he didn't. He needed, above all, a tormentor, and I had to take on that role to keep him up to the mark. I do not mind hurting as long as it makes a friend of a person."

"Didn't he appeal to you to stop this personal ballyragging? It was ridiculous to be competitive and personally comparative in old age."

"That's the schoolmaster in him; all the world's a school and men and women merely dunces. Now then, Shaw, you're in the sixth form now, no more ragging. From now on, your best behavior! But the man in the sixth form is only the undergraduate in university and the graduate is only the junior in a business. We've both hardly qualified to be undersecretaries, let alone sages. Wells described William Morris as a poet and decorator. William Morris might have got nowhere, but he was pretty near the truth when he said that idle capitalists were damned thieves, with the word damned not a mere decoration but a poet's prophecy. I'd rather be led by a poet than a scientist any day."

In the same way as William Morris would not have a word said against Burne-Jones, so Shaw grew furious when Morris was attacked. I could not help recalling the story of Tyrtaeus: how nearly two thousand years ago the Spartans, in their war against the Dorians, were advised by a sage to choose a leader from Attica. They applied to the Athenians, who purposely sent them a lame poet. His songs, however, so animated the Spartans that they won. The lame poet was Tyrtaeus.

"Well, Wells shouldn't complain. I've always been the sinister figure, urging him not to get excited nor to give way to eloquent exorcism. . . . He is determined to stay in London; I hope Hitler will have the common sense to spare him: martyrdom would have a disastrous effect on his works."

"You mean his provisional thinking and tentative proposals would be transmuted into dogma. . . ."

"I mean he would be canonized and some silly dramatist would have to waste his precious gift on writing a chronicle play called *St. Herbert*. Tolstoy was always hankering after martyrdom. If that had happened his *War and Peace* would be denounced as youthful excess, and all his nonsense would be forced down the minds of gaping villagers."

"But Wells was violently anti-Catholic."

"I know, but so was Marx and so was Lenin, but they have produced a church militant and an inquisition held together by a common faith and by vows of poverty and chastity."

"The true saints are not the people in the public eye," I said.

"That kind of thought leads us nowhere. It may be that full many a flower is born to blush unseen, but that fact should not take away from the pleasure we have in seeing the flowers which unblushingly reveal themselves. Wells is disqualified for canonization because he didn't use words not found in any decent dictionary. Accustomed to making his meaning clear to the meanest intelligence, he even corrected his spelling errors. Now, James Joyce was wise. You can't see his meaning for the words, and so there must be something deep and significant in what he says. People must spend their lives studying his texts and allusions, and even then they won't come to the fundament of his thoughts. I find that in every fifty words I write there are forty errors."

I could not help being flippant and suggesting that he makes a cult of these errors by making them seem deliberate.

"And charging a penny extra! In my case it takes fifty years for my thought to come through, and so I get the effect of mystery that way. Whenever I come across an original thought I turn to an old book of mine and find it always better expressed by myself. There's no need for me to descend to subterfuge; all I have to do is to live to a couple of hundred and see my heresies turn into orthodoxies. Only as I can't sit still and do nothing, and don't like to repeat myself, I have to contradict my early ideas to appear original and so it goes on."

He had really come in that day to take a photograph, just one, and one turned into six at least. This was the only sport that he permitted himself besides sawing wood.

"As I am not an artist," he explained this youthful excess, "this is the next best thing. When a person excels at something he should do something else in which he is a novice because that brings him down to earth. And I haven't a family to distract me and nobody likes a man of eighty."

Again he told me that he owed his ability to enjoy solitude to his mother.

"Apart from Lee, my mother never had a friend and never

made the least effort to win my affection, and I certainly made no effort to win hers. When my manuscripts were returned she wasn't in the least interested. I don't think she read a single one of them. She accepted me as a burdensome good-for-nothing, just what she would expect from the son of her husband. My father at least had satisfaction in seeing my work in print and actually praised, but she never referred to it. The only satisfaction I found in my parents was that neither of them were celebrities. Mozart's son was only a fair musician like his grandfather. Mendelssohn's father complained that he had begun as the son of his father and ended as the father of his son. Beethoven's nephew was a scapegoat, and none of the kindred of Shakespeare or Tolstoy achieved any eminence."

"There are one or two exceptions," I said.

"You will find that the exceptions in this case do not prove the rule. The parents had already prepared the soil by the usual process of ample means and ample opportunity. Look at Wells with his dreary schoolmastering, and look at me—after five years of commercial servitude I had to burn my boats and sponge on my mother. Even in the Civil Service, where gifted people tend to find refuge, I am told they have to work. That's a great pity; nowadays there are no employments which leave sufficient leisure to maintain a natural supply of geniuses. The only thing left is to have reasonable hours of work, say two or three hours a day, and then no genius would suffer much unless, like my mother, he's of the kind who prefers to work himself to death at whatever he is doing. Of course, the work should be so disagreeable that the genius will want to rush from his enforced drudgery and not spend a moment too much. Such work will at least save him from becoming a feckless nuisance living in an imaginary world and ignorant of the real one."

"So we've come back to the interminable wrangle about reality."

"Whenever I see a book starting with 'What is reality?' I put it down at once, knowing that the author doesn't know and I will never know, even if I read all the philosophies of the world. A philosopher and a matter-of-fact man might cordially agree with a half-dozen verbal propositions concerning the real while interpreting them in different and diametrically opposed senses. A philosopher opposes the reality of the things to its mere appearance, but to the matter-of-fact man the appearance *is* the reality, and things that have no appearance, like ideas, are less real to him than tangible, visible things. There is something convincing to him in a brick, when aimed at him, which he misses in Beethoven. He speaks of hard cash, nothing like leather, solid British oak, with a complete sense of security; even his heart is raised to being like oak. He feels completely lost when he is faced with something that he can't lay his hands on, like music or mathematics."

"Yes, instead of the matter-of-fact man, as you call him, admitting this lack of understanding, he prefers to think of the creative man as defective, or at least akin to madness."

"Most of them are," Shaw answered decisively. "Most of them are. I am possibly the only sane exception."

Before he left I told him that next time he came he would find a new friend to meet him. A look of petulance showed on his face.

"Then I'll avoid your place like a plague," he exclaimed.

"Just as you wish. He has come to stay, and you will find us inseparable."

He came somewhat earlier than usual next time. Eagerly he inquired about our new friend. But Tinkerbell himself came forward and would have no formalities. He barked his welcome, wagging his tail mightily, and then lay at the feet of G.B.S. in a line with the cat.

"I must admit I was frightened," G.B.S. said, "when you mentioned a new friend. Man is the only animal of which I am thoroughly and cravenly afraid. I don't want people; they waste my time."

"Is that why you instil fear?" I asked.

"I, do I?" He enjoyed this assertion. "When I was a little boy I was always playing the devil. My chief delight was to paint the whitewashed walls of Dalkey with pictures of Mephistopheles, and even Lee amused himself, at my expense, by decorating my face to look my future part. As a child dreams so he becomes. Though not perhaps by the ways and means he expects." As he spoke, his very eyebrows, mustache, and ears affirmed his words.

"Wasn't it Hazlitt who said: 'Man is the only animal that laughs and weeps: for he is the only animal that is struck with the difference between what things are and what they might have been'?"

"Well," G.B.S. retorted, "the quicker he stopped laughing and weeping and started thinking a bit, the better it would be for him."

G.B.S. folded his arms and swung his foot violently above

the prostrate form of Tinkerbell, who, with one eye on the sole of the shoe above, sighed deeply, and I was almost afraid of the impact on his trusting body, but the dog was wiser and jumped into his favorite armchair and listened from that vantage point.

Full of self-pity, he recalled his early struggling days again. He was older now and in London, pacing the National Gallery, poor and shabby and only able to enter on the free days! He said: "I, always on the heroic plane in my thoughts, had two disgusting faults which I did not recognize as faults because I could not help them. I was poor and shabby. And because I could walk into the National Gallery on 'free' days and enjoy Michelangelo, because I could suffer more by hearing a movement of Beethoven's Ninth Symphony taken at the wrong tempo than a duchess losing her diamond necklace, I was indifferent to the repulsive fact that if I had fallen in love with the duchess I did not possess a morning suit. That is why I am all out for the equality of income. The biological argument is all-pervasive."

I suggested that the duchess might easily have fallen in love with him just because of his cycling suit and pathetic poverty. This annoyed him. "I could never have kept her in the kind of life she was accustomed to!"

"But surely you never held that you 'keep a wife'?"

"Well, I wanted to marry May Morris, but she was accustomed to a way of life beyond my means."

"Yet she married somebody much poorer than yourself, didn't she?"

"Yes. My possibility of future eminence was unlimited. I

was already an unsuccessful novelist with not a single novel accepted and therefore an established genius frowned upon by the bourgeois publishers. What did Readers like George Meredith and John Morley know about good work? And as to May Morris, she knew too many geniuses to be taken in by another."

"In that case then the devil proved a good friend and prevented a disastrous marriage."

"I was foolish enough to believe that Woman did all the pursuing. I did not think it necessary to say anything or make any sign at all. I had no doubt that the thing was written on the sky for both of us, that all the material obstacles would melt away and we would live happily ever afterward. I had to consummate or vanish. I vanished."

"If you had vanished it would have been all right, but you joined the young married couple. . . ."

9

Often I had been this way before
And now it seemed I never could be
And never had been anywhere else;
'Twas home; one nationality
We had, I and the birds that sang
One memory.
They welcomed me. . . .

EDWARD THOMAS

G.B.S. told me that Robert Burns was his favorite poet, but I said that I felt more at home with Edward Thomas and Robert Frost. These were new names to him. He explained that he was really out of touch with the literature of the last twenty years or so. He was too busy with his own work and letter writing. He admitted that once he had ploughed through D. H. Lawrence's *Sons and Lovers* but found this dreary. At this time he was dipping much into Doughty and enjoyed above all his long poem. His chief interests were, of course, longevity and stories of saints; the *Life of Saint Bernard* was always by his side. He said: "In my *Back to Methuselah* the advocates of longer life all die, and the survivors find it just happens to them to their own puzzlement and surprise. As an advocate of a longer life for man I cannot expect to live to an old age myself. I have already left my old selves behind. They are dead and done with. However, I am still able to acquire a new self. With me the critical ages have been forty, sixty and eighty, and if I can leap over the hundred, a difficult stile to take, then I'll be well away for the three hundred. I will not admit a limit to human life except the fatal accident, of course. Death is not natural."

"In your case the circumstances are propitious; your parents lived long, you have disciplined yourself into cautious living, and you have all the things which sustain life, both materially and mentally."

But Shaw waved his tray of gifts aside with a wide sweep of his hand and exclaimed in a loud voice:

"You're talking absolute nonsense! I am not a free man. No millionaire is a free man. I would like to bake my own bread but I must not enter the kitchen. I'd like to take my coat off and help in the washing up, but what would my house-keeper say? She would walk out and refuse to work for a man who was not a gentleman. I have to accept their conditions. It was bad enough when I introduced the William Morris habit of no tablecloth for meals; for as you know I never use a table-cloth for meals."

"But that is almost a universal practice now."

"Is it? When I did it it was considered as immoral as nudism. I also wanted to introduce the Morris habit of hanging the carpet on the walls instead of on the floor, but the servants wouldn't budge on that point because I hadn't the physical attributes necessary for walking up the wall. To get my money I have to play up to the public and to spend it I have to play down to the servants. It's a hard life, mine, let me tell you, to be a *marchand de plaisir*."

I could not help remarking: "Especially for a person who takes life seriously."

"I have not yet reached my serious years. I'm still a child, boyishly interested in photography, pseudoscientific fairy tales, and pictures of imaginary life. Give a man a mere hundred years to live and he sings let us eat and drink, for tomorrow we die. But give him three hundred years and he becomes a new man, all his valuations change. You see our conduct is influenced not by our experience but by our expectation of life. I take life sufficiently seriously to want more of it even though I find it so horrible. We are told that when Jehovah created the world He saw that it was good. What would He say now? Tastes have changed, thanks mainly to me."

He did not for a moment convince me that he was finding life horrible, but when he seemed to be enjoying himself most he often came out with this note of self-pity to remind me that he was a human being after all.

Wasn't it Johnson who reminded us that there is a wicked inclination in most people to suppose that an old man decayed in his intellect? If a young man when leaving a company does not recollect where he laid his hat, it is nothing; but if the same forgetfulness is discovered in an old man, people will shrug up their shoulders and say his memory is going.

I did not notice such a decline in G.B.S. He was still as mischievous and wicked as ever. I often forgot his years and rather think he forgot mine. What he will be like at two hundred I will not live to know. . . .

When I heard that the rector had died I felt that a light had gone out of the village. His presence here was as native as the trees and the hills, and I knew that the flowers in his garden would miss him. G.B.S. told me of a vicar who had moved into a poor laborer's cottage because he wished to identify himself more closely with the poor, but at once he lost caste, especially with the poor. The bishop complained of the vicar's most irregular action, and though the good parson himself felt nearer to God, he found himself getting further and further from the Church.

"Very few people can afford to be poor. I have been living the simple life for years, but I had to marry wealth to afford it. That is why rectors are given mansions, which drive them into such expense that they are poorer than the poor. That is how I got my house, which is a rectory. There are certain tokens of wealth which one must show to be admitted into the inner ring; even if you are happy with a diet of bread and cheese, a table must be spread as for a Lord Mayor's banquet, an army of servants must be kept, and you must be called away on 'urgent business' so that you may eat your simple sandwich beneath the tree."

"The rector was a good man . . ." I began.

He almost jumped from his seat. "I tell you if I spent my time being good I'd soon be reduced to penury and dependent on evil people. I am besieged every day with begging letters from persons whose goodness has betrayed them into becoming unemployables and parasites. I find I have to print special post cards to stop them pestering me. Learn how to refuse giving and develop the gentle art of saying *No*. I have always gone about my business as if I had not a friend in the world."

This modest advice did not impress me much. I had learned to enjoy such assertions as I enjoyed abstract art, that is, without relationship to fact. I remembered the host of friends. I thought of Lee, of his mother, of William Archer, of his German translator, of Grein, of the Webbs, of the Murrays, of Granville-Barker, of William Morris, of Charlotte—only a few among hundreds. That very day he had received a generous parcel of unobtainable food from an admiring stranger.

He went on: "Of course, when I had already proved my worth they all came to me; but not as quickly as if I had been worthless." He refused to be sentimental about death and denounced earth burial.

"I know something about it," he declared. "I will not need an inch of soil to be buried in. As a nephew of the founder of Mount Jerome Cemetery, I know too much about earth burial to contemplate such a horror. It should be made a criminal offense."

When he heard that the Bishop of St. Albans was to officiate at the induction of a new rector he put on his black suit and sat right through the service. What he thought about it I do not know. All he said to me was: "The Bishop once invited Charlotte and me to dinner, and I had to tell him that like Daniel I was vegetarian but my wife was carnivorous. He is a very charming man; there is not a thing we agree about."

10

I heard in a talk on Bernard Shaw that you know his characters Joan, Candida, Eliza, Undershaft, Marchbanks, Tanner, better than your own neighbor and certainly better than yourself. In my particular case Bernard Shaw is my neighbor.

When I was a young boy at school I was given a ticket by a famous pianist, a friend of the family, and sat beside Bernard Shaw in the Queen's Hall. I liked his knickerbocker suit, though I had discarded mine by that time. His red tie must have been like a red rag to a bull to the pianist. I carried away his intent look and poise as he listened to the Beethoven Pianoforte Concerto. He must have been hearing it for the hundredth time; I was hearing it for the first time. Now we again sat together, listening to the Ninth: the same poise, the same intent look. . . .

He said: "I am highly susceptible to the force of all truly religious music, especially to the music of my own church, the church of Shelley, Michelangelo, and Beethoven."

I recalled my boyhood experience and remarked that he then seemed the happiest man on earth.

"Why not?" he answered, "I had achieved my greatest ambition. Everywhere I was considered the devil incarnate. I was abused, vilified, censored, and suppressed to the limit of possibility. I got nothing for nothing, and very little for a halfpenny. If that isn't happiness, what is?"

"I remember queuing up for hours to see your plays."

"You mean the Barker season at the Court when they did Murray, Barker, Galsworthy, Ibsen and myself. You could have had the stalls all to yourself. It gave me something to do, as I had just been kicked out of St. Pancras. I wasn't bottom of the poll; my colleague, Sir William Geary, had that distinction. I should have expected that result because in my election address I did not ask them to vote for me but to vote according to their judgment, and I made the outrageous suggestion that it was better and more economical for the ratepayer to pay a shilling more to the rate collector than a pound to the doctor. I even demonstrated that good sanitation can do more good than vaccination. I was innocent enough to believe that I could defy the superstitious reverence for the pill and the serum. I don't suppose I would have polled a single vote if it had come to the ears of any constituent that I was a playwright, that I had written *Mrs. Warren's Profession!* I attended the meetings so regularly and seemed so absorbed in drains that I couldn't possibly be interested in other things."

"I am surprised that you didn't stand for Parliament."

"I was too busy getting other people in to worry about myself. I have made it so perfectly clear in my tracts, articles, and books what was to be done that all Parliament has had to do was to read my works and do the opposite. I have never been a man for clubs, and I have always disliked talk for talk's sake, as I have condemned art for art's sake and food for food's sake. There was a certain councillor, a progressive like myself, who kept a tailor shop of the old-fashioned kind; he made up goods on the premises and sold them to the public direct. By the premises I mean a poky little shop with a workroom in the cellar underneath. He and his daughters worked by gaslight in this dark, damp room, and it never occurred to the man that it was murderous for those girls and suicide for him. I tried to bring him to his senses, but he couldn't see that there was anything wrong in working himself to death for a living as long as he was independent and above all could speak his mind. I used to call him the worst sweater in London and a scoundrel, though politically we agreed. However, he did install electric light instead of gaslight and cut down the working hours to eleven P.M. instead of midnight, though I shouldn't be surprised they got up a couple of hours earlier to make up the time. I couldn't make the man see that his daughters needed a holiday, and so did he, for the matter of that. Our movement was made up substantially of that kind of person."

As he spoke I thought of this family so typical in the slums, as Beatrice Webb had herself discovered by actually working in a sweater's den, eking out a bare subsistence, being ultimately crushed by a more ruthless competitor. What did that little hard-pressed tailor think of the bearded "terror," as he was known, who lectured him and swore at him and suggested holidays, of all things?

"I had just returned from Rome where I had seen the Sistine Chapel, and it horrified me to see one daughter, poor girl, from a charming young girl going fast into consumption. She had lost every vestige of color while I was away, and there was no doubt she could not live long. But the father would not see it."

G.B.S. did not tell me what I had heard from another source —that he was prepared to cover the cost of a generous holiday anonymously.

Twenty years ago, at the height of his fame, when *Saint Joan* established him as immortal, I took the chair for him at one of his large meetings, and I had the opportunity of watching the audience. It was a lecture on the literature of the drama, the kind of subject that ordinarily drew a few note-greedy students, but here a thousand people were held spell-bound by his voice. He would have held them even if he were reciting his new alphabet backward. When I thanked him he said:

"I'd rather be talking Socialism. I get invitations from all over the world to talk on the drama and I always refuse. But it is difficult to refuse to talk to a half-dozen people in an out-of-the-way industrial town on something to do with economics. If they want drama they can always go to my plays. Repertory theaters and amateur societies are all over the place now, but for Socialism I have to go to them. That's how I derived my education from the uneducated."

That was quite true. At these little meetings everything was thrashed out; they were convinced that the way to truth was through argument, and nothing was held sacred except this search for truth. They discussed morality, justice, freedom, sex, nationalism, everything. Bebel, the Socialist leader in Germany, had written a book on *Woman*, which turned, in its quiet, logical way, all our conceptions and prejudices inside out. Havelock Ellis had written his monumental book on the *Psychology of Sex*, banned in this country as immoral and considered by the progressive people as the greatest moral influence of the day. Then there was Edward Carpenter's *Love's Coming of Age* and *Civilisation: Its Cause and Cure*; and *Widowers' Houses* by that Museum bookworm, George Bernard Shaw.

"It was William Archer who set me going on the straight and narrow path of drama. We co-operated; he could work out plots, and I did the talking parts, but soon the talk left the plot far behind and, like Oliver Twist, I had to go to Archer for 'more and more and more.' He, however, was not equal to the strain, so I degenerated into leaving out the plot altogether and making my plays all talk. I discovered that it worked very well. For a man like myself who knows how to talk there is no need for a plot. It didn't take away from my enjoyment of the highly conventional form of the Greek drama as translated by Gilbert Murray or the well-made plays of Ibsen. I had something new to give and I gave it."

Those were the days of innovation and inner conflict. Salt and Joynes left their secure, highly respected jobs at Eton to do the far-from-secure and not-at-all respected propaganda for humanitarianism; Edward Carpenter, destined for a bishopric, made sandals while clerks and civil servants took to land work or crafts on "principle"; and in the Socialist movement the manual worker was venerated as a hero if he ever could pluck up courage and attend the conclave of intellectuals. It could almost be said that the intellectual, so intent on talking, had really no faith in intellect or talk and instinctively felt for the mechanic and the laborer. Shaw brought much laughter and gusto into the ranks and yet remained strangely unattached. I told him that a friend of mine who knew him well in those days summed him up as follows: "He is most convincing while he is talking, but the moment he sits down you find he has contributed nothing new to the discussion." G.B.S. agreed with this statement. He said: "This mania for originality appals me. An original thought only comes once in a century or so, if that, and they want me to do in five minutes what originally took five hundred years. It can't be done, for even I find that I have to repeat myself. Then again, an original thought doesn't sink in immediately, and you have to say it again and again, and it takes anything up to fifty years for it to germinate."

And yet, when we talked about Walt Whitman's *Leaves of Grass* and Richard Jeffries' *Story of My Heart*, he said:

"In the same way as I made it impossible for a dramatist to get away with the old kind of stuff, so these two people did away with any interest in rhyming and playing at verse. They proved that poetry is at its best when it is incorporated into prose, whether you split it up into line-lengths, as Whitman did, or let it remain prose, as in Jeffries' or my work."

Hyndman once spent a lunch hour with us denouncing Shaw as a man who would sell the movement for a laugh. But Hyndman held all laughter suspect. He was then the leader of the Social Democratic Federation, the proletarian wing of the Socialist Party, and he, with high hat, frock coat, and impressive white beard looked every inch a proletarian leader. It was the S.D.F. and not the bourgeois Fabian Society that attracted people like.William Morris, Walter Crane, Cunninghame Graham, and the Countess of Warwick. G.B.S. had a foot in both camps.

"Talking of the Fabians," he said, "they were Philistines. Ruskin's name was hardly mentioned. My colleagues did not seem conscious of Oscar Wilde's *The Soul of Man Under Socialism* or even Morris' *News from Nowhere* and seemed to suspect people associated with art. Perhaps it was better so. The artist should keep out of these organizations unless he can, like myself, tackle music, art, philosophy, science, and economics in his stride. For me they were one and the same thing. When I wrote music criticism for the *Star* I threatened my readers to take to playwriting if I could stoop so low. Have you noticed that when new repertory companies promise to do only contemporary plays they mean plays of mine written fifty or sixty years ago?"

"When I was young and full of years," he said, looking me right in the eyes, "I consulted a sage that I might achieve the formation of a perfect character. 'Young man,' he said, 'are you a vegetarian?' I promptly answered, 'Yes.' This took him aback; he asked a second question which surprised me. 'Have you mastered shorthand?' I told him that I could write it very nearly as fast as longhand, but I could not read it. That impressed him. 'Young man,' he went on, 'you are indeed high

on the Mount of Wisdom. There remains but one more accom-
plishment which as an artist is obviously destined for you: a
a life of poverty.' I fled without turning in case I was converted
into a pillar of salt. I was determined henceforth to prove that
it is possible to form a perfect character without poverty!"

I had never met Walt Whitman, but Edward Carpenter, who
stayed with him, told me much about him. He was, it seems,
an unworldly, unselfish, democratic man and full of charity
and goodwill to everyone, the impulsive writer who loved life
and all living creatures. I thought of this man as G.B.S. was
telling me about the burial of Thomas Hardy in Westminster
Abbey. He was saying:

"I had a chance of having a long chat with Edmund Gosse,
and a little flattery got him round far enough to tell me a story
of how he managed to see Walt Whitman with the aid of a
charming girl. Gosse was on a ferry when this girl offered to
take him to Walt Whitman because there could be no other
reason for his presence on the ferry. It must have been strange
to see this dapper Englishman in this out-of-the-way place.
When they found the door locked and could get no answer
she suggested that they climb the wall into a window and so
get into the house that way. Poor Gosse was shocked, but as
it seemed his only hope to get at the man he permitted her to
persuade him to rise to the occasion. They found Whitman at
his desk, just as she had said! Now, I have arranged for my
servants to guard me like bull dogs and I go down to my
shelter so that no one can get at me. It wouldn't do for a

stranger to discover me asleep with my mouth open. I would never have got through all that writing if I allowed curiosity mongers from all over the world to disturb me. Once, however, a man did overcome all obstacles. There was no attempt at climbing through a window. An Eastern had arrived at my door, in full regalia. When my maid answered the door he stood motionless and without a sound. The maid informed him that I was out, but he made no movement. She explained then that I was hard at work and not to be disturbed. He did not understand a word. Nonplused, she had to let him into the sitting room, where he bowed and stood in the way Easterns have, in those embroidered clothes of his. She had to come for me, and the moment I entered he shook my hand warmly and spoke perfect English as only Easterns can do!"

"Didn't Ellen Terry have a similar experience?" I asked. "When she was doing the sleepwalking scene in *Macbeth*, suddenly, on the stage, appeared just such a man, with a great bouquet of roses. He was so charmed with her that he paid the usual tribute. The audience, thinking it was Henry Irving in a new disguise, loudly applauded this celestial addition to Shakespeare, but the scene was not repeated."

This brought up the story not of a silent visitor but of a loquacious German. He came to their London flat.

"I asked Charlotte to prevent him seeing me at all costs, because I didn't want to be disturbed. Charlotte went out to him, and he started talking and she couldn't stop him. Every time she opened her mouth, she only accelerated his flow of speech. She had to give up and come for me to deal with him.

I meant to fling him out of the window, but he had already started his oration, and the upshot of it all was that he was given permission to translate my works into German, and that was the beginning of my great success. My failure in this instance proved my success."

11

When I told G.B.S. of the long queues to be seen outside a vegetarian restaurant and the large number of people who registered as vegetarians, he asked me if I remembered the kind of meals mentioned in *Pepys' Diary*. He said:

"They consumed the whole animal kingdom at each meal. Small wonder they were too old at thirty. Give Man a chance and he will do everything to destroy himself and laugh at his own imbecility. It is a good sign that corpulence and intoxication are no longer considered subjects of mirth but are now considered either a disease or a breach of good manners. I myself am seriously contemplating reducing my meals to two a day and perhaps have one fast day a week."

It is a long time since I have peeped at *Pepys' Diary*, but I had picked up a book of Tennyson. I was always picking up old books with the hope of repeating my first rapture. Here is his description of a picnic:

"There on the slope of orchard, Francis laid
A damask napkin wrought with horse and hound;
Brought out a dusky loaf that smelt of home,
And, half cut down, a pasty costly made,
Where quail and pigeon, lark and leveret, lay
Like fossils on the rock, with golden yolks
Imbeddied and injellied."

"That's just what I expected of Tennyson," Shaw said in disgust. I had to say something in Tennyson's favor. I reminded him how kind Tennyson had been to Ellen Terry, how he pointed out the beauty of nature to her and told her the names of birds and flowers.

"I should think so. She was an extremely beautiful girl and as innocent as a rose. When Watts kissed her, she took for granted she was going to have a baby. But to return to diet, I suppose I have stayed the course longer than any other vegetarian."

"There must be many Indians who have beaten you."

"I mean converted vegetarians. There are people who give it up in a week, others after twenty years. I haven't the least desire for meat or fish. When I dined out I tried to cause as little inconvenience as possible, but I made it clear I did not favor their delicacies."

I told of an American dramatist who was having a season of his plays in England. He was our guest while in this country and we were invited to dine with an editor. The table was spread with every kind of meat and fish. It was a gorgeous banquet fit for a king. My friend looked round anxiously and quietly said: "Have you a tomato? That is all I eat . . . with a piece of bread." The editor looked at his wife, and she looked hopelessly at him. They had to send for a piece of cheese and tomatoes while they themselves feasted to their hearts' content on fish and meat.

"I always regard a meal as a nuisance when people come to talk. Luckily the rationing has put a stop to all this entertaining, because people now accept such an excuse."

"The difficulty is that vegetarians, who are generally extremely social creatures, find themselves apart from their fellows because their diet is different. That is so in schools and colleges and in many boardinghouses. At Cambridge the vegetarian has to proclaim it each time a meal is served, and then he is given the potatoes and vegetables without the meat, but instead of the meat they double the portion of potatoes. Hospitals are even worse."

"What do doctors know about diet! They thrive on the ignorance of the people. When doctors themselves are ill they invariably go to a naturopath, but the trouble is they go back to their original diet when they are healed."

"On the whole there is a great improvement in diet. The war has taught people that it is possible to survive without meat."

"Do you know whether Prince Kropotkin was a vegetarian? General Booth was, and so is Churchill's chief scientific adviser, I hear."

"I am not sure of Kropotkin."

"I knew Kropotkin and I regard him next to William Morris as the saint of the century. His theory of mutual aid certainly put Darwin in his place. The Prince owed his first impulse toward a higher development to his teacher of literature, and this is how it came about. When he was in the Corps of Pages the inspector of the educational department hit upon a wise and successful plan of getting this rather uproarious class to study. Instead of indifferent teachers who formerly used to teach in the lower forms, he endeavored to secure first-rate men. He invited a great classical scholar and an expert in literature to teach a rather unruly class of juniors. When the professor came in for his first lesson he told them in a low voice that as he was just recovered from an illness he could not raise his voice and invited the students to approach nearer. They came, and as his voice dropped, they sat close to him and hung on his lips. The ice had been broken. When the inspector opened the classroom door he found them absorbed, and so he turned away lest he disturb them. The best teachers should go to primary schools. That's where we need them most. If we had proper teaching and pleasant schools, the inattentive and disorderly child could be sufficiently intimidated by the fear of being sent home, where a child is never happy."

Why was Tinkerbell so vociferous and why must he let the whole village know that G.B.S. was knocking at the door? The cat, on the other hand, was completely indifferent. She was lying snug on her favorite cushion in the corner of the divan, and nothing was going to move her. G.B.S. found his favorite seat occupied and stood contemplating the situation. He said resignedly: "Oh, I can sit anywhere, the harder the seat the better," and remained standing. Not for long. We lifted

Fuzzia bodily, rolled up as she was, and put her in one of the low chairs, and G.B.S. smiled happily as he sat down.

"There is a kind of understanding between animals and myself," he said. But we noticed that instead of treating them as wise, knowing companions, as Walter Pater did, and having them about him, G.B.S. chattered nonsensical sounds to them, and so they tolerated him as they would a child.

He reverted to the conversation we had had **previously**, as though he had been thinking much about it.

"Did the name of Prince Kropotkin," he asked, "ring a bell? Or is he, like so many of the people I mentioned, a forgotten figure of the past? I've been asked to write a key to my plays because I introduce so many people who were household names in my time, when the play was written, and they are now completely forgotten. I was asked the other day by a young person: who was Balfour? And as to Walkley and Gilbert Cannan, whom I use in *Fanny's First Play*, they might have not existed. I daresay it will not be long before people will say: 'Who was this Shaw?'"

"Hasn't one of the judges already asked that question in court?"

"I didn't know. Do you remember who it was?"

"It was some time ago, and I have forgotten *his* name."

"There is nobody," he answered, brushing the subject aside, "more ignorant than a person who is always right, and that is why I am sorry for judges and people of that kind. Now, Prince Kropotkin was a different kind of person. Though he was one of the great scholars of the day and certainly towered above

Darwin, and though he was a prince, he was the most simple and unassuming of all the people I had ever met."

"The name of Kropotkin," I had to say, "not only rings a bell but the very bells of heaven with me. As a boy I walked with him over the South Downs, and there for the first time learned of the difference between a newspaper conception of a man and the real man. He was built up by the Press as a desperate character, a terrorist with revolvers hidden in his pockets and all the time conspiring with similar criminals the downfall of all the things the world held sacred: property, royalty, government, morals, and freedom. I found him as you say, a man so filled with the social conscience that he could not bear the thought of anyone being poor or suffering. A tramp greeted us, and he took out all he had and gave it to him at once without question. When I remarked that this was not the way of solving the problem of poverty, he said: 'There are personal problems of conscience which are more important than all the great social problems. Tolstoy stopped his creative work because of a religious call, and I gave up my science because of the call of humanity, and how can a man help humanity if he is inhuman himself?' "

"Well, what was the result? He died in poverty."

"Why not? What does it matter how one dies? We are all the richer for his existence in the world."

"I suffer as much as he did, but I have taken the build-up of myself into my own hands. I shall leave nothing to chance."

"Have you ever heard, G.B.S., what Gorki thought of Tolstoy when he first met him and how disappointed he was that his hero should have used so many obscene expletives in his conversation?"

"That's interesting, because Gorki was a product of the doss house and the sweating den and Tolstoy of the Russian aristocracy, and it was Gorki who was shocked! You see, Tolstoy wanted to link himself with Gorki, while Gorki expected him to be the aristocrat and saint, and so the shock was all the greater! Now, W. H. Davies was a very refined man, and he came from the same class as Gorki."

"Yes, you must remember the poem Davies wrote on that very theme. I think he called it *Confession*:

'One hour in every hundred hours
I sing of childhood, birds and flowers;
Who reads my character in song
Will not see much in me that's wrong.
But in my ninety hours and nine
I would not tell what thoughts are mine;
They're not so pure as find their words
In songs of childhood, flowers and birds.' "

G.B.S. was amused. "Most poets and writers," he said, "prefer to show the ninety-nine hours nowadays and are ashamed of childhood, birds, and flowers. When I was on the Stage Society, James Joyce sent in his plays, and he always felt that they were not complete without a really good obscene act. That kind of thing bores me to tears. There are certain authors who have somehow been associated with obscenity; Oscar Wilde, for example. In all the years I knew him, I never heard him swear or say anything obscene. His wit was always a model of good taste. I always thought mine was, till the censor taught me otherwise. The poor old censor was shocked at the way I made a horse-thief talk, so unrefined. And yet the horse-thief came nearer to God than the almighty censor!"

"One of the most refined men I knew was the nephew of Sibelius who settled here in the Tolstoy colony. He was also a friend of Carpenter and the Garnetts, among many others. He said that the test of a man's character was best judged from his talk about women in private conversation."

"I don't think so. If one did that, there would never be any movements for world betterment, in the same way that you judge an artist's work by his talk and not his achievement."

"I don't think any artist can hide his personality. If he thinks meanly of women it will come through in his work. Look how the Italians deified their mistresses and made them immortal, as Madonnas."

"So you think," he chuckled, "that those good people who write pornographic plays or paint suggestive nudes do not lead respectable suburban lives! The distinction they covet most is to be appointed to the Watch Committee."

I brought out an old copy of a newspaper and read:

" 'Madame Grondhal is, in round numbers, forty; that is, she is in full maturity of her genius. And here you become curious about her personal appearance; you would like a little description. Well, she is what you would call, observe, what you would call, a perfectly plain woman. Her hair is not golden like yours: it is, I think, almost ashen: you would call it gray. Her figure and style are, well, quite slender, nothing in particular, nothing superb or Junonan; what can I say? Com-

Off to work

Going to lunch

*Fuzzia guards his hat
and muffler*

plexion? Quite Norwegian; no cream or coral, nothing to be afraid of there. Eyes? Well, eyes are a matter of opinion. I should rather like you to see them for yourself: they are *memorable*. A noble brow! But then, as you say, how unbecoming to a woman to have a noble brow! Would anybody look at you, if you were in the same room as she? Ah, there you have me. Frankly they would forget your very existence, even if there were no such thing in the world as a piano. For there is grace beside which your beauty is vulgar and your youth inadequate: and that grace is the secret of Madame Grondhal's charm.' "

"Who was this Madame Grondhal?" he asked. "Memory plays silly tricks with me nowadays." He held out his hand and I gave him the paper. It was a music criticism by Corno di Bassetto. He put the paper down at his side. Did his mind go back to the room with a piano and a crowd of primly behaved women in long dresses, and of men, bearded and formal? . . . But he said: "I remember being invited to an at-home of lions and lionesses, and there was one woman who seemed right out of it. A quiet, motherly woman she looked and very shy among these great ones. As no one else spoke to her I thought I would keep her company, but she found it very difficult to keep up conversation, and I had to do all the talking. Suddenly she interrupted me: 'I'm sorry I must go now, I am due to play at the Albert Hall.' She was the greatest pianist of the day."

A cold wind was blowing, and, wishing to accompany me, he went to the corner hat stand and from a whole history of hats and caps selected a black tweed cap; as to a stick, there were only a few to choose from and none of any distinctive design which we associate with the aesthetes of the nineties.

"Which way shall we go?" he asked, as if the selection were wide. There was the walk through the village and on through the park; there was the walk along the grove and back and past our house and across the fields, with wide vistas. "I'd like to see where the bomb dropped," he said. He referred to an incendiary that had fallen recently on a rainy night. When we came to the place there was no impression left. The weeds had made a rapid disguise, and no black blot on the landscape could be found.

"Ayot Saint Lawrence," I said, "already has its ruins, why do we need more?"

"Soon this country will be visited only for its ruins. There is one thing, they can't put down the demolition of the abbey here to me as they once put down a cathedral fire to the fact that Darwin had passed through the town. It is amazing how quickly people settle into a war and accept it as a matter of fact, as they once accepted bad drainage, in spite of the smells and the hideous deaths. There are some stupid writers who talk in a romantic way about the smells of a town, as a dog would if he could express himself while examining the excreta along the roads. I've spent most of my life smashing romance: the romance of poverty, the romance of love, the romance of home, the romance of suffering. The world will never be the same again because I have educated four generations to see things as they are, and not what they imagine them to be or want them to be. I can recall the moment when I shed poverty like an infected cloak. I had a speaking engagement and as usual dashed after a bus only to see it go off. I began to walk to save money and suddenly stopped short. I realized that I did not need to save twopence. I could now afford half a crown for a taxi. I jumped into a taxi and arrived in style. However much the Socialists run down the wicked bourgeois, they rather like to feel that, like the poor, the bourgeois are always with them.",

Suddenly he stopped dead and faced me. "Do you think," he asked, "the young are interested in my work?" He waited for the reply with stick in the air, as though to proclaim himself above defeat.

"The young and your generation have very much in common."

He dropped his stick, half in anger.

"So you think me typical of my generation? You have only to look at the copies of *Punch* of the day, to see how people like Annie Besant, William Morris, and John Burns were hated more than foreigners, and look up the files of *Truth* to see what lies they, the typical people, were prepared to print about us! I represented a small minority and was best when I was in the minority of one. Do you remember the mean tricks the respectable reactionaries resorted to to throw the progressives out of power in London? The horrid figure on the poster representing us, pointing a finger at every passer-by with the threat: 'It's your money we want!' I loathed and despised my generation. I have caused millions to laugh their way of life out of existence, and I have no doubt I shall succeed."

He pushed his cap over one eye, a way he has, and added: "I want to be remembered like Mozart and Michelangelo."

A farm laborer passed and greeted us.

"Who was he?" G.B.S. asked in a whisper. "He seemed to know me."

12

I had never seen G.B.S. so jubilant. He almost danced a jig on the lawn as he came tripping in. What good news had he to tell? Had Hitler committed suicide? Had we entered Germany? No. It was not long before he told me that he had succeeded in healing a person by post. An unknown Manchester man had written to him, asking about this vegetarianism, mentioning in passing that he was far from well. So many people have tried every other way to health and only when the orthodox doctor has failed do they turn to the radical change demanded by vegetarianism. In answering, Bernard Shaw advised the open window and brown bread. A month or so later he heard that the miracle had happened, because the man was cured of his trouble!

"I couldn't, of course, advise a real change of diet, because my diet may not suit the person in Manchester. Salads and fruit are no good for me because they produce in me the very symptoms they are supposed to cure."

He saw my look of surprise—for he had often grumbled that he could not get those very things at his own table—but he realized that he was not talking to the world at large and at once followed it up with: "Of course, you people know how to prepare salad dishes, but the other people are as frightened of fresh things as they are of new ideas."

I pointed out that the clinics and doctors were wiser now and not only was fruit advised but fruit juices were actually distributed free to mothers and children.

"Ah! And what about old people?" he asked, "Soon there will be few old people. Men are now much younger and more vigorous at sixty than they were at forty. It is nothing for them to expect people to stay on at their work till seventy. Women in fact are younger at fifty than they used to be at thirty. I put this down to the fact that they consume less and less meat and eat more sensibly on the whole. It needed a war to knock sense into people. A few more wars and we will grow into a nice vegetarian brotherhood. The quicker the better."

Whenever a voice was raised in the Commons bemoaning the lack of meat, the Ministry of Health came forward with statistics to prove that we were healthier and more immune from infection.

"I must tell you," I said, "that a man I knew who lived on unfired food challenged the hospitals to infect him with any foul disease and he would prove himself immune. This was tried at one of the hospitals and he came out as healthy as ever."

"I know. When I suggested these measures fifty years ago on the vestry, one old doctor shouted that the members should take no notice of 'that scoundrel over there.' Better to be thought a scoundrel than a clown. Margot Asquith, the woman with the big chin, insisted on regarding me as a clown even when I was the greatest political force in the world. I suppose it was because I did not drink. She was a strange woman. At lunch she would dig her chin into my shoulder and in that way made a very deep impression on me. Her husband will be remembered as a character in my play *Back to Methuselah*, but otherwise completely as characterless. In a Cabinet of scholars, John Burns, the worker, was the best-read of the lot of them. And his reading was only a form of snobbery. He liked to have books round him as a newly rich likes to have antiques. John Burns and I passed a restaurant one day, and we both saw a decorated menu. John Burns lost his head about a feeble little decoration of a robin and a bit of holly. 'William Morris would like this,' he said. As if it were the last thing in art! The poor man wept over Hood's *Song of the Shirt* and *The Bridge of Sighs*, as Asquith and King Edward wept over Marie Corelli's *Sorrows of Satan*. Those were the days, by the way, when we bred strong, silent men personified by Sir Edward Grey, who knew nothing about people and everything about birds. John Morley missed his chance in discovering a great novelist in my person and consoled himself ever after that with a mere secretaryship for India. Parliamentary speeches were so dull that newspapers gave whole pages to reporting them, often even condensing murder trials and divorces to find room for these trivialities."

The conversation was flowing rather inconsequentially;

Margot's chin bringing up a painful flow of memories and taking us away from his triumph in healing!

I could not help asking him something which has always puzzled me: "How is it that after all these years you, the most persuasive man alive, have not converted your own wife, nor any of the people in your service, nor any of your fans, to vegetarianism?"

"William Morris used to say: 'I don't know who are the best people to educate the young; but this I am certain, the parents are the very worst.' This is also true about husbands educating wives and wives influencing husbands, and it is doubly true about an oracle influencing his fans. Tell me a man is a Shavian and I will run from him as from a plague. Charlotte tried it out for a little while but she soon gave it up. You see, as Charlotte eats the standard diet I generally have to put up with anything that's going, leaving out flesh, fish, or fowl. Everything I eat has been proved by some doctor or other to be a deadly poison, and everything I don't eat has been proved to be indispensable for life. But that's also true as to everything I say and write. But I go marching on."

All at once he looked searchingly at me.

"You haven't a bad face, but you should cut your hair more often. Appearance is everything. I myself get my chauffeur to take me regularly to the barber, and he does it to my liking; just as I have trained him to do. As my face is known to the world and is part and parcel of my extensive publicity, it is most important that I keep it up to expectation. I almost think that if my beard and eyebrows and mustache had no face to hold them together, they would still get away with it. Appear-

ance is everything. That is why I have to live in Whitehall
Court, have a Rolls-Royce driven by a chauffeur, and a uni-
formed maid to open the door. We have a splendid view from
Whitehall Court flat, spoiled only by the Houses of Parliament,
which I have visited only once in my life and that in my capacity as an art critic to examine some fading murals. They
say appearances are deceptive, but deception is half the battle
for a sincere man who does not want to be beaten into impotency. Sidney Webb was the only man I know who was always against façade; it was he who declared that Ramsay
MacDonald was all façade and nothing behind it."

He sat down without a word. His face was white and drawn.
We guessed that he needed quiet and therefore brought out
books on art, which he examined with the greatest of care. He
knew few of the modern names, showed an antipathy to abstract work, and confused Picasso with Pissarro.

"Old Camille Pissarro was an excellent artist but [turning
to Picasso's work] what a son!"

He was obviously thinking of Pablo and not Lucien and
blamed the latter for indulging in abstract pattern to deceive
an ignorant public. He visualized Lucien Pissarro as a young,
irresponsible, irrepressible fellow with a great but indulgent
father. I showed him a photograph of Lucien with long gray
beard. G.B.S. smiled and said:

"That's where men have the advantage. They can always
grow a beard to cover a chin. I myself am not too good without a beard. I have a nasty jowl which needs softening with
natural hair." Again he denounced Lucien as one who ought

to know better. I explained that he was a personal friend, a hard, conscientious worker, the nearest person we have to William Morris in this country. I told G.B.S. of the wonderful friendship that existed between father and son and quoted a letter from Camille to Lucien:

" 'Remember that I have a rustic, melancholy temperament, that I am coarse and wild in appearance, it is only after a long time that I can appeal to anyone if the person who looks at me has a little indulgence. But the passer-by passes too cursory a glance and goes on . . . .' "

G.B.S. said: "When I was an art critic I recognized the moment I saw the work of the impressionists that a new vision and a new vitality had entered art. When an artist's work produces violent controversy people are apt to regard it with that sort of seriousness which is very appropriately called deadly. The same sort of thing happened in literature and the theater: they were almost done to death by the earnest disciples. Be earnest, certainly, but if you believe in a thing you can laugh at it. Atheists, whose religion is that there is no God, laugh at God and end up as theosophists. Do you remember St. John Ervine's story, when he and Galsworthy were watching a performance of my play? They were suddenly harangued by a funeral mute, an earnest student of the drama. He must have entered the theater after depositing a body in a cellar. He pointed to the dozen persons in the theater and exclaimed: 'And even these don't take it seriously!' Three blows of the mallet were heard, the artistic substitute for the orchestra, and the play was resumed."

I thought that the best bit of pungent criticism I had ever

read was of Courbet by Alexandre Dumas, fils; I read it to
G.B.S.:

" 'From what fabulous crossing of a slug with a peacock,
from what genital antitheses, from what sebaceous oozing can
have been generated, for instance, this thing called Mr. Gustave Courbet? Under what gardener's bell, with the help of
what manure, as a result of what mixture of wine, beer, corro-
sive mucus and a flatulent oedema can have grown this sono-
rous and hairy pumpkin, this aesthetic belly, this imbecilic
and impotent incarnation of the Self? Wouldn't one say he
was the force of God, if God, whom this nonbeing has wanted
to destroy, were capable of playing pranks, and could have
mixed Himself up with this?' "

G.B.S. laughed and thought it good stuff. "It was no doubt
the making of Courbet," he said. "Philosophically Dumas was
all wrong. God is capable of playing pranks, and He's always
mixing Himself up with artists. It's the only company He cares
to keep. All the same, I'm all out for a healthy Philistinism
which will laugh, though not urgently, at the mystic preten-
sions of our workers in paint, in stone, or in print."

"You prefer to think of yourself as a 'healthy' Philistine?"

He dropped his head and made up his mind quickly. "How
else," he answered, "is one to be free from the diseased lan-
guor of aestheticism?"

In that phrase I saw the *Yellow Book*, and the artists and
writers Max pilloried so tenderly.

"You know," he continued, "Dumas could have said all that
of Rodin's sculpture, or of my work, or, compositely, or
Rodin's sculpture of me. Rodin was an extraordinary man

really. He liked to work in his garden, and whenever he wanted anything moved he would call the nearest person, even the postman, to help him lift the sculpture, and the amazing thing was that he did it! We got on very well together. He could not speak English and I could not speak French, so conversation was smooth, as I did all the talking. He was really uneducated and like Anatole France had never heard of me before my wife asked him to do a bust of me. I don't think he had even heard of William Morris. He lived in grand style in a mansion with a large garden and a factotum who ran all his affairs very efficiently for him."

"You mean Rilke, the poet?"

"Was he a poet?" He was obviously taken aback. I waited to hear something about Rilke but he had nothing to say about him.

"Rodin was a very good draftsman," he continued, "and Charlotte, who managed to get round everybody, impressed him enough for him to give her one of his drawings, a nude, but he was delicate enough to drape this drawing before he presented it, in deference to my wife's modesty. Which reminds me of a sweet story about Ruskin.

"He had heard that a lady whom he had loved in his youth was dying, and he expressed a desire to see her. The reply came that he could only see her if he said that he loved God more than her. He did not go."

"It was well," I said, "that Ruskin didn't see her."

"I had a similar experience with Janet Achurch. My last meeting with her was at the Court Theatre. I had not seen her for ages, and I made an odd mistake. I went into the wrong room and found three women dressing; I went straight to the one made up as an old woman and kissed her hand. She was obviously surprised and quietly directed me to the next landing."

"Did Janet make you promise to put God before her?" I asked.

"No, it was I who was always preaching religion. Look how religion transformed Annie Besant. Mrs. Besant, the secularist, became coarser and stouter every year, while as a theosophist she became a teetotaller and vegetarian and looked quite attractive in her white robes. Annie had no taste. She bought an umbrella for me: it was so ugly that I wouldn't be seen at a funeral with it. I returned it to her, and she threw it over a fence in Regent's Park. To tease her, I did a drawing of the field with lots of little umbrellas coming through."

"You are inclined to ride roughshod over people's feelings," I remarked.

"Well, I had to show the cloven hoof even if it was on the foot that was in the grave."

G.B.S. had been living with one foot in the grave, on and off, for more years than I can remember.

He was back again in France, going round the galleries, Charlotte at his side or more likely far behind, striding from room to room, from building to building, for they had to see everything there was to be seen and photograph whatever could be photographed.

"I always made a beeline for the best and left Charlotte behind breathless. She liked pretty things, mainly water colors, but I looked for ability. It must have been very trying for her. On the whole, I don't think she has found me too trying. I have always managed to surround her with interesting young men who naturally adored her. She is so unobtrusively thoughtful while I am inclined to ride roughshod over people's feelings. Granville-Barker and T. E. Lawrence were particular favorites of hers."

"I hear that Lawrence was so afraid of old age that he deliberately endangered his life at the height of his powers to lose it."

"He was a strange fellow. He thought that by changing his name to Shaw he wouldn't be recognized, Shaw being such a common name. He refused to grow up and avoided adult interests like religion and politics and went in for boyish adventures, like dressing up as an Arab, as Tolstoy dressed up in peasant garb."

"He had a love and appreciation of modern art."

"Isn't that," G.B.S. asked, "a sign of youth? When I was young I thought Wagner and Ibsen the last and the best. In fact, it was I who put them on the map, but now I can fit them nicely into their proper places. The young think only of the strong and the pretty. As an older man I realize that some of the most irresistible women are what the young think astonishingly ugly. When I was in Russia, I was determined to see Lenin's widow. Every difficulty was put in my way, but I got there ultimately—I always get what I want when I want it sufficiently—and I found this terribly ugly person the most attractive person I had ever met. We had a most interesting conversation, and she enjoyed it thoroughly. Perhaps that explains why I have always proved so irresistible to females. One day I'll have to settle down to writing an *Intelligent Woman's Guide to Bernard Shaw*. By the way, do they still spend their years at the art schools drawing from the nude, getting to the reality beneath the clothes?"

I mentioned that I had been down to Oxford and visited the Slade, and they were certainly concentrating on the nude.

"They used to call it the 'life class.' Young women posed in ridiculous and painful attitudes. What on earth could they learn from it? Life doesn't yield its secrets for half a crown an hour, or whatever they pay these lifeless creatures nowadays. I've posed nude to a photographer in the manner of Rodin's 'Thinker,' but I only looked constipated. I would suggest that the artist, if he is to achieve anything, should do bodies at work, hands that work, faces that have been lined. . . . Then again, a quick glance at the model is often enough. I think I have told you before how, at the British Museum, I saw a young lady working at one of the desks. Her expression interested me, and I instantly conceived the character and wrote the description of Agatha Wylie. I had never spoken to her and knew nothing whatever about her, and yet you would say I must have known her intimately. I once even invented a servant for one of my models and found afterward that he had just such a servant!"

"The thing that amuses me in portraiture is that people expect the artist to see with the unimaginative eye of the cursory spectator."

"You mean the artist is the only one who has normal vision. I once went to an eye specialist. When I feel for a little fling, the privilege of the rich, I go to a doctor so that I can pay him well for listening to me. Mistaking the object of my visit, he commenced to examine my eyes and after the most carefully conducted scrutiny gravely informed me that I had most abnormal vision. I laughed and told him of the natural method and therefore the latest method of dealing with the eyes, but he was not interested. 'And what is wrong with my eyes?' I asked. 'Absolutely nothing. That is why they are so abnormal,' he replied, and asked for an autograph, which I inscribed on a check."

"Never believe anything a person tells you about himself," G.B.S. said before he had even settled into his seat. "A man comes to believe in the end the lies he tell about himself to himself."

I knew by this introduction that he had something interesting to tell me. The scottie smiled and cocked up his ears, and the cat kept far from his feet. He settled in the corner, brushed his eyebrows with a tiny brush, refused refreshments, and continued his conversation:

"I was invited to a meal and my hostess warned me, knowing my shyness in company, that I would meet a very interesting person. I had been working hard all day, and the last thing I wanted was to meet an interesting person, who generally turns out to be a bore. I was ushered into a large room, full of very beautiful things, and there before me was the man I had deliberately avoided all my life. I was turning to go when my hostess appeared. She said, 'What do you think of this wonderful mirror which arrived today?' and looked in the direction of my deadly enemy. What could I say? I answered sweetly: 'William Morris hated mirrors. He didn't want to see his wretched dial wherever he went.' 'Oh, did he? It's a pity he didn't live to see yours instead,' she said. By the way," G.B.S. added as an afterthought, "she wore the loveliest stockings I had ever seen, and when I remarked about them she informed me that she was not wearing stockings but that her legs were hand-painted."

I think it was the carved mirror in our room that brought up this "memory." He went up to the mirror, curled his mustache, and looked defiantly at his image. He again settled down and went on.

"The girl Leigh [Vivien Leigh] was round today."

"Lady Hamilton? I forget how many times Winston Churchill has seen the film. I understand whenever he's depressed he restores his spirits in that way."

"It must be Nelson that attracts him! I thought of walking through the village with her to attract attention to myself. I was staying once in an island off the Adriatic with Gene Tunney, the boxer, and Richard Strauss, the composer. When all three of us walked together all eyes turned our way, but when Strauss and I walked alone, nobody took any notice of us. Very few people have an eye for greatness. Beatrice Webb was a great woman, if ever there was one, but my mother was never impressed with her. You see, Beatrice had the nervous habit of tearing up flowers, and my mother was a great lover of flowers. 'I don't see what you find in her,' my mother would say. And yet Beatrice loved flowers. Whenever we walked on the Downs she would pick great bunches of wild flowers, and

when thirsty call at a farm for a glass of milk and always be
turned away because the farmers mistook her for a gypsy."

G.B.S. asked me if I had ever met Arnold Bennett. He
said: "I don't get on too well with snobs."

"I didn't like his 'shop front,' but to his friends he was not
so sure of himself. He laughed at the self he showed to the
public."

"I was amused to hear," G.B.S. said, "that he concluded
that the great world was not interested in Wells because there
were no A1 people at the funeral of Mrs. Wells. I was there.
The fact is Wells, like myself, is not particularly interested in
the great world and the small fry who inhabit Babylonia. It
was I who advised H.G. to enter the furnace room. I urged
him to take the boys with him because it was so beautiful.
Wells went and was glad he went. Did you know that Wells was
once a dramatic critic? He was appointed because he had
never been in a theater. That's how most art critics are appointed. That's how we first met. I was sitting next to him, and
he seemed to know who I was. We walked home together, and
I admired him for the way he picked my brains. We've been
friends ever since, in spite of the fact that I hold that literary
men should never associate with one another unless they want
their minds to produce abortions. It's unavoidable in the case
of politicians, but all the same, have you ever known of an
idea coming from the House? And as to religion, where two or
three are gathered together they invariably talk business, if
they are not up to mischief. In a church I must be alone. When
I put this point to John Galsworthy, he entirely agreed with me

and got me to become a life member of the P.E.N. Club, an association of literary folk. Galsworthy was by far the shyest man I had ever met."

"I always wondered what happened when two shy people met."

"That is why we did not meet often. However irreverent I am, I couldn't be irreverent in his presence. It was I who put him on the map; he sent his *Silver Box* to the Court Theatre, and I knew I had discovered a dramatist, as different in style to mine as possible. I liked him, but I don't think he cared for me. He has never forgiven me for not backing his proposal that aircraft should not be used in war. I called it pious piffle."

That was in 1914, and now we were enjoying the spectacle of cities being wiped out from the air. Every day bombers came swooping over our chimneys, not disturbing Shaw's work but probably putting a full stop to a Shelley and a Beethoven elsewhere.

The incessant noise of planes made sleep impossible. True, in this little village no warnings were sounded to add to the tumult, but we could not hear the owls for the planes. G.B.S. managed to get in a wink or two during the day and I found myself sleeping even on the early morning journey to London. The carriages were always packed to suffocation, and we were never certain that we would get to our destination.

"Do you know," G.B.S. said, "I was once recommended by Horace Plunkett to take to flying as a cure for insomnia? He tried it and it worked. He was seventy-five and did fifteen miles in fifteen consecutive minutes two thousand feet up. Very good, almost as fast as a car. Prince Paul Troubetskoy used to drive me faster because he found it safer to be fast. If I took to flying, I wouldn't be happy till I was doing three hundred; the danger is that I may fall asleep while driving, though Plunkett found it exhilarating and not at all fatiguing after a few lessons. I must go for a joy ride again to see if I have an air stomach and nerves. Plunkett took over the machine after he had watched somebody else doing it and found it as easy as dropping a bomb. He kept the machine the right side up, which is more than the statesmen can do. The only difficulty he found was in landing. I don't think Charlotte would approve. As I've given up driving the car and swimming, I need some form of recreation, especially as it is safer in the air than on land and it cures insomnia."

He asked me what the train journeys were like nowadays, and when I mentioned that King's Cross was out of action and I had to use Finsbury Park, he said:

"A man of fashion only knew Hyde Park. The Regent's Park held the Zoo and the other places the riffraff in my days. You did not walk in Hyde Park when the season was over. If you did, you were regarded as a man lost to society, and that was all that mattered. I was to be found every season of the year in Hyde Park, because that was where I learned my English. As a foreigner I enjoyed ideas, and every idea was thrashed out in the Park. You could learn much more by mixing with the riffraff at Marble Arch in one hour than by a thousand walks from Hyde Park Corner to Albert Gate in the season. Besides, you could take your lectures lying down at Marble Arch. The green sward is the natural couch of man, and the people for whose sake you had to avoid everything that was natural were not to be seen."

I think he was feeling homesick for the Park.

13

I thought as I saw him striding rapidly along the bee-loud grove of Lamer Park how well he fitted into the rural scene. He liked to think of himself as a walking tree, he told me, and it was not a bad description. He was rushing from an extended tea with his other neighbor, Mr. Cherry-Garrard, where he drank milk, ate nothing, and talked, and I was also in a hurry to get home and have a hot bath. I had been firewatching in London and wanted to get clean again and to find a little sleep, if possible. I had just heard that a young friend, so-called gay and irresponsible, had been shot down in a raid on Berlin. This death suddenly made me afraid of my own company. Humankind cannot bear too much reality; I was not ready to think about death.

G.B.S. said: "They taught me to fox-trot at Lamer: Cherry played the dance music, and at the other end, not altogether out of it, stood Christ pointing to the hole in his hand."

If he had told me that Epstein's Christ that stood there had stepped out of His bronze shell and joined in the dance, it would not have surprised me; nothing surprised me. I had seen so much suffering and bravery, quiet, unremarked, and anonymous, that the very generality of these things tended to make me indifferent. I used to think that the aim of life was heightened sensitivity, but I could now see that you can reach a point of dispersal and at that point to be left with your own company is a dangerous thing. Bernard Shaw could be extremely insensitive to another's mood. He continued:

"Cherry-Garrard came back with a beard as white as mine when, as a young man, he went out with Captain Scott to the South Pole. And all to get a penguin's egg."

"And now by plane you can get there in no time."

"And if he had asked you, would you have advised him not to go?" G.B.S. asked.

"It's very easy to be wise after the fact. Doesn't he say in *The Worst Journey in the World* that he doesn't want to see it done again and feels disposed to make it a crime to ship men for the ice in vessels more fit to ply between London and Southend? I suppose there is something satisfying in having one's moral and physical powers tested to the full."

"Heroics! The whole thing could have been done in reasonable comfort. In this country everything has to be done with the maximum of discomfort. If you enjoy a thing, there must be something wrong with it. The only acceptable religion is one which condones poverty and suffering and the only thing which provokes laughter is another's distress! Anyhow, a man will do anything to become a schoolboy's hero, even play cricket."

He told me that Charlotte and he were going to stay in London because their housekeeper had to have an immediate operation. I urged that London was no place for them, but he only laughed.

"Have no fear on my account. Let it get about in Germany that I'm in London and they won't touch the place. Haven't I said that I entirely agree to the *Herrenvolk* idea? By all means let the Germans think they are the chosen people; I want the Negroes to think that the black face is the mark of a superior people, I want the Chinese to be convinced that only those with yellow skins are human, and, as to the Indians, it goes without saying that they are the elect. The Irish already know they are nearest perfection and all that is needed is the universal use of Gaelic. Let each use his own tongue only and refuse to mix with contemptible inferiors, except to destroy them. Anyhow I'd like to see what London is like and to hear what they talk about at Marble Arch. Even if we do go, it wouldn't matter very much, we've had pretty long innings."

A woman drove her tractor toward us, stopped it, and asked the time.

"I think I'll do another couple of hours," she said when we told her.

"I have watched this woman," I said while we watched her circling the field. "She works much too hard. She leaves her house spotlessly clean before she starts out in the early morning. How superior to the women in the *Golden Staircase*, the degenerate women of the Pre-Raphaelites. When you see those paintings, you want to say:

'Has God, thou fool! Worked solely for thy good,
Thy joy, thy pastime, thy attire, thy food?' "

We had now reached the gate, but he wouldn't go in without telling me that the Pre-Raphaelite women were far from being degenerate.

"Mrs. Morris made a startling impression on me. When she came into her drawing room in her strangely beautiful garments, looking at least eight feet high, the effect was as if she had walked out of an Egyptian tomb at Luxor. She was the silentest women I had ever met."

He shook hands and walked rapidly into the quiet house.

In the late evening I went round with a book he had asked for, but when I got to the door I felt I couldn't enter. He was singing in the hall to his own accompaniment. Charlotte loved to hear him sing while she was in her bed upstairs. Though very ill, she yet spent a good deal of the day downstairs, interested herself in all his affairs as always, and went up to bed early. There at the foot of the stairs stood the piano, so that Charlotte could hear his playing and singing.

As I walked away and down the lane, I heard him loud and clear, singing with much gusto into the night.

14

There were moments when the enjoyment of one's own home seemed an extravagance to which no human being was entitled. There was too much suffering everywhere.

As our children were now away, occupied with their duties, we were free at last to give ourselves to causes which took us far away from the village. Our neighbors were away in White-hall Court, and this corner of the village was uninhabited. Occasionally, worn out with our duties, we would rush back to steal a little of the quiet and beauty of Ayot Saint Lawrence, so that we could go on with our work. Our scottie, of course, accompanied us everywhere, but Fuzzia stayed at home, being looked after by a friend.

On Sunday morning we would get up at five and catch a train to London so that we should arrive as early as possible at Ayot. Even at that early hour the trains were packed with sailors, soldiers, lying fast asleep and helpless. The blinds were down all the way, and it was pitch dark. One such Sunday, after a long week of arduous duties, when even sleep was out of the question and food had to be snatched in the form of sandwiches, we entered a compartment which happened to be lit sufficiently to show us that our fellow travelers were a stout lady, highly painted up from lips to fingertips, bejeweled and wearing on the top of her head an enormous hat, and in the other corner a young woman reading a tract on world reconciliation; my wife put our little scottie on the seat next to hers and went to help me into the carriage by taking one of the cases from me. When I sat down in the seat which Tinkerbell was occupying for me I heard a violent tirade against my wife and her scottie, now sitting on her lap, that there should be a law prohibiting dogs, and especially those "lazy" women who spend their days doing nothing but pampering pets.

"What do you expect from women who have never had children?" The stout woman was shouting above our heads to the other passenger, who agreed and added to this diatribe.

"Yes, that's why we have war. All these women who have nothing better to do . . . they think dogs are more important than people . . . and nothing better to do than make mischief."

Little did these two women know how far from the truth they were.

It was a corridor train, and so we went into the next carriage, but we heard their voices high and pungent in agreement. In spite of the high purposes for which men and women were giving their lives, the individual mind seemed to be contracting into littleness.

When we came to Ayot our cat came forward to greet us. Though we were always away for the whole week, she was always ready to welcome us by coming along the lane in our direction, often a mile away from home.

It was during one of these week ends that a call on the telephone informed us that the worst had happened. Charlotte had died.

We were away when he returned to Ayot Saint Lawrence. We were kept away for over a month on end, and when we returned I called on G.B.S. late one evening. He was delighted to see me. He drew a chair to the fireside and bade me sit down.

"Charlotte's chair," he said.

He was correcting proofs for his forthcoming book, and he thought of nothing else, it seemed.

"I am having an edition of eighty thousand for which I must do all the paying, and I don't suppose eight copies will sell, if that. Will my book manage to compete with war news, greyhounds, and the wireless? Young people go to the cinema as a matter of course and won't settle down to read my book, a completely dull and analytical book. You mustn't expect anything new in it, it is all a repeat of all the things I have said in my other books the last fifty years. It is very difficult to say anything new when you find that everything repeats itself. There is Hitler walking into the Russian winter just as Napoleon did."

All this time the wireless was on, programs changing from

talk to crooning, and neither of us paying the least heed; the fire was gradually turning to ash, and the proof galleys were lying around on the floor by his chair. He sat in his wing arm-chair, bolt upright in his black suit and white shirt, his beard well trimmed and his hair short and well brushed. Though G.B.S. made a point of changing every evening for dinner, he never had anybody to dinner. Suddenly he turned to switch off the wireless and turned to me:

"Where have you been all this time? Why have you been avoiding me? I have been round to your place several times, and you seemed to have left me in the lurch."

"Never," I said.

"I don't know. The only people who stick to me like leeches are those I don't care for. I suppose it is so in your case?"

"I don't find it so," I answered. "We have friends we have not seen for many years, and yet we know that the moment we meet time will contract and it will seem as though it were only yesterday that we last met. We always think that our friends are near. I think it must be the same with death."

"I don't know, and you don't know. It is no use talking about things we know nothing whatever about. There are so many things in this world that need our urgent and immediate attention that we can leave all these otherworldly problems to look after themselves."

And yet I could not help feeling that he was truly con-cerned about death at this moment. Thomas Huxley, who had similar views of death, in his advancing years hated the thought of ultimate extinction and surprised his agnostic friends by directing that the following words be inscribed on his tombstone:

"Be not afraid, ye waiting hearts that weep,
For still He giveth His beloved sleep,
And if an Endless Sleep He wills so best."

And had we not often gone looking at literature engraved on tombstones? And I even had in mind that his reason for coming to live at Ayot Saint Lawrence was due to a tombstone inscription.

G.B.S. poked his fire and said:

"Taking things philosophically is not philosophy. It was an insult to humanity for St. Paul to say that if the dead rise not, then all that is left is to eat and drink and be merry for tomorrow we die. If a person who is dear to you has been taken away, why should a man turn into a beast? As for Charlotte, it was better she should have gone. She had suffered more than a human being can bear. I have never been much good with illness. I always get out of the way."

The conversation stopped dead. Consolation would obviously have bored him, and death was not a subject he cared to discuss. Not at that moment. I changed the conversation by recounting a story I had recently been told by a mathematician about a professor of mathematics in the United States, knowing how interested he was in mathematics. The professor was accustomed to walk to the university reading a book, and in the course of his walk he had to go through a square in which was a circular garden surrounded by a footpath. He was so absorbed in his book that he was found by a student one day

wandering round and round this path, completely unconscious
of the fact that he was not moving in the direction of his college at all.

"I am getting as absent-minded as that," he said, "but not
because I am absorbed in any particular subject. Mathematics
is the most interesting subject of all, and I still hope to dip into
it though I don't know the difference between a tensor and a
vector. The other day I had a similar experience. I was in
the shelter, after breakfast, when I needed a paper. I walked
up to the house, and by the time I entered the dining room I
had completely forgotten my original intention and, seeing
the breakfast things still on the table, I sat down and thought I
had to have my breakfast!"

It was obvious to me that it was the statistical side of mathematics that he was dipping into at this moment, for at his
elbow were bits of paper with notes and figures giving the
number of letters, the number of sounds, the number of words,
the number of lines on the different pages, with the trium-
phant heading: "Words in Book, 181,536."

"I have to clear away the accumulated rubbish and nonsense of centuries," he said, "I must get hold of the young."
And when he said "young," how very young everybody looked
to him.

"You see," he explained, "I want to get hold of the young
so that I know I won't be forgotten quickly."

I had to assure him again and again that his book will
especially appeal to the young. I pointed out that the soldier
and sailor of today were far and above in character and
knowledge those of 1914. Our new responsibilities kept us

very much in touch with them, and we knew. He laughed and said that all generations were very much the same. They were all bloodthirsty.

"I don't find them bloodthirsty in the least," I said. "They're bored with war and do not play at heroics. They can't even be got to hate the enemy. Whenever they have a chance they show interest in books and music. They are dance drunk, it is true, but that is only natural to the age. I think as a whole they regard war as a 'nasty bit of business' which should be forgotten as soon as it is over, as a young mother does after birthpangs."

"Don't introduce birth into this silly business. Nothing is being born. This idea of something good coming out of plague, poverty, war, is nonsense. It isn't a struggle between one conception of life and another. The only ideas that come into this business are the scientific ideas; which side will come out first with a universal slaughter machine. This war will be a glorious victory for science even though the whole human race perishes. My book is an ignorant old man's attempt to knock sense into a young and foolish world."

"Do you remember Samuel Butler after years and years of argument coming to the conclusion that the best way of dealing with those on the other side is to pretend to agree with them? It piques the opponents far more and makes them far more uneasy if we make them see that we do not care one straw what they think. This makes them suppose that we must feel strongly enough not to want their support, and the more they think this, the more of their support will they give us."

From
Bernard Shaw   13th June 1946

Phone & Wire:
CODICOTE 218.

AYOT SAINT LAWRENCE,
WELWYN,
HERTS.

Dear Winsten

If the League desires to add a bust of me to its exhibition there can be no question as to which to choose. All the famous ones are on view in the Tate, the County Hall, the R.A.D.A., and have been there for years. They are out of date, and are laborious modellings from studio settings rather than spontaneous works of art. There is no novelty about them.

My own choice would be your wife's bust of me. It is entirely new to the public. It is up to date. Made without sittings it is a work of imagination as well as a portrait, and is more like me than my bare portraits are, besides being a technical masterpiece.

I know of course that you cannot recommend it or even suggest it yourself, nor can Mrs Winsten bear being implicated in any such suggestion.

But it should be made clear that if the choice were mine I should not hesitate.

G. Bernard Shaw

Childhood is unknown territory to him

Village scene

"I know," G.B.S. said, smiling, "but Samuel Butler was getting old when he was talking like that."

There was a flicker, and all the lights went out and we were left with the faint glow of the wood fire. The housekeeper brought in a couple of lit candles, which were placed on either side of an early photograph of him in the Mephistophelian pose.

I had only to mention a name to bring forth many a tale. He came in with information about Samuel Butler whom he knew well:

"When he completed *Erewhon Revisited* the trouble was to get a publisher for it, as there was a real danger of people wanting to read it. Longman's turned it down because it might offend the High Anglicans, not realizing that the secret of success is to offend the greatest number of people. He wrote to me as a last resort to recommend him to a man in whom he could have reasonable confidence. I invited Grant Richards, my own publisher, and Sam to lunch, but only after preparing the ground. I told Richards that he would meet a shy old bird, and I told Butler that my publisher would quake in the presence of so eminent an author, and so I could look forward to an enjoyable meal. Result: Grant Richards agreed not only to publish *Erewhon Revisited* but a new edition of *Erewhon*. There is one point Butler made which is worth bearing in mind: 'A little levity will save many a good heavy thing from sinking.' I myself cannot always successfully subdue my tendency to seriousness, and that is why, I suppose, that profound statement must be taken seriously to heart by those who want to save many a good heavy thing from sinking, especially when the heaviest thing of all nowadays is the heart. He told us an excellent story about Richard Garnett. A Siamese prince was taken round by Garnett and Butler to see the British Museum reading room, and naturally Garnett as the chief wished to impress the prince. They showed him among other things how the place was heated. Neither was mechanically minded, but Garnett felt that our good relationship with Siam depended on the successful heating of the reading room.

" 'And how does it work?' asked the prince, more interested in engines than in books. Out came Butler with: 'Damnably.' What on earth did it matter whether the prince was offended or not? The British Museum was built to house revolutionaries who generate their own heat."

Once on Butler, there was no stopping. He continued:

"You know Butler thought of becoming a pavement artist, as he could put his expensive university education to no other use. In that way he resembled William Morris. He got the idea from one of his tenants who made a good respectable living that way and turned one of his rooms into a studio. I myself might have come to that if the office had been the only alternative; there are so few openings for people who don't want to work. Well, as I said somewhere else, Butler had no style at all, which is the supreme sort of style."

We went for a walk across a field path toward Codicote, and I told G.B.S. that I came across a lane in that village called Cowards Lane, and I asked a villager how the lane came to be called in that way. It was an old man, and he remembered how dangerous it was for a Welwyn man to venture on the road to Codicote because of the hatred one village had for the other. Codicote youths would attack Welwyn people and vice versa. Cowards Lane was the way of circumventing the road and avoiding trouble.

"That's the lane for me," G.B.S. remarked. "I was coming out of a meeting in London one day when I overheard a lady asking Cunninghame Graham who this fellow Shaw was, and I heard his reply: 'The coward who left William Morris and me to face the police in Trafalgar Square.' So you see what path I would have taken if I had to walk from Welwyn to Codicote. Have they come to terms by now?"

"I think they have both combined against any encroachment by that newfangled city, Welwyn Garden City. They seem to have strong words to say against garden cities."

"If it were not for the Garden City, where else could I have my haircut? My address is a Welwyn one, my telephone number is a Codicote one, and my barber is in Welwyn Garden City, so if war breaks out, my way will have to be down Cowards Lane. Mine has always been the lonely track. We are fortunate people, we have lived to see wars fought on a really large scale for similar causes; but what talk and what weapons!"

Hobbes, the philosopher, at the age of ninety sang to strengthen his lungs and prolong his life; but he did it only when the doors were barred and he was sure nobody heard him, for his voice was none too good. G.B.S. often fell into song to illustrate a point, and his voice was a good testimonial to "The Method." We were listening to the singing of Paul Robeson, on the wireless, of course, and he joined in, almost drowning Paul's voice. I told him of Paul Robeson's visit to Frank Harris in Italy and how the old man boasted of his editorship of *The Saturday Review* when he had three of the most promising young writers in the world: Wells, Bennett, and I think the third was Max.

"Frank Harris was really a mild and inoffensive character, the kind of person one should guard against. Those three haven't done too badly."

"The other G.B.S. called on Paul Robeson one day, and only his wife was in. Mrs. Robeson seized the opportunity of praising her husband to the skies: the grandest man in the world, the most intelligent, the most gifted, a great artist, and yet so modest, so simple. . . ."

"And who is the other G.B.S.?"

"G. B. Stern."

"I can't call myself Bernard Shaw because there is a musician by that name, and I daren't call myself G.B.S. because there is a professional writer who uses those initials. What on earth can I call myself? Charlotte was like Mrs. Robeson, you know. She married a genius and she wouldn't have a word spoken against me. It makes it very difficult for the husband."

I switched off when the singing stopped, and he said:

"I get cables from everywhere asking me for articles on this cursed war, as if it were being run for my benefit. They are willing to pay me whatever I ask. I'm a poor hand at pushing and meddling in things that don't concern me; I haven't got the parochial mind and am therefore not up to the great issues involved. They'll go on shoveling men and money down the drain until men are worth more than money and then they'll stop. I feel like the Arab who was so ashamed of our civilization that he took out his European false teeth and crushed them to bits."

He helped himself to chocolate and grumbled, "Nowadays they make soap and call it chocolate, they give you paraffin and call it fruit juice. This war will be the death of me."

He put another chocolate into his mouth and continued: "I once had a project of releasing people from reading my books if they paid a small fee. Hitler by throwing a few incendiaries on my books has hit on a better idea. Insurance companies now pay me because the readers can no longer get hold of my books. Books are always the better for not being read. Look at our classics; it has always been my ambition to write a play which nobody whatever would want to act and so establish myself as an immortal. Samuel Butler almost succeeded in writing books which nobody read, and he, you will admit, is in the front rank of writers. He, however, had a consolation which I never had. You will remember that when his friend Fuller Maitland rebuked him for being so hard on his sister, because she was really a very good woman and she would go straight up to heaven whereas Samuel Butler was destined to the other place, Samuel replied: 'I am not afraid of anything of that kind. The Almighty's taste in literature is far too good to allow of his committing such an error.' "

The days were shortening rapidly, and even though the clock registered an early hour and two hours earlier than the sun-dial, G.B.S. had to shorten his visits because the darkness blinded him.

"One day I'll fall and not be able to get up," he said to me as I saw him to the gate. "Luckily for me I had theatrical training and can stage-fall; that avoids any real damage to myself. I fell this morning in my garden and stayed there quite a time, and when I eventually did get up I found there was nothng wrong with me because of this stage-fall. It involves much presence of mind, though with me it is almost automatic. You know, as soon as we know how to do a thing exceedingly well, consciousness in respect of it vanishes; swimming, for example, and cycling. However difficult it was to acquire these things, once mastered they become part and parcel of you, and children are born with this unconscious knowledge through their ancestors. Breathing and walking were acquired through the efforts of our ancestors, and so were the upright posture and balance. Only, as Lee discovered, all the established methods were wrong, and therefore these things had to be learned all over again. When I was taught to relax by an American lady I discovered how heavy the head really is. She made me lie down on a couch with my head hanging off the couch. For all these years I had not known how to relax at will and, as she told me, I must have been sleeping without proper rest. I was a timid young man when I first came over to England, and by the way, I thought, like all Irishmen, that every Englishman was an aristocrat, and Lee advised me that

if I was to do anything at all in public I must create a voice
that even if I spoke rubbish the people would still be en-
thralled. I am the most spontaneous speaker in the world
because every word, every gesture, and every retort have been
carefully rehearsed."

The night was upon us, and the lane was lost in complete
darkness. He leaned on my shoulder, and I went with him to
his own door.

He was convinced that he was one of the few people who
could control his temper in emergency. Compared with Hyndman and Morris he was as cool as a cucumber.

"By giving myself a bad reputation," he said, "my few acts
of goodness cause such astonishment that they become the
subject of praise, and the rest is forgotten. And so I get a
reputation for being the kindest of people and the gentlest.
Whenever Charlotte and I missed a train, say, she was helpless
and would stand for at least ten minutes as though stunned.
She could not stop bemoaning the loss of the train for long
afterward and naturally blamed me. But I always took the
situation in hand and pointed out that we had only to get a
porter to call a taxi. I never lose my nerve. But once, in Africa,
I was driving, and the car took it into its bonnet to go its own
pace and where it willed. Charlotte was sitting beside me, and
she was quite unperturbed because she always thought that I
could do anything, but suddenly the car flew into a ditch,
jumped, and overturned. Charlotte was hurled out and mi-
raculously escaped with only a few bones broken."

"Cars can be like that. The other day I had a lift to London by a neighbor in a nearby village. He was a good driver but a bad debater, having to use his hands in order to prove his points. At one moment he got so excited that he forgot he was driving a car, and at full speed at that, and to drive home an argument let go the wheel and used both hands on an imaginary map of Europe to place the different armies and to show how our strategy had proved inefficient. When a concrete post stopped us from flying into a ditch, the argument yielded to caution, and we continued sedately into London."

"I never speak in a car and fortunately have a chauffeur who never utters a sound, not even about the weather. I didn't even lose my head when I was actually drowning when out swimming with Robert Lorraine. I simply wondered what Charlotte would think if I were late in getting home. She could not believe that a mere ocean could extinguish a light like my own."

We were ploughing through a luxurious crop of nettles in the much neglected ruined church and came upon an arch of carved stone vitalized by a pretty pattern of ivy carving.

"William Morris would have liked this. Like all atheist revolutionaries he was all out for preserving churches. That little bit of carving is worth more to lovers of beauty than all the pretentious tombstones put together."

He went round examining all the tombs most carefully, as though he had never seen them before, now and then stopping to take a photograph.

"I hear," I said, "that William Morris's tomb is sadly neglected."

"All tombs are neglected sooner or later," he said, "that is

An argument

His shorthand to be transcribed by his secretary

why cremation is such a good thing. My ashes will be mixed inseparably with Charlotte's, which are being kept for that purpose, and then when that is done neither of us will concern ourselves with what happens to them afterward—most likely they will be scattered over the garden."

15

"Don't talk to me about that hackneyed myth, the Irish race! There is no Irish race. We are a parcel of mongrels. Spanish, Scottish, Welsh, English, and, as to the purity of the Huns, weren't they born of evil spirits who mated with witches in the dreary deserts of Asia? All this talk of purity of race leaves me cold. The more mixed it is the better, and the quicker that happens, the sooner shall we get some sanity in the world." He spoke like this because the Russian Government had discarded the International and had frowned upon any suggestion that the past had not been glorious if sometimes unhappy, and it was obviously a definite reversion toward extreme nationalism.

"I am a cosmopolitan by temperament and have always found that the so-called national is an imposture which only impresses an audience as a comic character. I have laughed these people out of court in *John Bull's Other Island* and in

Geneva, but they still have the impertinence to exist. I told the German ambassador when he congratulated me on my seventieth birthday, there is a supernational republic of thought and art, of which I am but a very humble member. Anybody who had worked in the British Museum, as I have done, among people of every nationality, cannot shut out the rest of the world."

One of the De Havilland's latest planes screeched over our heads, shook the house, and whisked over the trees and away into the distant clouds. Then there was silence. Not a sound could be heard in this little village of ours, this very isolated village.

I broke the silence. "Years ago I went for a long walk with a German professor of English literature who did his best to make himself agreeable by comparing the literature of both countries, ours and his. To bolster up his own superior claims he suggested that it was to Germany you owed your recognition in Europe as a thinker and dramatic poet."

"Perfectly true. In England I was regarded as a dangerous and disreputable person. My debt to Germany is incalculable," G.B.S. interrupted.

"Good. It was a day like this, gentle and quiet, and we settled down by the river at Kimpton and enjoyed the extraordinary peacefulness of our countryside. He was all out to impress me with Germany's greatness and to what depths of despair Socialism had reduced his country. There were evil influences, such as Ernst Toller, Thomas Mann, and Wassermann. . . .'

"Great writers are always evil influences," G.B.S. interrupted once more. "Second-rate writers are not wicked enough to become great."

"That was exactly what he made a point of proving. He told me that Ernst Toller stole jewels from passing ladies, and when I treated this extravaganza with the laughter it deserved, he was insulted. With him it meant a long sulky silence. He was a Junker of the old school and was not accustomed to be contradicted. He made statements which were to be taken down by his students as gospel facts. However, he thawed more quickly that time and was willing to enjoy a lunch with us by the river. We talked religion then, and as I did not want to spoil his meal I refrained from argument, and so he continued with his statements. I now learned of another great philosopher, Professor Lipp, whom he knew personally and whom he regarded as the greatest thinker that ever lived, greater even than Goethe.

" 'To prove to you,' the professor said, 'how original Professor Lipp is, I will tell you of a wonderful statement he made: "Do to your fellow man as you would wish him to do to you." If people acted up to this wisdom, then the world would change and become what God intended it to be. You have no such philosopher in your own country!'

"I could not help pointing out that I had heard that saying before. He would not hear of it. He stood up—he was a very tall upright figure of a man—and I thought he would challenge me to a duel forthwith."

"Conrad challenged me to a duel," G.B.S. said. "Unfortunately Wells got in the way, otherwise Conrad would have taken his place among the saints. My answer to him would have been that it is unwise to do unto others as you would that they do unto you. Their tastes may not be the same. For example, if a meat eater like G. K. Chesterton wished, as a good Christian, to do unto me what he would like me to do to him, he would send me a roast chicken and some whisky, but they would be as acceptable to me as water would be to him. Our tastes were somewhat different."

"The statement of his which has stuck in my mind was that in an age which has nothing to say, the loud-speaker was invented."

G.B.S. looked at me quizzically. "I thought it was I who said it. Doesn't matter, let it pass. Nobody, however, could call G.K.C. a loud-speaker! He never grew up in spite of that huge body of his. Anyhow, we enjoyed ourselves together, standing on our heads and proving that black was white."

"You both dramatized yourselves very well."

"So well, that when I appeared at a rehearsal where the poor dramatist made a desperate effort to include me as one of his characters, the stage manager, not expecting my personal presence, thought I was the impersonation and rebuked me for being nothing like the man Bernard Shaw. He shouted: 'What he would say if he saw this weedy old thing, I daren't say.' Or something to that effect."

As he spoke, he pulled himself up and mocked the movement of the stage manager. "You would have done well as an actor and ousted Henry Irving, no doubt."

"A man of intellect makes a bad actor. I was unfortunately endowed with a brain, otherwise, like Shakespeare, I would have fitted quite well into a touring company. There is one thing in my favor, I can work with other people. I was always a poor hand at pushing and struggling, but I might have been able, if permitted, to improve on the text, as I did in *Cymbeline.* . . ."

"I am surprised that you should have permitted yourself to improve Shakespeare, when you do not permit even your film producer to alter a word of your own text."

"Give me a person greater than Shaw and I'll permit him to spoil my work beyond recognition." He brought out his watch, scowled, then immediately smiled happily.

"Of course, I needn't hurry. You know, I feel dreadfully hungry these days."

I knew that this hunger was mainly due to his loneliness, which he tried to cover up even to himself.

He now came almost every day because we were working at home.

"I was looking through Charlotte's papers and discovered that she had considerable literary talent. There was a bundle of letters, correspondence between herself and T. E. Lawrence. They were great friends, which surprised me. I did not know that she could write as she did. She might have made a good romantic novelist. Anyhow, Charlotte married me as a genius, and there is no room for a couple of geniuses in one house; one of them has to give way to the other."

"But what about the Webbs? They were equals, working together. . . ."

"The Webbs are an exception. Nothing like it has ever happened before. Wells didn't know them; I did."

"The Brownings!"

"The Brownings. Any amount is written about the romance of the Brownings, but though their story is among the romances of the world, I doubt whether they are read at all. Gossip there will always be about them, but with the Webbs there can be no gossip; they will be remembered by their work. As I have said, the prophet of the race will be the political economist. There is nothing like prosaic work. I had a grand time on the vestry worrying about drains, dust destructors, and instituting women's lavatories. The Webbs made a romance of reality, and when I want good literature I go to them and know I get the whole truth. When a person takes you aside and asks you what rent you pay and whether your boots pinch, you know that he is interested in you. The Webbs had that curiosity about life in a magnanimous spirit; they missed nothing and saw everything. Charlotte got to know them because she wanted to do something with her money."

"I always think that you would never have written as well as you did if it were not for Charlotte. In the future a Samuel Butler will come along and prove that it was Mrs. Homer and not Homer who wrote the *Odyssey*, that it was a Charlotte Shaw and not the fabulous Bernard who wrote the plays and prefaces!"

"You know how he hit upon the Mrs. Homer idea, which put out every authority and pedant and made him an Ishmael among them? He wanted to compose music when he gave up art and hit upon *The Adventures of Ulysses* by Charles Lamb. When he referred to the original poem he felt sure that the man who wrote it was drawing the whole thing from life. It was so good that he felt it must be the work of a woman and not by an old man. He had the highest opinion of women, and I believe he didn't marry for that reason. Of course, Butler could never have afforded to keep an intelligent woman."

The new rector was sitting with us when G.B.S. came in.

"I'm Bromley-Bourne," said the rector, standing respectfully.

G.B.S. was puzzled. "Are you quite certain?" he asked.

"Well, as far as one can be certain in this world," the rector replied.

"George Lansbury was unmistakably Bromley born. When I helped in the strike of the matchmakers sixty years ago I got to know the accent very well. I'm Dublin, you know and Ayot by adoption," G.B.S. explained.

"It was very good of you to be present at my induction," the rector remarked.

"Oh, you mustn't mind me. I'm a sort of unofficial Bishop of Everywhere. I qualify because I was a freethinker before I knew how to think. When my friend, Dr. Inge, was made Dean of St. Paul's, somebody remarked that he was the best man for the post because he was a Buddhist. The first moral lesson I can remember as a tiny child was the lesson of teetotalism instilled by my father. One night when I was still about as tall as his boots, he took me out for a walk. In the course of it I conceived a monstrous, incredible suspicion. When I got home I stole to my mother and in an awestruck whisper said to her, 'I think Papa's drunk.' 'When is he anything else?'

she replied. By the way, I found the church door closed the other day."

"There have been so many robberies in churches lately that we decided on taking precautions."

"Oh, that's not my motive in going to church. I go for recreation. I like the solitariness. . . . When Queen Victoria was eighteen, they came to her and told her she was Queen of England. She asked whether she could really do what she liked, and, when this was reluctantly admitted by her careful mother, Victoria considered what wonderful and hitherto impossible happiness she could confer on herself by her new powers. And she could think of nothing more delightful than an hour of separate solitary confinement."

"Then for your sake the doors must be left open," the rector agreed.

"Oh, no, not for my sake. There is the danger of having people praying all over the place. A pious Frenchman, visiting Westminster Abbey, knelt down to pray. The verger, who had never seen such a thing before, promptly handed him over to the police and charged him with brawling. Fortunately the magistrate had compassion on the foreigner's ignorance and even went the length of asking why he should not be allowed to pray in church. The reply of the verger was simple. 'If we allowed that,' he said, 'we should have people praying all over the place.' The fact is I'm a moralist. You see, the stage works as an instrument of moral propaganda because it exhibits examples of personal conduct made intelligible and moving to crowds of unobservant, unreflecting people."

I recalled the dispute between Laurence Housman and the

Lord Chamberlain when permission to perform *Pains and Penalties* was refused. The censor insisted on the omission of the word "adultery." Housman pointed out that the word in question was uttered in the churches every Sunday before women and children. Came the reply, "in church it meant nothing, but on the stage it meant everything!"

The rector stood up to go. He said, "We consider you here a pillar of the Church."

"I know exactly what you mean," G.B.S. answered, winking an eye. "There is already one ruin in the place, we don't want two."

It was difficult to carry on a conversation in the evening at his own home because he sat in the dining room and the wireless was always on tap.

"I have to have this wretched noise in the room so that it can be relayed into the kitchen. I'll try and make myself heard above the dance band and the crooner. I've had training in the open air, where I had to fight against brass bands and every kind of interruption. Often I felt like stopping my speech and conducting the band instead."

The proofs were lying round him, a greater heap than ever. They lay like foam round his feet; books and papers and manuscripts lay scattered on the dining-room table, seemingly neglected.

"I thought that you had finished with this book at last," I said.

"I never finish anything. At a certain point I have to say: full stop! Otherwise I would get nothing else done but rewrite my work all over and over again. One must put a limit to the time to be devoted to a piece of work. This wretched thing has taken me years, and I won't want to see it ever again. People are always surprised that I only go to see my plays once, but my own work is put behind me once I have finished with it, and I never want to hear about it. William Morris always hid his work behind a curtain."

"Did you like William Morris all the more after you had seen him and known him intimately?" I asked.

"His presence vitalized his work as he vitalized everything he touched. What about you? Have you read any of my work since you have known me so well?"

"Some authors I have met have made me lose interest in their work, others create a new interest. In your case, the latter is true. There are many things in your works that I would have missed without this intimate acquaintanceship with you. In fact, when I see any of your plays done now, I always feel they are far off the mark."

"That's a great pity, because I am dying of the fatal disease of being Shaw, and soon the plays will have to go on without me. With Galsworthy and Bennett the plays stopped dead as soon as they died, but with Chekhov they only began to make themselves felt after his death, and I am glad, because Chekhov is the greatest dramatist of all."

"Such nice people, so cultured and so futile!"

"The point to remember is that Chekhov in giving us Russian life gave us the life of every country house in England, in the same way as Ibsen gave us every provincial house in the world. Tolstoy blew up such homes with his fierce language, but Chekhov gently let them go to the bailiffs! To be gentle is to be very wise—not an easy thing, I can tell you. To be wise is to be misunderstood."

He asked me to examine a manuscript on the table. He said:

"I glanced through this, and it reads quite well. Who on earth sent it, I don't know. Why do all the budding dramatists presume on my generosity?"

I, too, glanced through it and thought it very good. I imagined a young author hopefully posting his work to the great dramatist, eagerly awaiting every post. Perhaps an immediate invitation . . . perhaps an introduction to a theater manager. Such things were known to have happened. Had not William Archer done so to the very great man himself?

In a modest corner of the cover of this manuscript I found the name of the author in very small hand:

Charlotte F. Shaw,
10, Adelphi Terrace, W.C.2.

I said nothing.

"Getting a play produced," he pronounced, "is all a matter of chance. A manager may be at the moment hard up for a play, and in his overcoat pocket there lies one which he did not mean to look at. He suddenly comes across it on a dull train journey to Aberdeen and he reads it because he may not have anything better to do. Perhaps the famous playwright whom he has asked to write for him has nothing ready and he has the theater on his hands. It is better to risk failure than vacuity, and that is when the new playwright steps in. I have only to commend a playwright to make him the butt of every manager and later of the pawnbroker! I have myself made many an author by tearing him to bits, as the lions assured Christianity by tearing a few harmless fanatics to shreds. I've never helped a soul by praising him."

16

On the whole he was a man of equable temperament, and he gave me the impression when he lost his temper that it was premeditated. Discipline was part and parcel of his nature, and every gesture studied, probably with the help of a mirror. I remember once surprising a politician before a full-length mirror while he was practicing a speech which he was to deliver at a large gathering; he was being advised by a specialist in gesture and enunciation. G.B.S. lived even in his most secret moments as if the whole world were watching. Or did he, like other great men, have a haunting spirit to keep him up to the mark?

One Sunday when I had just returned from a Friends' meeting, he and I talked about the Quaker faith. He said that he was a Quaker by temperament but not by faith. He could not define his faith and did not want to, but the accepted mythologies did not appeal to him. He said:

"What an amazing title for a religious organization: Friends! That in itself was a stroke of genius. I believe in the discipline of silence and could talk for hours about it. There is nothing more impressive than spontaneous prayer, because it involves long and arduous preparation. I have always given my speeches an air of spontaneity and in that way achieved something of a reputation as a wit, but I was an actor saying his lines like any other Quaker. How well the words of the Scriptures sound when uttered spontaneously by a Friend, and how well my words will sound when, in the near future, they will be uttered in every place of worship. I am all out for healing through art, and the Quakers, by denying these things, deny the very essence of religion. There is as much healing power in a Beethoven sonata or a painting by Constable as in the excerpts from the Bible. I have always agreed with Samuel Butler that we need soul doctors, or, as he called them, straighteners. I have always found that the best healers were the artists."

I could not refrain from smiling at the memory of an acquaintance, who, having similar views, painted her small sitting room, as a book on color told her, each wall a different color to suit her moods. She would sit facing the wall with the appropriate color and was thus uplifted. She happened to be a neurotic woman, and her illness did not improve, but she for a while had all the satisfaction of knowing that her semi-detached house was different from all the others in the neighborhood.

"She should have consulted an artist and not a book. What

is the use of books? Did she know anything about color, or perhaps she was color-blind?"

"Most likely, judging by the colors she inflicted upon herself."

"Anyhow it was a sure way of securing the room to herself. No sane husband could keep her company in such a room."

"Luckily the husband was a sailor!"

"To go back to the Quakers," he said, "in the Great War, Number One, I pleaded before a tribunal for a fellow-Fabian and almost converted the military representative—at least I made him laugh, which was more than this representative deserved—but unfortunately this pacifist friend was represented by counsel who insisted on giving a long and wearying account of the history of pacifism, starting with Cain and ending in disaster. It was dinner hour, and an Englishman automatically stops thinking at one o'clock, but this stupid, inconsequential lawyer insisted on ignoring this fact. The result was the wrong fellow went to prison. Talking about hunger, I remember once, at a Socialist conference, calling at my hotel and finding all the leaders standing disconsolately around a fire, looking as if the social revolution had come and left them far behind. They were silent for a change, and so I could hear a rumbling which I ultimately located as coming from their tummies. Then Hyndman spoke up at last. 'The Countess of Warwick has invited us to dinner and has forgotten all about it.' "

"What would you have done," I asked, "if you were young enough to fight?"

Painting in oils by Clare Winsten
(In the possession of Gabriel Pascal)

Drawing in pencil by Clare Winsten

"In fact, I never was young enough. In the next war, when the old men and women are called upon to do all the fighting, I shall be eligible. That will be a testing time for me, because everything I have uttered will be used against me; not only my own utterances but the sayings of all my characters."

The relationship between an author and his characters, between a man and his words, between a man and his conscience. . . . I quoted William James as saying: "Man, biologically speaking, is the most formidable of animals, of all beasts of prey, and, indeed, the only one that preys systematically on its own species." It certainly looked like it. In spite of the amazing courage and solidarity shown in the war, we were inclined, all of us, to take the lowest view of human nature. In these days of faith, that is all we had to depend upon at that moment; we all affected a complete lack of belief. How could one believe in a beneficent power when a chance bomb could make a laughing stock of any sentient, dreaming creature?

"Let us treat the men and women well: treat them as if they were real: perhaps they are," I pleaded.

G.B.S. said: "I turned a person, now an M.P., into something real by incorporating him as a character in *The Doctor's Dilemma*. He came to see the play and then sent me fifty pounds in payment of an old debt. He thought that I had written the play only to get the money from him. No person is real until he has been transmuted into a work of art. That is why I can lose my temper when it comes to art."

"Didn't you say that if you believe in a thing you can laugh at it?"

"Did I? There's a lot of truth in it. But when it comes to art I cannot be sane. I am always being asked: If I were God how would I have created the earth? As a fellow-artist I would no doubt have made a similar mess of things, but I would not have made the mistake of making men without art to live in a world of art. I would have ruled out from the very beginning pain, poverty, and piety."

"You call this a world of art; yet it is the evil things that are infectious and not the good things. Illness and persecution, greed and lust. . . ."

"Because the men without art got the upper hand of the world. As I have said: sanitation is aesthetic, economics is aesthetic, as Ruskin proved conclusively, and religion is aesthetic. The difficulty is that people have got so accustomed to having life seasoned with crime and poverty that they cannot contemplate a life without it. Like the peasants who are so accustomed to having their feed smothered in condiments that they find the simple food quite uneatable, tasteless, in fact. It took me years to get accustomed to the natural taste of things."

"Exactly, and these people you call peasants consider our diet as 'tasteless,' just as you consider theirs. All because . . . ."

But I realized at once that I had made a mistake. The word "because" always irritated Shaw. He was not interested in reasons. Reasons given may be right or wrong. He wanted to get down to facts. He said:

"The people objected to Venus de Milo without corsets and high heels. The simple thing is the most difficult thing of all.

I would have made the simple thing the most natural. But like God I would soon have lost patience with the world and drowned everybody. It was stupid leaving a single family. What happened? The progeny of the family reproduced all the vices of their predecessors so exactly that the misery caused by the flood might just as well have been spared. Man, as an experiment, has proved a failure."

There was a knock at the front door and I went to open it. A young man, looking like a Shelley, handed me a leaflet and quietly informed me that I would be pleased to hear that the reign of justice was at hand, that millions who had died would be born again and all that was good was on the way. Was I ready? If not, here was a book, priced five shillings and six-pence, which would not only show me the way but would be a pass to this delivered world. I offered him a cup of tea, but he informed me that he only drank water, which his spirit turned into wine!

When I returned, G.B.S. reached out his hand for the book and said:

"I am pestered every day with the literature of the insane. Here is a note from a university proposing to set up a Chair of Gerontology: the object is to develop a synthetic food to enable persons to retain in their nineties the mobility and resiliency of nineteen. Among the materials to be used are horseblood and the lining of pigs' stomachs. The idea is for me to subsidize it."

G.B.S. had his long white mackintosh on, his old gloves, and a slasher in his hand. We were going for a walk along the gloomy lane at the back of his garden. Smothered with nettle and briar, the track led to Mr. Cherry-Garrard's private estate. Here, in the Adam house, lived Epstein's Christ. When I first saw it as a youth it made a deep impression on me. Here it stood in an illumined alcove, with one hand pointing at the scar on the other. There He was, this sculpture of the Man of Sorrows and acquainted with grief, shut away in a wealthy country-house. Whenever I passed this house I could see the pitying eyes. Here was the symbol of a very real thing, aware of all that happened in the heart of man.

G.B.S. said, "Beatrice Webb had a physical antipathy to Him."

"Have you?" I asked.

"The problem of today is not how to bear the burdens, but how to get rid of them."

I suggested, "Both, surely?"

He slashed away a line of nettles, while I used **my secateurs** on the overhanging branches.

"The Christian has been like Dickens' doctor in the debtors' prison who tells the newcomer of its ineffable peace and security, no duns, no tyrannical collectors of rates, taxes, and rent, no importunate hopes, nor exacting duties, nothing but the rest in safety of having no further to fall."

I could not accept this concept of Christianity. All of us had to live within very narrow confines, but the fact that we were thus restricted did not prevent us from living a good life.

He answered: "Quite. If all people were like you the world might be quite tolerable, but what the world would be like if all were like myself, I daren't contemplate. There is room in the world for one Shaw only, and, as we have proved, there is yet no room for a Christ. His followers would be the first to disown him if He appeared."

"Especially if He came as depicted by Holman Hunt."

"He would be crucified, and I, Barabbas, the agitator, would swing by his side. People are so wicked that their life would be miserable without the consolation of religion. The press would, of course, be there, all clamoring for interviews and articles at reduced rates!"

There was no sight of sky, the crowded young conifers created a dead stillness, and not a bird was heard. We walked on in silence, he slashing at the resisting nettles and I repairing the frail wire which is supposed to prevent the entrance of never-present trespassers. A fat rat darted across and was soon lost in the wood.

"I used to do this regularly, I had to create this path for my own use," he said. "Thirty years ago it was just a wild mess here. I had quite a job to clear it. Somebody must take the Garden of Eden in hand and weed it properly."

"I don't like the thought of your walking alone along this path."

He pointed to the murderous slasher and laughed.

"As a matter of fact, I had quite a fall once and remained helpless on the nettles for quite a time. Have you ever tasted boiled nettles?"

"Yes, it tastes very much like spinach and is an excellent cure for nettle rash," I answered.

"Oh? No doctor would ever say so. For every illness there is a natural cure, but it wouldn't pay a doctor to admit it. I have always claimed that if the doctor were only paid when he actually cured you, or at least kept you in good health, he would not exploit illness. I hold the extremely unorthodox view that to write well one should be well. I know men who cannot write until they have drugged themselves into insensibility by drink, tobacco, and stale air. I've found that I write more when under the influence of drink; but it is only quantitative and not qualitative. I had to eliminate most of the work I had written as well as the stuff I had taken. Only an experiment, of course."

"I myself can work anywhere and under any conditions, but I am happiest in the country."

"It makes no earthly difference to me where I am, as long as it is away from people and I can devote the morning to writing. Dickens stopped thinking in the country, and all the best nature poetry has been written in town. I have always been a solitary person and most solitary in crowds."

"But you have always seemed extremely happy in crowds."

"Leave the word happy out of it. I can tackle crowds and twist them with a word."

We now reached the stile which leads to an open field. I expected him to step over the fence with those long lean legs of his, but he proved most cautious in climbing over, grumbling at the rickety crossbar and the barbed wire. We now walked in the warm glow of the sun among the golden stooks.

"I'm happiest in the open fields. I have more in common with the lark than the nightingale."

"I am more at home in a wood, which has something of the cathedral in it."

"I have always liked to escape into a cathedral when I could. William Morris did some of his best work in defense of cathedrals, and there wasn't one which he had not entered. I have always avoided people. In town they leave you alone, they don't know you from Adam, but in a village they know all about you and much more than you know about yourself. There is nothing more disturbing to the writing of a play than knowing lots of people. When Charlotte and I were in London recently I lost my way walking in Southwark and not a soul cared who I was. The children were playing among the ruins, the gulls circled round my head, and the policeman let me pass without asking me for my identity card, which I have always carried about with me. A young man noticed my predicament and offered to show me the way. He told me as we were walking together that he was studying medicine. I advised him to read *The Doctor's Dilemma,* as there were so many cute things said about doctors, and I told him that I number many of the greatest doctors among my friends. He said that he had seen the play many times, and that he thought it gave a fair and sober view of the profession. I quite liked the word sober. It so justly describes the commonplace originality of my work. There is nothing more striking than a platitude. I am very popular among doctors and teachers; they are like nettles, you know, the more you slash at them the better they grow. . . ."

A laborer, bent double with rheumatism and toothless, greeted us.

"Nice day," he said.

"Do you think so?" Shaw asked, straightening to his maximum height and swinging his stick, gloating over his "youth" and vigor.

Ninety plus—for this laborer was reputed to be well over ninety—stood for a moment with ninety minus, and they had nothing whatever to say.

In spite of the upright walk, the swinging of his stick, the grandiose talk of high finance, the desire to be alone, we knew that G.B.S. was lonely, very lonely. He would never admit this even to himself. When he was lonely he became anxious to place himself among the gods he despised. He spoke about his wealth, Charlotte's wealth, the high taxation, his unique position in the world of finance, of literature, of science, of the theater, films, and, above all, philosophy. It looked as if he doubted his prestige and had continually to remind himself that he was wealthy and famous. It was rather hard, for the war was taking some attention from him, and he knew too well how easy it was to be forgotten.

He came in and summarily asked for lunch. We were glad of this mark of friendship, and though it was already midday a meal was soon forthcoming. He told us, as if he were eating with us for the first time, that he disliked conversation at meals, that at home he had the wireless on and read his letters or his newspaper, that people did not look their best when feeding and he looked forward to the time when we would all live on air and get rid of the sanitary preoccupations so unpleasantly aggravated by our present diet.

It was quite a simple matter for us to remain quiet, brought up to regard silence as significant as speech. We took it as a

The author and G. B. S.

Every evening
   Drawing by Clare Winsten

test of friendship to be able to remain silent together. But there was conversation all the same. We told him of the self-help cafés which had sprung up all over the country, of the British Restaurants. G.B.S. was impressed.

"Now, I would have liked such places years ago, when I used to eat out. I like to take what I want, consume it in silence, and get out of the way. In my day you could get a permanent heartburn for a few pence when much literature was included in the meal to justify it, when lentils and beans were considered the meat of the vegetarian. The rage then was to live on sixpence a day."

After the meal we retired to the sitting room and he said: "It was Shelley who converted me to vegetarianism. I must have been the only man who took his poetry seriously, because it was mainly women who attended the Shelley Society. You see, vegetarianism to Shelley, like marriage and atheism, was a form of poetry. I am always asked how it is that my opinions have changed so little since my youth. It is because I got to them by poetry. As I always say, the aesthetic is the most convincing and permanent. Shelley made his ideas sing; I make them dance. I'm a little more mature: youth is driven by despair, old age by hope. Despair will serve a reformer as well as hope. He played the devil with all our convictions and will be considered, with Morris and the Webbs, the most effective propagandist the Socialist movement has ever had. He converted me not by his suffering, but by the sheer logic of his poetry. There is no falsehood, no calumny, no torture which the mere expression of a simple truth does not provoke."

But when I mentioned Harriet, G.B.S. quickly said: "He proved himself a gentleman. That action was understood by the other gentlemen. In fact, it gave me the right to suggest to the authorities of University College, Oxford, that a mural, representing Shelley in a silk hat, with Bible in hand and leading his children on Sunday morning to the church of his own parish, would be quite a worthy memorial to the man they expelled. It would have been as true as most memorials to celebrated people and certainly better than the pathetic image of a dead and helpless figure erected at Christ Church Priory. That's the kind of memorial they'll put up to me if I don't look out and do it beforehand."

As he was talking, I began to wonder what Shelley would have thought of this disciple of his. "I risked everything on his behalf," Shaw continued. "At the Shelley Society I shocked them all by publicly declaring myself a Socialist, an atheist, and a vegetarian. What chance had I of getting a foothold in polite society after that? Only by going all out and giving society no quarter. I praised it for the very qualities it despised."

Yet I could not help wondering what would have happened if a despondent Shelley walked into his den. I am convinced that he would have mocked at his unworldliness and sent him away weeping. But I am wrong, for Shelley was of good birth and wealthy, and these qualities appealed greatly to G.B.S.

He went home to his usual rest on the couch in the bay window of his dining room, where he threw his head back and completely relaxed.

17

Rationing became a pretext for unsociability with many people. You called upon a person, found him consuming an austere meal without even the thought of breaking bread with you. Even if offered, you were expected to refuse. Times were hard, domestic service difficult to obtain, and many a busy wife found herself having to do all her housework, to queue for food, and to do war work into the bargain. The strain on physique and temper was unendurable. Money was easy to get but could not ease the burden of existence. Yet if the enemy had offered us leisure, luxury, laughter, we would have refused. We meant to see it through. We fought for the things that meant most to us at the expense of these very things. G.B.S. was fortunately cut off from the mood and temper of the people. Ours was the only society he had, and, of course, the wireless. There were occasional visitors and occasional visits to other places, but with us he was almost a daily companion. There was one woman I heard who complained of his high spirits so soon after the death of his wife, but that only proved how little she understood him. For weeks at a time we were reduced to worrying about his difficulties in getting indoor help. He even suggested living in one room and letting the rest of the house go hang. The thought of being left without a servant was certainly frightening. "All these servants tending a senile man makes me uneasy," he said. But in a moment he was talking about increasing his staff because it makes a good impression.

"I don't want to be relegated to the rank of field marshal when I can still be an active general."

I enjoyed the pun, for it recalled a vision of D. H. Lawrence in shirt sleeves doing all the washing up after a talkative meal. He always insisted on things being washed up immediately so that the "troubles" shouldn't accumulate. Lawrence was a perfect general, a maid of all talk and work.

But Shaw did not mean general in that sense. He was thinking of Napoleon moving armies on their stomachs and of Montgomery meeting desperate situations.

Then there was a change of mood.

"I'm going to die in my bed tonight," he said.

"You will outlive most of us," I assured him again.

"You had better take me seriously for once. I tell you I'm going to die any day now. I didn't wake once in my sleep last night."

I laughed. "Of course, it is a sign of good health. You have not looked so well for a long time."

"That is also a sign," he insisted. "Isn't there Beethoven on the wireless?"

"No. There's a play of yours."

"Then we can go for a walk. My plays make very good radio. Have you ever listened to one?"

We sat down to listen, and soon his eyes shut, and it seemed as if he were asleep.

G.B.S. had no intention of dying. There was nothing of the too-old-at-ninety feeling about him. With the book safely behind him, he could give his time to his correspondence, which had by now mounted to giant proportions. All kinds of people were giving him advice on how to grow older still, how to dispose of his money, how to enjoy his solitude, how to invest, what gods to invoke, how to breathe, how to bathe, how to grow his food, what to do with a new moon, and how to face the sun. There were people from the other end of the earth who offered him the very apparatus proved to have doubled the life of rats that might prolong his if he invested in its manufacture, and there were ladies who knew that they were destined to look after his last years. Some of these people couched their letters in such literary language that they obviously spent much time in the composition. There were those who wanted autographs, and there were those who had personal problems which only he could solve, because he showed such wonderful understanding and knowledge of their own particular situation in his plays. In fact, he might or must have had them in mind when he wrote them.

All this time, while he was answering letters in a humorous

and lighthearted manner, what seemed a little cloud was reaching storm proportions, blotting out everything else. International and national affairs were forgotten. Every day now he spoke about this coming catastrophe, and all his ingenuity was of no avail. If I offered any suggestion he would brush it aside as if there were no possible help for him. We knew that he had hardly spoken to his servants, had never, in fact, entered the kitchen and did not know in what condition they lived. These two, the housekeeper and her husband, the head gardener and valet combined, had been with the Shaws for over thirty years and accepted as inevitable all the old duties and conditions. Modern inventions which had made housework bearable were not introduced. They never asked for amenities, were thrifty, kindly, and reserved and followed the dictum of their mistress that one should not mix with the village. Mrs. Shaw hated gossip of any kind and would stop the first hint of such from anybody. And yet it did not prevent G.B.S. from knowing everything that was happening in the village. How he gathered his information had always been a mystery to me. He himself rarely spoke to anyone in the village and had no contact with the villagers. He liked passing on his knowledge to me with touches which can only be described as Shavian exaggeration; like Duvallet in *Fanny's First Play*, he enjoyed the exhilarating, the soul-liberating spectacle of men quarreling with their brothers, defying their fathers, refusing to speak to their mothers. Yeats said it was an Irish characteristic, this perfectly disinterested, this absolutely unselfish, love of making mischief, mischief for its own dear sake. There was no doubt of it all being perfectly dis-interested.

And now he was faced with his own domestic issue for the first time. Until now it had been his mother, his wife. . . . It was staggering, especially as he hated change of any kind. However unsatisfactory things might be, he preferred them to continue rather than have the worry of new adaptations.

But the two old servants determined to go, for, as they put it, they had the means and were independent enough to live their own lives. They had nothing to lose but their chains. For years they had looked forward, dreamed of this moment, but loyalty to Mrs. Shaw had kept them meek, submissive, and impersonal.

"Why not," I suggested to G.B.S. at one of these anxious meetings, "why not turn this opportunity to your advantage? At last you have the opportunity to employ a woman with experience in vegetarian diet. Until now it was difficult, as Charlotte was not a vegetarian, but now at last you can have someone who will not only understand how to feed you but, what is more important, the aesthetics of it."

"I won't have cranks in the house. It's bad enough with me in it. I want a *normal* person who will not think of herself as more important than myself. And anyhow, you can't get a vegetarian cook."

"But you can," I insisted.

"I say you can't," he shouted. "I've been told that you can't."

"Who on earth misinformed you? There are many who would be only too glad to serve you."

"Those are the very people I want to keep out of the house. I want a person who knows her place and will not be interested in my ideas or read my books. I can't stand Shavians. This is a lonely place, and it would be fatal to me to have to entertain her. She must not think that she can rely on my company. As you know, I never come up to expectations. I want a person to come, not in the spirit of self-sacrifice, to do me good, but for the few pounds she can get out of me. No servant is a heroine to her own master."

"I was thinking of your welfare only."

"I'm not an invalid. I'd rather die. And anyhow a vegetarian cook would soon land me in Carey Street, I know."

The solving of this problem in the most ordinary fashion released his spirits and he became less self-pitying and more sprightly. He was talking about Granville-Barker now; the remarkable collaborator, Shakespearian scholar, and producer who became a great friend of both the Shaws and then suddenly went out of their life completely.

"Aubrey Smith played in my *Admirable Bashville* and wanted to make up as me. Nobody has ever succeeded in doing that, not even myself, and nobody could say what was wrong. But Granville-Barker came on the stage, saw what was wrong at once, and dabbed some white here and some white there on the beard, and Aubrey was transformed. On the first night my mother came with me. When Aubrey Smith walked on to the stage, there was loud laughter, and again laughter, which held up the play. My mother was quite bewildered. She turned to me and asked what the laughter was about. I told her that this actor was impersonating me. 'You?' she said, 'but this man looks so elderly.' "

"I always think that when you put down your comedic sense to your father you do an injustice to your mother. It is from her that you have inherited it. You owe everything to her."

"Perhaps you're right. The comedic sense is more closely related to gravity than levity. I rose by the force of gravity. I made the laugh into an intellectual thing."

I told G.B.S. of a visit to an exhibition where there were paintings by Picasso and Burne-Jones. The crowds flocked round the former and deserted the latter. He said:

"Burne-Jones was a great artist and will come into his own again. I heard a delightful story about his magnificent studio in Kensington. I was never there but I heard from Morris that he lived in grand style. He used to employ models, and, of course, whenever a visitor came these would run away to hide behind a curtain. One day a statesman and his wife called with their son of ten. The artist and the two visitors got talking, and the boy slipped away to explore the studio. He came back quite excited to his father, a pillar of nonconformity. 'Dad, I've just been talking to Eve!' "

"That kind of thing would not happen in a studio today. The model would remain sitting and would probably be introduced and make one of the party. There is no shame in the nude in an artist's studio."

G.B.S. smiled. "An actress had to come on the stage in a long loose robe, and for a moment she forgot to hold it up and it fell to the floor. She had nothing on underneath, but being a great actress she pretended that it was all intentional, and the effect was instantaneous. It was so wonderful that we were all spellbound! However, that was the only time it happened. She never repeated it."

We all clung obsessively to our varied interests to keep our minds off the war. Shaw's interests were all-comprehensive, but he was giving a great deal of his time to the drawing up of his will.

"Where's the hurry?" I asked.

"It's the only fun permitted nowadays. There must be many expectant benefactors who think I've kept them waiting too long. Some have died of the lingering illness of waiting. I suppose I ought not to keep them dangling so long—they'll be suggesting that there is malice in my survival. Many have given up all chance of earning an honest living and are living in the lap of penury, boasting of their wealthy relative far away in foreign England. It is not a good thing for people to wait for money to be left to them. There is quite a lot of it in Ireland. They live without the least knowledge of my desires or interests. I shall not leave my money to individuals if I can help it. I am leaving it to such institutions as I am interested in, and I haven't yet made up my mind which. I am getting hundreds of letters advising me as to what to do with my money, that I should support poets, unrecognized artists, unpublished authors, and, of course, I am to finance every crank organization in the world. I'll do just what I want to do. Still, I like people to write to me about it; it makes the humblest deal with large sums for a moment. Do you think other wealthy people receive so much gratuitous advice?"

"I rather think you are favored more than others because you have associated yourself with causes which are too unpopular to become wealthy, and also because they think that you have a kind heart."

"I thought that people generally concluded that that part of my anatomy was missing! I have deliberately hidden it from the public eye."

"Can one deliberately hide one's heart?" I asked him.

He looked keenly into my eyes, waiting for a retort rather than a revelation. Nothing came, so he turned his eyes away and said simply: "I never knew love when I was a child. My mother was so disappointed in my father that she centered all her care on my sister, and she left me to, fend for myself. If I had not returned to the house I don't think they would, any of them, have missed me."

"Your mother, then, was the perfect educationist."

"Yes. I see it now. My gratuitous meddlesomeness must be a reaction to her nonattachment. With me, when a person comes upon the scene I immediately give her the benefit of my advice on how to do her job if she is a specialist, how to bring up children if she is a mother, how to treat a husband. . . . I treat all people as malefactors in the same way as doctors treat all people as invalids, with the hope that they are chronic invalids; especially if they live better and seem happier than I."

The moment you agreed with him he thought there must be something wrong with his argument, and he was prepared to put the case for the other side. He liked to be in a minority of one, and so he insisted with all the pertinacity of a fanatic, and a rich fanatic at that because it ran away with much money and much time, on a new alphabet. Rich people have a way of discovering drains down which they can throw their money almost unnoticed. His new alphabet was to consist of no less than forty-two letters, and each sound was to have the distinction of its own particular symbol. He had to confess that the interest aroused in it was negligible, but that only meant that he was right. This alphabet was essentially a timesaving device. The time saved would be phenomenal. In fact, if his arithmetic were correct, ninety minutes would be saved in each day. As always, he asked the advice of phoneticians, statisticians, and even politicians, and discarded their information if they disagreed. I wasn't quite certain what people were to do with the time thus saved. In spite of the handicap of an illogical and confusing alphabet in use at the moment, G.B.S. has managed to complete quite a handsome number of books, and it would have been worth while for our sake if his output could have been trebled by the economy of his new alphabet.

His statistics satisfied him if they satisfied no mathematician. He argued as follows:

"In any fair and simple test between two experts copying the same text for a minute in the present spelling and in the phonetic, the time saved will come round about twenty per cent. Such a figure impresses nobody, we might as well attempt to move the Himalayas with a spoon, but the figure leaves out the time factor. We are used to read 'per cent' as 'per cent per year'; but in the test 'per cent' is 'per cent per minute.' Now, there are five hundred and twenty-five thousand minutes in a year; therefore, the twenty per cent per minute means a labor saving of two months' working days prescribed every year. Multiply this figure by the number of persons, and the total is astronomical! The mere suggestion of it is enough to sweep away the notion that we cannot afford the change. I am the first to present this overwhelming calculation."

All this was done to win a young Cambridge mathematician with us at the time. G.B.S. waited for a response, but there was no response.

"Is there a fallacy in my argument?" he asked humbly.

"There are surely more pressing issues at the moment than creating a new alphabet?"

"Nonsense! To a person with a toothache, even if the world is tottering, there is nothing more important than a visit to a dentist."

This reminded me of another famous person spending a whole week of my stay with him proving that if poetry were written prose-wise, there would be a terrific saving of paper, especially if all people took to writing poetry, a consummation he had set his heart upon. The young mathematician, taken aback at the fanaticism of sheer logic, fell back upon the time-honored timewaster by suggesting the appointment of a Royal Commission to investigate all the different ways of saving time. G.B.S. took this suggestion to heart and himself thought of financing such a committee of experts, and even to make arrangements for this alphabet commission to continue after his death.

"It will be of immense benefit to everybody, from the child

having to learn to read and to write to the oracle who has to advise thousands of people."

The alphabet then gave way to the coupled vote. My wife let the proposal slip in the course of a conversation, and he appropriated the idea in the twinkle of a Shavian eye. He was saying: "If public affairs could be managed by one sex only, I should vote for leaving them to women."

"Women would make the same mess of it as men. I suggest men and women equally, surely. The home is run that way, why not the country?"

He brushed the idea aside and next time came as newly inspired. He had a new plaything in the shape of a new legislature to consist of an equal number of men and women!

"I gave serious offense," he said, "when I warned the suffragists that votes for women would not secure the return of even one woman to Parliament, and would certainly do a great deal to prevent it. It is true that ultimately one Irish woman and one American woman, both titled and both very ignorant of English ways, were elected to the English House of Commons, and the Irish woman even refused to take her seat. I have sat on a vestry myself on which women sat with men. I have seen the effect when women were excluded by the substitution of the new borough councils for the old vestries, and when the women were brought back by the new municipal franchise. I have seen a male health committee laugh uproariously when one of the medical members raised a question about a woman who was expecting a confinement, as if this were the primest of jokes! I noted that when women appeared on the same committee these very men behaved decently."

"Women know only too well that things must be done; they have no patience with men's trick of avoiding everything and calling this practical."

"Think what cowards," Shaw agreed, "men would be if they had to bear children. Women are an altogether superior species. Now that they have acquired the genuine good manners of their freedom instead of the tricks they practiced in slavery, they are irresistible. The trouble is that women refuse to vote for women; they prefer to vote for an incompetent man where they might put in a fine woman. The result is that the best women keep out of Parliament and take to literature or the arts."

We fell into easy masculine gossip about the women we both have known: Mary MacArthur, the politician who could rouse maid and mill girl; Annie Besant, the atheist orator turned mystic; Ellen Wilkinson, who, as Shaw put it, might have sat, when young, for the Mona Lisa.

"I sent Annie Besant my *Intelligent Woman's Guide to Socialism,* and she was quite flattered because I regarded her as an intelligent woman."

We played about with the names of women who were in the front line, and we found it difficult to name many.

"When women can get into the House of Lords in their own right, like Lady Rhondda, then we might get great administrators at last. The men today couldn't even run a whelk stall, and the women will find scope there because the House of Lords is a more democratic organization. In these days of universal education we are all peers, and every laborer boasts of his descent from Adam. Autocrats find themselves elected to the House of Commons where, chained hand and foot by their morality and their respectability, they insist on each man toeing the party line. A democrat should never vote on a question otherwise than on its merits."

Only an old man carrying a scythe passed us as we walked. He greeted me, as I knew him well. G.B.S. asked who he was. I told him that he was the aristocrat of the place, the only one who does job gardening, and he comes when he likes and goes when he will, and if there is the least complaint he leaves, never to return. There are neglected lawns everywhere dying to be scythed because they are beyond mowing. He states a price, you have to agree, and he fixes a day but never turns up.

His eyes shone like a little boy's. He folded his arms as he settled himself on our couch and at once proceeded to tell us of his new discovery.

"Do you know that I found a box of trinkets belonging to Charlotte and I have never known that she possessed any or was in the least interested in these things. I was looking in the chest of drawers in her room, and I came across this in a little hidden drawer. I don't think I really knew Charlotte."

"Why not? All women like jewels, surely?"

"I have, of course, no use for such things. I have sent them away to be disposed of."

"Your wife liked pretty things."

He smiled and said nothing.

"I like some jewels, for I regard them as works of art," I

said. "In fact, I have an eye and a feel for them. More than once, when on a bus, I felt that I was passing a shop which had something to sell which I would like, a piece of pottery or a jewel . . . ."

"William Morris was like that. But I hope you were more businesslike than he. He did not care a scrap what he paid for a thing he liked as long as he could get it. He put the thing under his arm and asked the price afterward."

"Quite right. Why should one bargain over a work of art?" I said.

He laughed and then told me this story:

"When I was in China, I was on the way to catch a boat when I saw a chair I liked very much. It was a work of art. 'How much?' I asked. 'Five pounds,' the Chinaman answered. 'I can only give you five shillings,' I said. He looked me up and down, sized up my capacity to pay, and agreed to let me have it for one pound. But as I moved away, he called me back and let me have it for seven and six, saying that it was a gift because I seemed to like it, and promised that it would give me much happiness. I took the chair and then wondered what I would do with it and decided to return it to him for the money I paid him. 'Give me seven and six for it,' I said. He smiled and offered me half a crown and would not budge. Ultimately he agreed to give five shillings, but only as a kindness to me. I let him have the chair and the five shillings."

"I know a man who carries about jewels in his waistcoat pockets. Whenever he sees a jewel he likes, he buys it and puts it in his waistcoat pocket and then lets his children play with them as though they were marbles. The most precious diamond may roll against a Roman ring, a bunch of keys, and a pencil. He was a Jewish merchant, and when a customer turned up, especially if he were an artist or writer, he would give the jewel away for nothing. 'Like to like' he would think, and feel happy that it made another happy."

G.B.S. laughed. "I suppose," he said, "he is in the work-house by now."

"On the contrary, he has won an international reputation, and when people want anything beautiful they come to him. He even considers that he is doing the world more good by selling his beautiful things than political propagandists."

"Well, I sell my plays and articles . . . but I am better off because they remain mine even after they are sold."

I went in one afternoon, and there was such silence that it seemed the whole house was asleep and the tiniest movement would wake it. Ultimately I discovered G.B.S. in the drawing room arranging most lovingly the busts of himself. He did not notice my entry, and I saw him put his hand on the Rodin as though giving it his blessing and blowing away specks of dust. Then he went over to the Troubetskoy and turned it to catch the light. I slipped out of the room and waited in the dining room, which is by the sitting room. I had ample time to compare the different aspects of Shaw as done by a Belgian artist, De Smet, and a British artist, Augustus John.

When he came in he said, seeing my eyes on the De Smet: "I know that this drawing of me must be correct because it is so much like my father, a quiet, spineless fellow, while John makes me out the inebriated gamekeeper."

We sat down by the blazing fire, burning up the wood which he had cut.

"It is amazing," he said, "to what expense and trouble, even to the point of losing all one's liberty, a gentleman will go to have the freedom of an inconvenient house. All the wealthy people I know have always dreamed of a log cabin to themselves."

"I know mistresses," I said, "who did all the dirty work of the house behind the backs of the servants in order to retain their services, and I know men who are afraid to step into their houses lest the servants complain of the mess they might bring in."

G.B.S. boasted of his skill and diplomacy in outwitting the witless.

He took off his outdoor shoes and put on a pair of black slippers which had been given to him as a Christmas present. He put his feet on a low stool before the fire and sighed wearily. I could see how well De Smet had portrayed him. De Smet, like his fellow impressionists, did not work according to a formula but preferred to give a sincere rendering of the subject. It is the general custom of G.B.S. to get his own rendering of himself if at all possible, and to do this, while the artist is painting him, he talks about himself, the particular aspects he wants emphasized, and is most unhappy if the artist is not amenable to his authority.

"I shall never sit for another portrait, because I have been done by the two greatest artists in the last forty years, Rodin and John. Besides, there is no more room here for further portraits of myself. I have been called the finest model in the world, therefore artists should pay me for the sitting."

"Are there still people who want to paint you?" I asked.

He was really hurt. "I get any number of requests for sittings. If artists had their way, I would be sitting for the rest of my life. There are far too many portraits of me already. I have to reply that I have already been done by Rodin and Augustus John and I cannot be done by anybody else. Think of Pope Julius II sitting to anybody else after being done by Raphael and Michelangelo!"

I was worried by the look of fatigue on his face. I switched on the wireless, knowing how music healed him, especially the old favorites, each of which could bring up a whole history of association. He saw Grieg conduct this . . . and Wagner conduct that; he was the first to recognize the merit of that fifty years ago; he remembers his mother and Lee singing this together eighty years back . . . and he joins in, forgetting his weariness. But this time he wanted to talk.

"I enjoy talking with you," he admitted. "Don't think that you must get out of it by switching on the wireless. If I want it I'll not hesitate to tell you so. When I was young I suffered fearful headaches, but at seventy they went just like that," and he flicked his finger and thumb into the air. "Now I am looking forward to see what ninety will do. My diet is very monotonous. It can't be helped, I suppose. If there were a Woolworth, or a cinema, or a dance hall, I might have had a wider choice, but then I would not have been here. I am an old man, and that is all there is to it. Who wants to spend their days with an old man! There are some things, however, gained in old age which compensate for the loss of physical powers and which the young will never understand and cannot understand."

But his interest in outside affairs was unflagging. In spite of appearances to the contrary, he declared that the stage was now set for German defeat. I listened to his analysis with the greatest interest.

"They always make out that Stalin is a grim, dull kind of tyrant. I assure you we'll soon know him for what he is, a statesman of unique experience, and, what is most important, I found him to have a sense of humor. Now, Hitler has no sense of humor. I was pleasantly surprised to find when I met Stalin that he has a wonderful smile, somewhat like mine. We understood one another, though we could not converse directly together. You see, being myself the most foreign of all foreigners, an Irishman, I understand him. Stalin also can listen, and made me feel that even what *I* was saying was important. I never met a man who could talk so well and yet was in less of a hurry to talk than Stalin. With Hitler, the slightest contradiction threw him into a fury of impatience; that is why he is surrounded by brutes and degenerates. In fact, Hitler is the stage Bolshevik, and Stalin, if we but knew it, the English gentleman. The quicker we get to understand the Russian way of thinking, the better it will be for all of us. Do you realize that Labor had no foreign policy until I came along in 1913 and urged the declaration of the pact made years afterward, when it was too late and no expert believed in it. . . . Even the Webbs ignored foreign diplomacy until the Russian Revolution turned their eyes abroad."

"You must have enjoyed your meeting with Stalin," I said.

"I would have enjoyed his company even if we were silent together; like Stalin, my bane has always been modesty."

18

The housing problem was frightful. In the ivied wall on the north side of the house, as many as twelve wrens lived in a single nest left by a house martin. As the snows had come in early, the feeding problem had become equally difficult, and no sooner did we put out food for them, it all disappeared almost at once. We found that the minute wrens drove off, through sheer impudence, all the other small birds, and we had to devise methods of feeding the latter, who ultimately became so tame that they came right into our porch for food. Much to our anxiety, because we felt our cat would let us down. We hung up baskets, tin lids upside down, and trays in trees and bushes, and every variety of bird flocked to our garden.

"I am cursed with a strange temperament. I soon give up anything I cannot do easily, and when I do discover that I can do a thing easily I am disabled by the thought that everyone knows as much as I do and can do it rather better." G.B.S. had come in spite of the weather. He had no overcoat on but was wearing a Harris-tweed suit, and the only part of him dressed as for a wintry day were his feet. These were in sheepskin boots, in which he shuffled along.

"The cold never worries me. I am better off in cold weather, and I can't stand very hot weather," he continued as he spread out his hands to an electric fire. We always lit this, even on summer days, when he came in, though we might already have had a wood fire burning.

"I have been reading my new book, and I am thoroughly depressed."

"All creative artists are depressed when they contemplate their work," I suggested.

"Because of the mixture of the permanently bad and the transiently good, I suppose. There is so much padding one has to put into a book."

I demurred. "The compound surely, not the mixture. An entirely new substance has been formed, having entirely new properties, which we must call, for the want of a better name, Shaw. Your book is good fun, and what I enjoyed most was that it upheld government by dissent."

"But I attack democracy," he reminded me.

"Exactly," I agreed, "and democracy will survive attack. You would never have attacked it if you did not think it invincible."

"William Morris was converted to Socialism after reading Mill's attack on it."

"Wasn't Mill always right, having no sense of humor? I can

quite see Morris enjoying himself contradicting the omniscient. Everybody knows that you are always prepared to take up a line of argument for the sake of being in the wrong. The thing that I note in your new book is that you are still finding it fun to contradict everybody, even after you have converted us all to Socialism."

"I must get rid of the notion that *tout le monde* has only to vote for socialism and socialism at once comes into being; instead of the chaos of capitalism, we institute liberty, fraternity, and equality, and there is nothing left but to live happily ever afterward. What really happens is that capitalism collapses and the socialists have to take over and build on ruins, and so the ultimate edifice is not what they expected. Instead of fraternity, liberty, and equality, it is restriction, austerity, and dictatorship, however disguised. Stalin has revealed to us what reserves there are of organizing and administrative ability in the masses, and these are the people who will be able to effect the social transformation. It is sheer ability that we will have to fall back upon."

"Morris would turn in his grave to hear this," I said.

"Morris fell back upon a utopia. I have to face facts as they are. The great point is that there must be no unemployment, and poverty must never be taken for granted."

The mere mention of William Morris was enough to change the subject.

"The weakness of the artists in the time of Morris was that they were afraid of ugliness, and they turned to a visionary world where nothing was ugly and all people were strong and good and happy. Works of art that go deeper than the surface are always considered ugly. My work was considered inartistic because I insisted on showing the unpleasant side of truth. You must admit that artists have a great advantage over playwrights. We can only represent God by a hole in the ceiling, but the artist need only paint or model his best friend and call him Christ and everybody will say: 'What an original painter or sculptor he is!' In the medieval mystery, Cain was a funny man, a coarse farmer type who talked to God just as he talked to his laborers. Then they had no hesitation in representing God on the stage, but in the Victorian times it was considered sinful to do so; that was because the Victorians were never sure of their belief, even though they filled the churches on Sunday. They probably filled the churches on Sunday because they did not believe. However, they permitted the Devil, and that gave me my opportunity. I took the trouble of reading the gospels, and I have drawn in my mind's eye as close a picture of Jesus as I could of myself. I have discovered, to my great relief and to the horror of every Victorian believer, that Jesus was an artist; in fact, He was a Bohemian in His manner of life. He supported my contention —there is only one way of teaching the people, and that is through art. That is why He spoke in parables. As all artists have been, He was quite misunderstood by His followers. If I were ever allowed to portray Jesus on the stage as Da Vinci has done on canvas, I would have Him as a convivial man who indulged in neither pity nor humility and was quite willing to overthrow conventions when they were in the way. I see no sign that Jesus glorified martyrdom."

"I understand Da Vinci," I said to G.B.S. when he paused,

"left the Christ head to the very last, in his 'Last Supper,' because he never felt equal to doing it, and he almost left the painting unfinished, with the mere triangle to represent the Christ. He was teased by his fellow-scholars that a person occupied with airplanes, drains, and wheelbarrows could never understand the soul of Christ."

"If he were painting now he would have used me. When I went to the festival at Oberammergau they suggested that I might represent Jesus."

"You would not have been just a hole in the ceiling!" This made him laugh.

"But a great hole in their pockets," he answered. "I am the first philosopher to make truth pay, and like Jesus I went among the sinners by getting my articles printed in the Tory and Hearst press. I found more freedom of expression in those papers than in the Labor press."

"You mean you brought more readers to the Tory press?"

"The Tories like hearing themselves called thieves and liars in the same way as churchmen like hearing themselves called miserable sinners. I soon discovered that the more blunt I became, the sharper the rise in circulation."

"The amazing thing is that your writing did not deteriorate in the least by translation into the Tory press. Everything suffers by translation."

"Except a bishop," was his speedy retort, "and I am something of a bishop, because I need the support of a crook."

We had got on to his favorite subject of money again, but it was low finance this time and not high finance. I said:

"You mentioned before that the artist has an advantage

over the writer, but he also is at a disadvantage. His work is often bought while he is unknown at a ridiculously low figure, stored away in cellars while his reputation is being forced up. That has been done with many."

"Only the worst painters are put in the best-cellar class."

He liked being frivolous about art at times. He continued: "I am not a collector. I never buy paintings. You see, I am not certain whether Picasso is the name of the latest car or a horse. Now, in the days of Cimabue they created gods, not abstractions without significance. Cimabue's colossal Virgin is not a mistress but is frankly a goddess. Nature abhors a vacuum and gives us as many gods as we can cope with. *Chacun à son goût.*"

"This petrol shortage suits me down to the ground," G.B.S. said. "It keeps off people. I don't want people, they waste one's time, they give more work to the servants, and with food at a minimum I am not in a position to feed anybody. Besides, what is there here to entertain anybody? Why should they want to come? Here, at last, I can escape from the false good fellowship of the town."

I said: "I went up to London and slipped out of the complete blackout there, where the lights of torches held were like rats' eyes in a pit, and entered a theater to see a play of yours, *Heartbreak House,* and there I heard laughter. Everybody thoroughly enjoyed it. All your quips and all your onslaughts went down like fish down a penguin's mouth. They laughed the whole way through."

"Good, then they had value for their money. I meant *Heart-*

break House as an extremely serious warning to humanity, but it is only the very great who can afford to be solemn, Beethoven in his Ninth, Ibsen in his *Peer Gynt,* Wagner in his *Parsifal.* The fact that I make people laugh doesn't mean that I do not take life seriously. Now, when people think of my plays all they remember is their own laughter, and then it comes to them as a shock that there were any ideas in my plays."

"So you found it necessary to write long prefaces?"

"Nonsense. I am in the classic tradition. The combination of preface pamphlet and play is the classic tradition in English literature, but nobody has given such good measure as I. My plays do not need prefaces, but the people who buy my books need variety and quantity to last them at least a year. I want people to be amused and sufficiently discontented to feel there is something to live for. Those who like political essays and don't like plays can skip the prefaces. Those who care for neither can still buy me as a classic, that is, spend more on me than the merely intelligent person by insisting on a luxury edition. The road to ignorance is paved with good editions. Only the illiterate can afford to buy good books now. The silly people who are ignorant of the literary tradition and who read neither my books nor anybody else's imagine that the prefaces which they never read explain the plays which they never see."

I made a point of bringing home and showing him the catalogues of all those exhibitions I visited. He was interested and studied these carefully but would not submit to the contemporary movements.

"One fashion follows another before even the previous movement has started moving. Nothing is worked out to maturity," he complained. "The dealers demand of the artist to repeat himself *ad nauseam.* When I read my work I find it as fresh as when I first wrote it, in fact, it has improved with time. But with contemporary paintings they become meaningless as soon as you get to know them. All the same, as a concession to modern art I did present a Roger Fry to Virginia Woolf, and one of the last letters she ever wrote was to thank me for the painting and to say that it appears more beautiful because of the person who gave it."

"I regard Virginia Woolf as the greatest of contemporary novelists."

"Anybody can write a novel. When a novelist cannot pad a story, she puts in a few hundred pages of psychology. Ricketts used to say that writing was very easy because everyone knew how to talk and write letters and so there is no technique to learn, but in painting you have to master a new technique, and every weakness is immediately exposed to the eye. The fact is the arts are exhausted. I thought when I arrived in London that it was the center of literature and art, but I got nothing for nothing and very little for a halfpenny. I was abused and vilified. I soon realized that a mighty harvest had left the soil sterile. From the habit gained in my commercial work, like Trollope I worked daily at my writing without waiting for inspiration. By sheer persistence, repetition, and self-projection I managed to get myself not only read and seen but also canonized. Now the time has come for me to go: an eclipse of reputation always becomes visible at Greenwich soon after its possessor's canonization. I will probably live to hear myself called vapid and old-fashioned as the Restoration thought of Shakespeare and the Victorians of Mozart. You must expect a depression to settle over Ayot Saint Lawrence in the not-too-distant future and to stay for a considerable time."

While he was talking I noticed that there was a huge hole in his thick woolen stocking. It was the first sign of personal neglect I had seen.

19

I received a letter including a story about Shaw. It was as follows: G.B.S. was not feeling well so he decided to stay in bed and to send for a doctor. This was a typical Harley Street doctor, who came up fat and puffing from his long ascent to the top floor of Whitehall Court, the lift being out of order. G.B.S. asked him to sit down in the most comfortable chair and immediately sprang out of bed to give the doctor a tablet for his fatigue saying: "This will help you immediately! But the main cause of your trouble is overfeeding. Stop having butcher's meat and take to vegetables and fruit. I am twice as old as you and a hundred times as agile. Did you notice how easily I sprang out of bed?" The doctor admitted noticing his agility. Then Shaw asked the doctor whether he could dance. No, the doctor could not. Then Shaw switched on dance music and began to dance. Then he gave the doctor this advice: "Dance every day for at least a quarter of an hour, then you will become as slim and agile as myself. You doctors are too ready to give advice which does not suit the patient. You tell a postman to walk more when he spends his energy by walking, and you will tell me to stop writing when it is by writing that I keep so well. If I don't write every morning I fall to pieces. And now that I have given you this expert advice I want you to pay me the usual five shillings."

The doctor smiled. "You must give me two guineas," he said.

"Oh, why should I?" asked Shaw.

"Because I have been successful in curing you. By pretending to be ill myself you forgot your own troubles, you have danced and called yourself agile."

Shaw laughed because he had been beaten at his own game.

The unbolting, the turning of keys, and the sighing! It might have been a castle in the Middle Ages with its drawbridge and heavy gates. I was the only visitor at night. The dark was a heavy wall which shut off the house from traveler and intruder. But why the fear? Why the bolting and the bars? All the years I have lived here I have never heard of anything being stolen nor of any assault.

He was sitting in his dining room in his wing armchair beside the wireless, which was full on, and, as usual, a jar of sweets and a load of press cuttings by his side.

"I am glad you came," he said. "I have been worrying. I don't remember switching off the light in the shelter and there is no blackout there."

A symbolic moth was noisily buzzing round the lamp. We

both went across the moonlit garden held by the silence of the evening. But there in the south it was obvious that London was again having it. Death was taking advantage of the beautiful night. We found the shelter dark and locked. He was naturally a cautious man. Back to the house again, across the wild grass of the lower lawn, a sky full of stars spread overhead so low that one could almost reach out to them. Suddenly we heard a crash, the house shook, and it seemed that a load of bombs was upon us. Our sheer helplessness amused us. What a relief it was to know that it was miles away.

"If that bomb had got me," G.B.S. said, "it would have been considered a natural death, as natural as death by illness or starvation. If, however, I took my own life, there would be an outcry which would send the war news into the shade, just because it is not the accepted mode of departure. War, disease, and starvation have always been accepted until I came upon the scene. It won't be long when dying of illness will be rare, and starvation, disease, and war will be considered most unnatural, and declared crimes. All the same, all this talk of the sacredness of human life sounds piffle to me. As soon as lives become a burden to the community the State must be unsentimental and dispose of its lunatics, its criminals, and its misfits. The means, however, must be humane."

"The only lunatics in this village," I pointed out, "are ourselves, and we are also dangerous criminals because we do not frequent the local, and we are both obvious misfits. We are, in short, mere artists, and so unclassifiable."

"I don't think I have ever been in a local," he said. "A comparison of the works of our carnivorous drunkard poets with those of Shelley, the vegetarian, or of Doctor Johnson's Dictionary with the teetotal Littré's is sufficient to show that the secret of attaining the highest eminence either in poetry or in dictionary compiling—and all fine literature lies between the two—is not to be found in alcohol. All the same, I insist on teaching people that they must reform society before they can reform themselves."

"I sometimes wonder, G.B.S., how much of your teaching, years and years of it, has reached the merry-makers a few yards away."

"None, I hope," G.B.S. answered. "That is why they keep well away from me. It would be fatal to live in a village where they thought me a great man. Much better that I am considered rich. In a village a rich man is respected, a great man suspected. I am sure I would have lost my sense of humor if I took to drink. These things act in an opposite way with me, and so I would have lost my livelihood. My father never laughed when he was drunk. On the occasion when he mistook the garden wall of the Dalkey Cottage for the gate and made a concertina of his hat by butting at it, the laughter that could be heard did not come from the drunken father but from the sober son. I do not mind in the least making a fool of myself; I am built that way. There is a professional reason for not drinking alcohol: the work I have to do depends for its quality on a very keen self-criticism. Anything which makes me easily pleased with myself instantly reduces the quality of my work. Instead of following up and writing down about two per cent of the ideas that occur to me on any subject, I put down twenty

per cent if I go to work under the comfortable and self-indul-
gent influence of a narcotic."

"In most jobs, of course, people don't use the whole of their
minds. The work is so automatic and uninteresting that they
long for the emotional side of their lives to be used up at the
local, the cinema, and the theater."

"Well, they have me to talk about," G.B.S. said. "They
haven't far to go for their heroes. My clothes, my meals, must
be a constant source of amusement. But now that I have a big
house, a Rolls-Royce, a piano, and a maid to open the door,
they respect me sufficiently to hide their contempt."

"I was invited once to give a poetry reading at a local," I
said.

He lifted an eyebrow as a dog cocks an ear.

"I found a very appreciative audience," I continued, "I
read Oscar Wilde's *Ballad of Reading Gaol.*"

"And how did they swallow the synthetic stuff?" he asked.

"They stopped swallowing while they listened," I answered.

"I meant the poetry. Irishmen excel in laughing and crying;
that is why they talk so much. When you hear an Irishman
crying, then you know that he is laughing at you; and when
he is laughing, he is hiding his tears. Oscar and I were born
the same time. He died crying; I'll probably die laughing."

I wondered how would G.B.S. have taken years in prison, as
Oscar Wilde and many of his fellow-Socialists and suffra-
gettes had?

> "And all the woe that moved him so
> That he gave that bitter cry,

And the wild regrets, and the bloody sweats,
None knew so well as I.
For he who lives more lives than one
More deaths than one must die."

He continued: "I have been very fortunate. The gift of ridicule which I have inherited has proved to be my most precious possession. Being naturally of a serious disposition I soon saw the world for what it was and was not in the least deceived by the peace and prosperity of Victorian days. The peace was the peace of a lunatic living in the world of fantasy, and the prosperity was the prosperity of the vulture. I laughed Victorianism out of existence. When I was young, George Eliot was thought to be the greatest writer of the day. I had to go to a young Fabian meeting held in the Hampstead library, and as I came twenty minutes too early I took down a novel by George Eliot and shall never forget how disappointed I was. I could do that kind of writing, I thought. Until then I had never thought of writing for a living, but what was I to do? I had discovered that I could never be a Michelangelo, and I was without means, so I wrote a novel, and it read like a bad translation. When, after trying five novels, I discovered that I would never become a George Meredith, I resigned myself to playwriting. I could make people talk but could not think of any plots, so I decided that plots were not necessary to my kind of drama. I persuaded the critics, the gallery, and later on the stalls that I was the last word in dramatic construction. In *Misalliance*, for example, the action is a discussion lasting three short hours. The curtains come down only for the sake of the bars. And yet I have convinced everybody that it is a very amusing play. How did I contrive to get so many people together where I wanted them, too? A man falls in the garden from an airplane, a charming but simple expedient that neither Sophocles nor Shakespeare had ever thought of. I never hesitated to introduce the most outrageous coincidences, knowing that they would not be noticed. You can get away with anything nowadays except the truth. Dare to tell the truth and you are at once accused of being an outrageous liar. If, however, I were not a gloriously successful person, in England they would have dismissed me as an Irishman and in America as a Socialist."

"It is all a matter of income. In the eyes of the world Barnato was five million times as great and good a man as William Blake and Henry Ford on a far higher plane of respect than William Morris. They all praise me now because praise saves them the trouble of thinking and gives them the credit of profound opinions. Money represents health, strength, honor, generosity, beauty as undeniably as the want of it represents illness, weakness, disgrace, meanness, and ugliness. Not the least of its virtues is that it destroys base people as certainly as it fortifies and dignifies noble people."

"And yet," I said, "it is the people without money who stood by you. The people in the market place and in the street corners; the galleries were full, but the stalls were empty!"

"Think of me now in my old age without money; where would I be? To lead the simple life that I need for my existence I must have wealth. I would rather die like Samuel

Butler calling for a checkbook and asking if the drains of the new freehold he was purchasing were all right than like Mozart and Molière and Beethoven. I would rather die the gentleman that Shakespeare ended up with. To make myself secure for the next ten years, I am arranging an annuity for myself, and after that I'll probably have to start all over again. William Morris died weeping for the poor; I'll die denouncing poverty. Lee knew the secret of sucess; when he left Ireland he took a house in Park Lane, then the most exclusive and expensive thoroughfare in the West End, where rich peers and millionaires lived. There he could charge anything he liked, and all he had to promise was to make them sing like Caruso, Chaliapin, Tetrazzini, and Patti in one. Well, if he could do it to my mother in Ireland and make her his chief disciple, he could do it to peeresses and peers. That is how I met such people for the first time when I ultimately followed my mother to England. Unfortunately there are fashions in these things as there are clothes. A new fashion drove Lee out of the ring, and I had to draw up a circular for him to show that he could cure clergymen—sore throat. That was my first attempt at a preface. Now if Lee and I had put our heads together, we might have thought out a pill, and we would have become millionaires without the effort of creative work. Lee was still in Park Lane when he dropped dead in the act of undressing himself. He died without a penny, and he died as he had lived, without a doctor. I took to heart the lesson in the value of London fashionable life and to this day look to the provincial and the amateur stage for my chief source of income. You will notice that there are no elaborate sets in my plays, for I always bear in mind the Muddleditch Repertory Company that can afford only one set, a few players, and a small crowd only is attracted."

"I take it," I suggested, "that you are avoiding elaborate sets and keeping expenses down to the minimum in the film you are now doing, in *Caesar and Cleopatra?*"

"You must understand that people who understand nothing about art, and that is the very vast majority, judge a thing by its cost, and the cost of the film will determine its popularity. You see, there is no sex appeal in my film, and we have to make up for it by tonloads of sand and appealing sphinxes and great crowds. The Muddleditch Repertory could never afford such things. If I were starting my dramatic career again, I would run to every extravagance in production and stop at nothing, because I know the films can go to any length, anywhere and everywhere."

When we do talk in the train, strange subjects crop up. Huddled together in the dim light, fatigued, self-centered, and cautious, conversation like hospitality falls into the tradition of a lost art. A few connoisseurs continue, and the others listen suspiciously behind their papers. I was telling my neighbor almost in a whisper that when I left my home to catch this early train the lane was so dark that I did not even know which way I was going and suddenly I tumbled over a huge, warm, moist mass. I heard deep sighing, and my hand clutched a horn. The cow was a gentle lady and moved out of my way, but this little incident had made me lose all direction, for I thought that I could not be on the lane and

With Devadas Gandhi in the author's garden

An autumn walk
      Painting in oils by Clare Winsten

must be careering across a field. I went on, however, and soon found my instincts had led me in the right direction after all. He was a civil servant, and he countered my story with the following: "I'm in the civil service, and my office is flooded with rats. Why? Because all the girls they are now employing bring their lunch to the office, and they not only leave their crumbs about but very often their sandwiches, too. The rats come from all over, miles around, through the sewers, up the lavatory pans, and we men have to hunt them and get rid of them. I expect rats were made for some purpose or other . . . but I do not really think there is any purpose in life. How can I when some of the best minds of the world are being slaughtered?" The dim lights of the carriage went out, and the train came to a standstill. We ourselves might have been rats in a hole. Someone was saying, "We got stuck like this for a couple of hours the other day. Hope it won't be so today."

But the train did move before long, and when we neared our London, the sunrise lay over it like a blessing, and it seemed impossible to think that people were still lying asleep in shelters, or were going home after a night's firewatching, or were lying under rubble.

After a busy day in London, back at Ayot it seemed impossible to think that I was in the same world, that it was the same world. What was this madness called life which could give us, in a single day, sordidness and splendor, horror and happiness? What was it in life that gave us this knowledge of immortality and yet made living so dreary and meaningless?

I found Shaw sitting at my place when I returned. The rat hunt by the civil servants amused him. He laughed, and of course he had a dictum ready to hand: "The rats came as a warning to the civil service in the same way as pain comes to a human being when he needs an overhaul. Sir Almroth Wright once remarked that sanitation was aesthetic, and I saw at once that he had hit upon a great truth. The artist must join with the politician and the scientist to eradicate filth and squalor, otherwise the rats will overrun the human race and the Life Force will have to bring into being a new creature with aesthetic sensibilities, something better than Man."

"If the Life Force treats the rat, as you say, as a discarded experiment, how is it that it can still be a menace to the more successful experiment, Man? If the Life Force is an artist, then it should scrap completely the inferior work," I argued.

"I don't know. We can only see a little way ahead. Probably even the superman won't know why the discarded elements survive. I myself am against any cruelty to the less developed creature because cruelty in itself degrades man. But when they are a danger to man, they must be got rid of, otherwise they will get rid of us. I myself am not responsible for the coming of life, we must face up to facts and within our limited compass try to solve our difficulties."

"I agree, but who on earth can face up to facts as they are; one daren't think of the slaughter, the misery, and the outcome of it all. Facing up to facts has led to sanitation, it is true, but it has also led to the bomber. If it were not for the consolation and the healing effect of the arts, we would not have survived. It shows the regenerative effect of the Life Force that the arts survive even in the midst of the vilest war. We were sitting in a railway refreshment bar one day at dawn having, like all the people there, traveled through the night, sipping stewed tea, the only thing we could get, and a more depressing scene one could not imagine, when suddenly someone struck up a tune on a mandolin and heads were raised, smiles appeared everywhere, and we joined in. There was an immediate sense of recovery."

"I knew a doctor," Shaw said, "who wanted children, but they died soon after birth. As a last hope he took the last baby that was born alive into the garden and there placed it in a little bright red tent. The baby survived, just like that. Now it is a grown-up man with children of his own, no doubt. And all due to a spot of color. I have always urged that the aesthetic element in life is a fact which has been too long ignored."

"Didn't Darwin complain that his scientific concentration meant the loss of literary appreciation? In his youth he had loved Shakespeare, but in later life he could only pass his leisure time in the reading of light novels with happy endings. He said that the mind dwelling on the tangible and definite lost its sense of the mystery and fascination which hung about the meaning of life."

"In spite of Chesterton's prophecy years ago that invention would cease and the hansom cab would still be in existence a hundred years hence, science has turned the romantic hansom into a ponderous museum piece, and every child looks to the heavens to name the latest plane. Mankind stands bewitched by the helpless rush of science, and only art will waken it to reality," G.B.S. answered.

"You would have the poets trained in the sciences instead of in the classics and the scientists trained in one of the arts?"

"If the stuff taught were not hundreds of years behind the times. . . ."

Keeping fit was a very serious business with G.B.S. There were all kinds of exercises he performed: this was for the spine, that for the eyes, and the back of the neck must not be neglected. He must never forget to stretch himself to the utmost and to sit bolt upright, movement after meals, the splashing of eyes with cold water, and especially appearance: the training by gentle combing of beard, mustache, eyebrows, hair. Nothing was left to chance. He must rest after lunch in a special position, relaxed completely, he must walk in the open and not give way to weakening legs, he must write letters and change his clothes into his black suit for the evening.

I mentioned a friend's way of keeping fit. Every morning he stood on his head while a waiting robin perched on his toes expecting to find a crumb there. Shaw was not going to be outdone. He said, "That's how most people think I do my writing."

"You should follow up," I said, "your *Sanity of Art* with *The Sanity of Living*. What advice would you give?"

"Never to take advice. To do everything they were told not to do, to break away from the tyranny of the past, and to enjoy being old." He was beginning to take off his old gardening gloves and his miner's eyeshield. His wood was neatly piled up, and now he was ready for a walk. I noticed that the tree overhead was an old elm, and I did not like it. I suggested that his sawing should be done elsewhere and as far from the elm as possible.

"I like to be well away from the house," he said, "and on my own." He would not give way. He had been there for years and had rooted in to that corner.

"When you are on the land you soon grow into it," he said. You can't transplant an old tree."

But I would leave nothing to the treachery of an elm. I knew them. I shifted the paraphernalia to a far part of the garden where it was open to the sun and far more suitable. Besides, it was within reach of the house.

Next day, when I came in he asked me how I liked the new place where he did his sawing! Of course I thought the spot was admirable. He looked up at the elm tree and told me that the tree should have been cut long ago, but it was impossible to get anybody nowadays to come to this out-of-the-way place.

"I believe in being ruthless with trees," he said. We walked round the orchard, and I suggested that we both pitch into the trees, let in light and air, and give them a chance to grow. He was as enthusiastic as a child with a new toy. He at once started planning the time and the tools and discovered that he needed new gloves and new secateurs. But he was sure that these were unobtainable. Whenever he wanted anything, he told me, he was told it was unobtainable. "Civilization has reached the point when you can never get anything you need. Money buys nothing."

However, the things were obtained, and I taught him the art of pruning. He had certainly not lost the desire to learn. As he had said, he enjoyed being ruthless. Branch after branch came down, and the trees were more naked than I had wanted them to be. When I could not come he went on himself, and I felt that the trees must have trembled at his approach.

One day I found him contemplating a great branch in the damp dell where he once sawed his wood. He said:

"I was thinking there is nothing that looks more dead than a fallen branch, except an outworn theory like natural selection and survival of the fittest. If I had been foolish enough to stay there," and he pointed to the old base, "I would have been underneath that heavy branch. Not that it would have mattered; who wants to go on living in my state?"

The sight of the branch shook him, and he wanted to be out of his garden.

"Would you mind if we walked toward the post office? I have two letters I want posted, and they must go today. One is a letter to *The Times*. A very solemn letter. The path of glory leads but to the grave."

He chose his cap and stick very carefully, put on his embroidered gloves, thrusting aside some tattered ones which he usually used. He lifted himself to his full height and was ready to go out. A girl of about seven appeared in the lane and looked up at him with a "Hullo, Mr. Shaw!" but he passed on. His eyes were at the moment on the clouds. Again she repeated a little louder still, "Hullo!" As he did not answer, the child's face puckered up, and she ran away. He did not refer to the child. There was not a soul visible in the village; he threw his letters into the box and wanted to stroll on.

"I have not been to the lane down there for years. Is that sycamore still there? We are contemporaries, you know." The sycamore was not very far away, and there were many other sycamores standing by, forming almost a little spinney. He spoke with authority. "They do neglect their trees down here. They will be a danger one of these days."

I told him of a branch that fell only recently and just missed the road sweeper. "Who is responsible, sir, for falling trees?", the road sweeper asked me. "It's called an act of God," I informed him. "Act of God, act of God, then I must talk to the Vicar about it! I've never done any harm to a soul." He put it down to the rigid upbringing, glad that his father had beaten him severely when a boy. "There was a God in those days, but that does not seem to mean anything nowadays."

"I once said," this official told me, "to a Chinaman that they did not believe in God because I used to think in those days that only we white people believed, and what he answered has made me think. The Chinaman said to me, he said, 'Why, don't things also grow in China?' And so they do, sir, don't they? They do. So there must be a God in China."

G.B.S. was not interested. At the moment he was walking round the sycamore to see how much greater its circumference had grown.

He turned away, happily, swinging his stick.

"Shakespeare," I said, "had a marvelous knowledge of flowers. There is a special part of Waterlow Park devoted to flowers mentioned in his plays, and it takes up a very considerable space."

"Oh, is there? Mine wouldn't take up an inch. I'm not knowledgeable in that way even though I may be called a country gentleman. In Ireland a man is considered ripe or mature when he has a good knowledge of beasts. I would be considered very deficient in that respect. I can talk intelligently to a horse but have always failed to talk to a cow."

We were back at his gate, and both of us admired the copper beech beside the dark cedar at the entrance.

20

Three miles from my home I was greeted by a sight rare in this part of the world. An Indian approached me and asked me the way to Ayot Saint Lawrence. There were, of course, no signposts to help him, and none of the people seemed to know how to direct him. Who was to know whether he was not a spy and would cause bombs to shatter the peace of this part of Hertfordshire? Fougasse had done his work well. Boys cycled past and had never heard of the place. And most likely they had not heard of Ayot Saint Lawrence. For why should one village know about the other? I was going home, and the Indian asked most courteously, as Easterns do, whether he could accompany me. He said something which enchanted me: "Perhaps I will disturb your contemplation?"

I learned that he was on a special mission to the Sage of Ayot. Had I ever met him? Because it was well known that he was unapproachable.

He said: "I am going to ask Mr. Shaw to intercede for peace." He explained his presence here politely. "I am a Buddhist, and he is a Christian, and both religions have the same creed of nonviolence." I must have shown that I was surprised he should call Mr. Shaw a Christian. "Only a Christian could have written *Androcles and the Lion,* also *Saint Joan.*" Out of his pocket came proof that he had read these works; an Indian translation of *Saint Joan* was underlined and with many commentaries in the margin.

"I cannot understand," he continued, "that such an intelligent people as yours, with such a wonderful religion of love and goodness, can permit the world to fall into chaos and nothingness."

I suggested that most people here thought that if evil were not resisted it would only invite aggression and conquest.

"How can a civilized person of the twentieth century talk like that? I am shocked. The man who enjoys marching to kill other men has received the brain by mistake. The spinal cord would be sufficient for his purpose. I would rather be smitten to shreds!" But he immediately apologized for his outburst. He said:

"In England you do not express your feelings. You are so much absorbed in doing things that you cannot get far away enough into your own soul to see what is coming to pass."

We walked on silently, and I noticed how very tired and sad he looked. I tried to assure him that the village he was going to was a homely and unspoiled place. He stopped, looked in my face, and placed his hand on my shoulder reassuringly.

"What a beautiful world, what radiance, what joy! I am a man of great wealth but who cannot feel at home in a world of suffering and dumbness. I want to ask Mr. Shaw what he thinks of life. Why it has come to this pass. He must be a wise man, for his words have gone across the world and he is very old. You are a wise people; let me tell you why, because I have no doubt that you don't know it. After the last war, you put up a monument to a kind woman with the inscription: 'Patriotism is not enough.' Even in the heat of victory you knew it was not enough. What will you put up after this war? Possessions are not enough, Beauty is not enough, Happiness is not enough, Love is not enough. . . ."

"Who cares? Inscriptions are of no account!" I interrupted, but he ignored my remark.

"We in the East believe in venerable old men, that they understand that which we are mystified with, the things that trouble us."

Again we walked in silence. We were at the foot of the hill at the top of which stood Shaw's house. He looked up eagerly, hoping to see . . . what was it he wanted to see? An Indian temple or a minute straw shelter open to the world, such as the holy men are wont to live in? He said: "You are silent, you think me strange." I assured him that I did not think him strange but that I hoped he would not be disappointed in his visit.

"I could not be disappointed. See, I come to a strange place and meet a stranger who immediately takes me to the very place, who listens to my talk so courteously. No, I can see I am right, and I shall get Mr. Shaw to join with our Mahatma to intercede with the evil forces, the Hitlers, to stop this slaughter." I was on the point of leaving him as we reached Shaw's Corner, but to save him from officious handling, I conducted him personally. Unfortunately the van of the local butcher drew up and a large plate of meat was carried in, and, as if arranged to shock this Indian, Mr. Shaw's secretary in her long fur coat came out. I saw the look of astonishment and then of sorrow in his face. He said nothing, however, but followed me round the house and across to his hut. G.B.S. was sitting with his account book in front of him. I tapped to make him aware of our presence. He greeted the Indian warmly.

"How I admire your simplicity. This little hut reminds me of the places where our men of wisdom and holiness retire," the Indian said.

"You know that I am the Mahatma of the West, so I have much in common with Gandhi. When I met him in England I had a very nice chat with him. He was very considerate, because at the end of the talk he asked me how I was going back. I told him that I was going to pick up a taxi outside. He wouldn't hear of it and insisted on arranging for my transport himself. It was a fine car with a smart-looking chauffeur, well-groomed and very neatly dressed. When I got to my door I wondered what to give this smart man. I felt he deserved something more than the sixpence you tip the usual taxi-driver, and so I decided to give him five shillings. To my surprise he wouldn't take it. I thought he considered it too little, but I wasn't going to spoil him. The next day he came and sent in his card. I thought he had come for the tip, but he told me when he came in that he had called to say how he had enjoyed driving me and that he was a millionaire prince. Of course, we had a very agreeable conversation about cars, for anything mechanical always interests me." Just then the dinner whistle went, and Shaw looked up.

"Oh, dear, this is calling me to dinner and I haven't even changed for dinner. This is shocking! Ah, well," and he held out his hand to say good-by. The Indian was taken aback, but quickly said: "May I make a little request?"

"I won't sign autographs!" G.B.S. answered petulantly. He walked at my side up to the house, with the Indian on the other side of me. I explained the reason for this visit.

He laughed aloud.

"Lansbury, who was so successful in converting the Serpentine in Hyde Park into a Lido, thought he could equally convert a serpent into a lamb, in fact, he told me personally that he had succeeded with Hitler. They all thought they had succeeded with him. You see, he kept them standing while he shouted at them at the top of his voice, and when he calmed down through sheer exhaustion they thought he was giving way. They were taken in." He winked with mischief at this and then consoled the other with the assurance that Hitler had no earthly chance against Stalin. He went into the dining room, where his Irish maid stood by the table ready to serve the food.

On the way back the Indian said:

"I have failed in my mission. If I were a perfect man I would have compelled conviction by the force of unchallengeable Truth in me." Then he added, to show that he was not ungrateful, "My visit has been well worth-while for the lesson it has taught me."

"Those wonderful eyes," he repeated, as if to himself, later on, "how very frail and white he looked. Our Tagore was equally impressive. In India we go in for the things of the spirit and venerate our seers and poets, but in this country, if I may respectfully say so, you spend fortunes on education and show contempt for the educated; you hide your goodness, as if you are ashamed of it; and your great people, too, they pretend that they are businessmen. Am I right?"

The next time I met G.B.S. he said: "These Indians always make us look small. I think if I had my birthplace to choose again, it would be Ceylon. The people there seem to be the original from which all the rest of us are only bad mass-produced copies."

G.B.S. has not a good voice on the telephone. He tends to shout and to be on the defensive. He rang up and told me that he wouldn't be able to come along because he daren't show himself. He was suffering from peripalpebral ecchymosis. I told him to have a hot bath immediately and then went to the medical dictionary to find the two simple words which covered his ailment completely: black eye. He had fallen against a tree and had received a blow which would not have hurt a boxer, but in his case it was a bit of a shock. I was relieved to find it was a retributive tree and not H. G. Wells, his sparring partner. I had only to say "H.G." and G.B.S. would spring into position at once; these two giants agreed about nothing, and the world accepted their bickering as it accepted thunder and lightning. This is not at all unusual among the great and successful. Keats tells us that Reynolds and Haydon were always reporting and recriminating and parting forever, but we think of them as inseparable: "men should bear with one another: there lives not the Man who may not be cut up, aye, lashed to pieces on his weakest side. The best of men have but a portion of good in them, a kind of spiritual yeast in their frames, which creates the ferment of existence by which a man is propelled to act and strive and buffet with Circumstance."

"Wells teaches everything and never learns anything. People who begin with a thought that man can achieve anything that he sets his mind upon invariably end with the delusion that man is worthless and will never achieve anything. Those scientifically minded people have no self-control; they start with destroying or torturing animals for the sake of humanity and then end by destroying humanity to try out new inventions."

Having rid himself of his complex, we could now go on with the pruning in his orchard. I noticed that he himself was not too eager to exert himself, and I wondered whether the fall had really shaken him. He preferred reading all the books he could get on the subject of fruit trees and suggested that if one does the opposite, the result would be equally good. He became a watcher and talked.

"My tree needs pruning," he said. "It's all branches, intertwining, crisscrossing, and there's a lot of dead wood. One day I must sit down and do a little radical pruning on my own. I wrote about music, I wrote about art, I wrote about the theater, I wrote novels, I wrote plays, I preached at the City Temple, I professed atheism, I was a funny man, I was a dangerous man, I was an agitator, I was a Fabian, a vegetarian, and now

I am a millionaire! All unconnected and uncollected odds and ends. It is time I became an individual."

"The pruning will have to be very drastic in that case."

"Well, that is as it should be," he answered with a twinkle in his eye, "then only a clothesprop will be left!"

He was not in this happy mood long, however.

"I am expecting a visitor," he said gloomily. "She rang up to say she wants to come. The trouble about her is that she lacks the power of conversation but not the power of speech, and, what is worse, she always insists on bringing a crowd to hear her talk. The result is that I am dragged into this, and I am exhausted in the end."

"Have you forgotten how to say no?"

At the Winstens

Ninety

21

The Germans were ahead of us scientifically; from secret bases on the Continent and obviously only from across the Channel came rockets, doing away with whole areas at a time, causing people to disappear out of existence, not even leaving a single trace for identification. There was no chance of warning. The machine did its work. G.B.S. was quite excited when he saw something come flying in the sky toward us. He pointed upward across the lawn and was sure it was a rocket. But it diverted its course and went in a southwesterly direction.

"It was a rocket," he insisted; "it was not intended for me, but I am sure it was a new kind of rocket! If they go on like this London will disappear out of existence. It won't matter much because they'll have to build a nice clean place. There is no other way of getting rid of the slums. I tried my hardest when I was on the vestry at St. Pancras to clear away the slums, but where I didn't succeed the rocket will. I wasn't sufficiently explosive, it seems."

"There are potential G.B.S.'s living in those very slums."

"Ah, well, one G.B.S. is enough for three hundred years. Anyhow, these mute inglorious Shelleys and slum Tolstoys should know better than to live in slums. They should insist on Garden Cities. I was amused to hear the other day that within a few years of the death of Saint Francis, two or three of his friars were publicly burned at Marseilles for adhering to their Founder's ideal of poverty. That's what we should do to the people who insist on being poor."

I laughed almost against my will and said:

"Not all people have it in them to grow out of poverty by sheer gravity, as in your case."

"My books are read in slums far more than in Mayfair, which is not a good thing for me, because one library book reaches a thousand, and that means that a thousand people read it for the price of one. I made it easy for them at one time to get a whole collection of my plays. The only condition I attached to the purchase was that the man or woman had to be a regular reader of the London paper which held the most extreme views, that is, first making sure that every morning the potential reader of my plays was fed with the same political stuff as I. The danger was that as it was a gift they would read all my plays in one go, if at all, and then put it under the leg of the piano or some piece of heavy furniture as a prop. Even then, I think I would be of some use eventually because I would bring down their most substantial edifice round about my plays."

"Those were the days when young men knocked at your door and offered you a suite of furniture, a life insurance, and a trip to the other end of the world if only you would become a regular reader of the particular newspaper!"

"I hear that this book is most difficult to come by. One of them went at fifteen guineas the other day. When the *Daily Herald* announced that I would be thrown in with the regular news, many people thought it not enough and asked for the book to be autographed by me into the bargain. I had to explain that my signature was already in the book and so was my portrait, smiling and cute, just as the labor people like it, to prove that I was not to be confused with the jabberwock and the bandersnatch which I was supposed to be at the time. Now that I have retired to Ayot, I cannot prevent myself becoming entirely fabulous. Why, the other day, I had to take out my set of teeth to show a Chinese gentleman to prove that I was not a dragon but simply a toothless old man."

"I personally have never heard that a Loch Ness Monster inhabits Ayot Saint Lawrence. . . . On the whole, people here think of you as a harmless, unobtrusive gentlemen, and, as you notice, they do not run away."

"Yes, but my size and ferocity grow in proportion to distance. When I die you will have your work cut out to prevent G.B.S. becoming a myth. There is already a Saint Bernard, a Saint George, a Saint Lawrence."

We were now coming to the greenhouse. He pointed out, as we entered it, an inscription I had never noticed before. The letters G.B.S. and C.F.S. engraved on the windowpane of the door. Unfortunately the window was loose, and there was a crack in it.

"I wanted to show you this," he said, "because I would like

you to tell me whether you think it can be repaired. I am told that one can get nothing done nowadays. Look at those cracks. I do not wish this to be destroyed, because it has Charlotte's initials as well as mine on it."

G.B.S. asked me very shyly what would happen if he asked my wife to paint his portrait. He said:

"She is the only artist who has not asked me to sit. All others would jump at the opportunity."

I said that the wisest thing would be for him to ask her personally.

"You see," he explained. "Troubetskoy promised to do me in half an hour and took half a year, and, as for Rodin, I had to stay there for a whole month, and even then he did not finish. I got painted by John because I happened to be staying at Lady Gregory's in Coole when he was invited to come down. She commissioned him to paint her grandchild and so got what she really intended. When John painted, he took off his coat, put the canvases on the best chairs, and painted many at one sitting. When he was dissatisfied he just washed off the whole canvas clean and started another on the same canvas. He painted with large brushes and used large quantities of paint. I was also painted by Collier. He painted with a very long brush like a broomstick, to keep well away from the canvas, and his wife always came in to tell him what to do. He took her instructions without question."

He did ask Clare if she would like him to sit.

"I will come and sit for you every day if you like, as long as you can bear my company. I warn you that my repertory is very limited, and as soon as I start repeating myself you will, no doubt, not want to see me again. However, when will you start?"

He was surprised, when he came to sit, that a large canvas awaited him.

"This is a large canvas," he said. "Isn't it waste? John only did a few small canvases. I warn you that it will never be hung in the Academy. Once, a portrait of mine was provisionally accepted, but when the P.R.A. appeared on the scene and saw it, he shouted, 'Take that beaver out of the way!' "

He was a born sitter. And he had obviously decided as to what he wanted to go down to posterity. At the end of the first sitting he thought the head already complete, though it was but sketched in.

"I am not as magnificent a figure, surely? It is a pity that I have always refused honors and degrees, for I would look well in academic robes. I have this in common with Quakers, that I despise honors. It is enough that I am a Bernard Shaw, and that is the highest order of merit. O.M. just stands for Old Man, and I am not that yet. Wells has a fondness for academic distinction. It is the boyhood in him, respecting the professor and wanting to beat him at his own game."

"My son says that every young fellow while at school dreams of being in a position of power, that is, becoming a teacher, and that dream goes when serving in the army. Then you begin to think in terms of brigadier general."

"I must be of the latter kind," G.B.S. said, "for when I met Montgomery at John's studio, I advised him how to run the war. John was painting his portrait and asked me to come and amuse the sitter. I gave him a few hints on strategy and told him that each war demands its own approach and that something different would throw Hitler into confusion. And the best thing that I could advise him was not to become too professional." My wife was dissatisfied with her painting, and when, next day, he appeared in his long burberry, she was only too glad to have that as an excuse to begin afresh. "Will this burberry do?" he asked humbly. "I thought it would do as my regalia. The knickerbockers made me look too boyish, as though I had long grown out of my clothes and not worthy of the Michelangelo head you have painted in. Here you will be able to disguise my thin legs with folds. I spent the morning looking for something worthy of your canvas, but I could only find this." He arranged the folds himself, held up his head erect, and his legs were almost completely hidden in the folds of his burberry. Every day he assumed this pose and kept it without effort, whiling away the time with lectures on high finance, art, and politics. He was now an Undershaft, Napoleon, and Caesar, all in one.

Clare would rather not talk while she worked and so was only too glad to have a sitter who was willing to talk to the world at large. Whether it was wet or fine, blazing with sun or pouring with rain, he would come dressed in this heavy mackintosh, tweed cap and gloves much the worse for wear. Punctual to the minute, he was most businesslike, going straight for the chair prepared for him and assuming the pose. Though when in conversation he would sometimes forget, he would soon return to the character he was enacting at the time. Clare would often stop the sitting when she saw that he was tired, but she had to pretend that it was she who needed a rest because he would not admit fatigue.

"I may not live to come tomorrow," he said, "so get as much done as you can."

"You will live to sit for another painting," Clare said.

"I shall never be painted again. I have no desire to sit for anybody else now that you have painted me. I have a lovely alcove in the dining room where I sit, and this painting would fit like a mural. As it is all going to the National Trust, let the world know me at my ripest."

22

The lifting of the blackout made little difference to Ayot Saint Lawrence. The war was not yet over, but the result was now fortunately a foregone conclusion. As there were no lamps in the village, the change meant a vision of warm homes. One villager actually suggested that a lamp suitably placed and lit in the center of the village would make a suitable war memorial, but such a revolutionary proposal needed consideration, and that meant time. Besides, there was nobody here who could afford such an expensive innovation.

We enjoyed taking down the horrid blackout curtains and left the windows uncovered as a mark of restored sanity. It would not be long before peace would break out. Within a day or two, however, the lights were taken for granted and not even noticed. The realized dream has a way of losing its magic with familiarity. When peace came at last it made practically no difference. It is true that business people who traveled to

258

The mirror

With Gabriel Pascal and Vivien Leigh

London felt certain that their offices would still be standing and the staff would not have disappeared out of existence over the night or during the day.

G.B.S. came in on the day the Germans surrendered. The heroism of the Second Front rarely came into our conversation. It was too huge an event to reduce to words and to bring into the orbit of this secluded village.

He was sitting for his second portrait, this time in a pose of the writer and philosopher, his blue pad before him, his eyes reflective, and he changed every time into the dark suit he wears in the evening.

It is strange that we talked mainly about methods of agriculture. Not that he was, like many a writer, taking to farming. He treasured his leisure and would not find himself preoccupied with that which others could do equally well, if not better. But that did not prevent him giving them the fullest advice. Food was going to be the world problem and, if we were not careful, the world killer. We were going the wrong way about everything and always had done. Because of the extensive use of chemical fertilizers, the soil was being exhausted and the food grown had no nutritive value. He had been trying to eat the whole-meal bread and vegetables, and they had no taste. This scientific nonsense has taken the taste out of everything, he would assert, and that was why we were all physically and nervously exhausted. The consequence of abusing the soil was disease. This did not make any difference to the methods adopted in his own garden; at the same time as he theorized, he told us of the amount of money he was spending on chemical fertilizers as required by his gardener.

I must say that the figures he quoted were most disturbing. To him, statistics were everything; ever since he had disputed the value of figures with Karl Pearson, the famous biologist, he regarded statistics as one of the major discoveries. "Figures," he said, "cannot lie as much as figures of speech. It is the analogy which misleads, not the fact."

Two hundred and fifty million acres in the United States of America, that is, more than sixty-one per cent of the total area under crops, had their fertility completely lost or partially destroyed. A very serious position in view of the world's dependence on America after the war. Almost everywhere the same dismal story could be told. And this subject led to the harnessing of the tides to make electricity.

"When these wretched scientists can make themselves useful, they go on grubbing for power in the coal mines. They do not seem to know that our tides, almost unique in the world, exist. What a cleaner place England would become. I know that it is the fogs that attract the tourist, but we can do without the tourist if we can manage to survive our meals and our winters. I suppose the people here are so convinced that they have arrived at godliness because they have won the war that they won't even consider the next thing to it. It's pure lack of imagination, this desire for impure air and impure food."

And this led to the question of eyeglasses. For here again we were going the wrong way about it. Seeing is an art, and the eyes of today were as exhausted as the soil because we were relying on optical glass instead of being trained in the art of seeing. Organisms like the soil and eyes must be provided with the internal conditions most favorable to the exercise of their own restorative powers. I had only just received a letter from Aldous Huxley, who had once been on the point of blindness but, through the practice of the art of seeing and natural curative exercises, had recovered sufficiently to dispense with glasses and write with such a clear hand. "I discovered early in life that the sanction of authority was to be mistrusted. I even left my window open and survived."

"What would you have done," I asked, "if open windows were forbidden? As nonrepresentative art was in Russia? Would you have waited until you had converted the majority?"

"The law is always wrong, but I obey it all the same. If I went to prison there would be no windows to open. The choice is not between right and wrong but between one evil and another."

"Talking about prison," I said, "I was the other day at Bedford and saw two sumptuous memorials, one to John Bunyan, who wrote his *Pilgrim's Progress* in Bedford Prison, and the other to Howard, who prevented writing in prison as part of his reforms. If sanitation is aesthetic then prisons should be considered the most aesthetic institutions in the country. I had to lecture at Pentonville Prison on your work somewhere around 1930, and I shall never forget the clean, whitewashed cells, the clean faces of the prisoners as they faced me in their thousands; everything was silent and orderly; it was a living death." G.B.S. adjusted his glasses and laughed.

"My Joan was right in preferring the flames to life imprisonment. I could never do without air and free movement."

And so we considered what would happen to a young person who took Bernard Shaw at his word: that all property is theft, that wealth can come only through the exploitation of the worker, that incomes must be equal. . . .

"I have never known a Shavian to alter his way of life in the least!" G.B.S. said gloomily. "I do not expect anybody to carry out what I preached. I expect the very opposite. I would no more dream of ———— giving up his obscenities, or of ———— denying himself his raw meat and cigarettes than I would expect that cat to stop torturing mice. However, the first task of my idealist is to make good in this world, that is, to become a gentleman. A gentleman is a man, more often a woman, who owes nothing and leaves the world in debt to him. It is better to die a gentleman than a martyr. A gentleman, you see, makes certain claims for himself: for instance, that he shall be able to live a handsome and dignified life, a life that will develop his faculties to the utmost and place him in a respected and honorable position. In return, the gentleman is willing to do the utmost for his country that he is capable of, and would scorn the idea of a money value being put upon his services. I want to be thoroughly used up before I die, and I want to die gloriously solvent, intellectually, morally, and financially."

"I myself," I said, "want to see this used-up world gloriously solvent." He folded his arms and sat back smiling, assured of himself.

"My advice to you is," he said decisively, "do not stay too long in contact with a world which is not a natural world but an artificial world, created by a catastrophic convulsion called war. You have to see children dying of starvation and not share your food because you can only add to the general misery by disabling yourself. That is not human nature; it is utterly repugnant to it. You have to see morality reversed by hunger; nothing can be less natural. You can learn nothing from it except that it happens when war happens, just as drowning happens in floods and scorching in fires. Keep a grip on this and don't let it overwork or starve you, and you will come through without losing your faith. Poetical vision will lead you into a wrong relationship with life as it is reversed today, and it is political capacity which will determine the course of events."

He found Clare working at a head in clay.

"When Rodin was doing my head he found the ears all wrong in spite of his meticulous measuring with callipers; he cut the ears off just like that," and he swept his hands like a knife cutting air, "and put new ears on without sentiment or sensitivity. My ears have always been a trouble to sculptors because they are not normal. My nurse must have lifted me by the ears when she wanted me to do anything I did not want to do."

When I walked with him, he said: "Clare must know my face better than anybody in the world. She should do a bust of me, and I will sit if she needs me. My Rodin is at the Royal Academy of Dramatic Art, my Strobl is with the London County Council. But all those were done in my nonage."

"My greatest happiness is to watch Clare at work," I said.

23

All kinds of communities were springing up of young people determined not to be swallowed up in the routine of a capitalist society with which they had no sympathy and which denied them all opportunity and outlet. They were to live by growing their own food, making their own things, and working in co-operation. Instead of being actuated by the profit motive or becoming wage slaves, they preferred the principle as expounded by Prince Kropotkin in *Mutual Aid*. Aldous Huxley was now the chief living exponent of this way of life and himself was his chief disciple, quoting such heretics as Jesus, Tolstoy, and Gandhi. As Tolstoy himself put it: "If the arrangement of society is bad and a small number of people have power over the majority and oppress it, every victory over Nature will inevitably serve only to increase that power and that oppression. That is what is actually happening."

When I showed this statement to G.B.S. he said it was so true that it might have been made by himself.

The manifestoes of these co-operatives were a mixture of the Sermon on the Mount and Shaw's Prefaces, and all they needed was a little capital to set them going—the purchase of a suitable estate, no easy matter in these days of premiums, inflated prices, and building restrictions. They meant to practice what others preached and had to fall back very often on the man who proclaimed to the world that he was now a millionaire. Little did they know that these letters were invariably thrown into the paper basket. I was with him when one of these appeals arrived.

"All people are free," he said, "to commit suicide. They can do it en masse, as these young people propose to do, or they can do it as individuals, as Hitler has done, and Göring will, no doubt, do. A self-righteous community soon forgets its righteousness and remembers only the self, becoming the slaves of the cabbage and finding itself without the leisure to recall why, and the money to know how. In our desire for liberty we all sympathize with the tramp and are even prepared to give him our tattered garments and leaking shoes. But what if a man of self-respect wants to be free, wants to wear his own clothes and shoes that fit, and to sleep in a bed, supposing he is not as romantic as George Borrow and Robert Louis Stevenson; then he has to fit into a system of society which will provide him with these things if he is prepared to do his share. The tramp wastes his leisure and is miserable, and these small communities will soon waste their treasure and begin to quarrel. If it happens, as it has with one or two communities, that there is a man in charge with a flair for business, then the community knows prosperity in a capitalist sense, having a host of text-driven slaves never worrying about leisure or the ordinary decencies of life. In other words, these communities prosper under the rigid dictatorship of a Sunday-school capitalist. When he dies, the community dies with him and becomes a backyard slum inhabited by illiterate savages, and the children, not having had the benefit of a stable existence, grow up like wildcats."

"If there is only one life to lead, why should not these enthusiasts contribute their little bit by teaching us how well men can live together? Living together is the problem of the day: people are thrown together in factories and cities, and there is no community spirit to bind them together. You did everything to keep out of an office and even sponged on your mother, and for all you knew you might have failed."

"I did not fail, and that's all there is to it. In fact, I have been the most salutary influence in the last hundred years. Now, coming back to capitalism. Capitalism can justify itself as an economic principle only on the express ground that it provides selfish motives for doing good. The fact is, and I use it to the utmost advantage, rogues are often highly effective persons of action, while these idealists are hopeless. There are two ways only of avoiding the evil effects of capitalism: one, to do as I have done, become wealthy enough to be independent, and the other is to find an outlet for its frustrations in successful agitation. Every capitalist knows that it is the Socialist who makes the best worker; dog racing and football are not enough."

"It is obvious from what you say that the primary object of social organization is to create a wide public for your work, and to make it easy for you to continue with your work."

"How can there be more than one primary object?" G.B.S. demanded.

"In England alone," I answered, "there are more than forty million primary objects."

"You mean subjects, and that is an entirely different thing. The vast majority have no objects. They just take what they find for granted and strongly object to people like you or me. If, like T. E. Lawrence, a sensitive man if ever there was one, they find themselves overwhelmed by the callousness and treachery of the machine, then they can lose their identity in the crowd and not think of themselves as separate egos. How did Lawrence end his last days? By drugging himself with speed, by doing sentry-go over petrol dumps. Never anything worthwhile. And the little time he had left to himself he collected Air Force obscenities, which he published privately in *The Mint*."

Once on the question of Lawrence, he forgot economics and went into anecdotes. He said:

"A number of friends met at Martins Bank to consider a memorial to Lawrence. One suggested that his face be carved on the rocks of Arabia, but he had overlooked the fact, which I had to point out to him, that the Moslems object strongly to the making of graven images. Then came the suggestion that there was a certain book of which he had heard privately, which could be published as a memorial to its author. He told us that Lawrence had told him about this book on the understanding that he was not to whisper a word about this to anybody else. Of course, we soon discovered that Lawrence had mentioned the book to each one of us on the same promise. I had to show my copy to convince them that I, too, was in the know. Lawrence had that habit of making each feel that he alone was in his confidence. Need I say that the book suggested was none other than *The Mint!*"

Standing on my lawn I saw in the distance, in the spinney at the far end of the garden, a dark figure busily intent. He seemed to be shifting things into the lane skirting the garden.

He did it quite methodically and without hurry. There was his perambulator laden with sacks, and as soon as he saw me he moved toward me and at once started talking. He was a thin man, upright, bearded, and clothed in good-quality clothes which were in a very sad state. He had slept the night in the spinney and had already breakfasted in the true Stevenson manner. He thought an explanation was necessary and so started from first principles on a long philosophical discourse. He expressed his belief in the all-kind sun, the Futurer, as he called it, the Giver-of-light and warmth and food! The word Futurer was new to me, and when I asked him to explain it, he said that "the sun worried like a mother about my future, your future." He recited, he sang, and made movements with his hands as in a static dance. He told me that he was born in Dublin, he was not sure how long ago, and refused to fit into humdrum life. "I am a poet," he said, "if you know what that is, and a poet must be near to nature." While he drank the tea and ate the sandwiches we brought out to him, he talked without ceasing, as if he feared interruption. "This isn't nature. You should see Ireland. There's nothing in the world like it."

It seemed that he had tried his hand at many things, had been everywhere, and had even "had the grace to see the Sistine Chapel, which had transported me into the infinite glory of the heavens, and from then on I could not at all harness myself to anything but the star."

This he followed with a sad Irish song, and then I left him. But he followed me and would not let me go.

"I will wash soon," he assured me. "I will wash in the water along the ditch. Water is the substance of life, for we are all mostly water."

I went back to our house and later saw him carefully inspecting our garage and as carefully shutting the gate. He walked off with his perambulator before him, singing to himself, and a little way off he stopped and bent down to collect water from the ditch, filled with the night's rain. Then he knelt down, threw the water into his eyes again and again, after which he lifted his hands to the sun and made movements. Then he passed out of my vision.

I described this visit to G.B.S. when he came along in the late afternoon. He listened carefully, then said:

"Did he steal anything?"

"I have missed nothing as far as I can see," I answered.

"Never trust an Irishman with the gift of the gab. An uncle of mine, who made it a rule to offer tramps a job when they begged from him, naturally very soon became familiar with every excuse that human ingenuity can invent for not working. But he lost his temper only once; and that was with a tramp who frankly replied that he was lazy. This my uncle described with disgust as cynicism."

I speculated as to who was getting more out of life at that moment.

"Clive Brook," he continued, after a long pause, "played the respectable tramp in Gorki's *Lower Depths* very well. That was well before he became a film star and young Lawrence Irving, Sir Henry Irving's second son, was all out for down and outs. There was a time when it was considered the thing to romanticize poverty. The Russians were at the back of it; Tolstoy, Dostoievsky, and Gorki, having lost faith in the rich, fell back on the soul life of the poor. I, of course, put a stop to all that. Starvation, overwork, and dirt are as immoral as prostitution and as unromantic. There is no security for even the wealthiest while there is poverty.

"The man, 'once passing rich on forty pounds a year,' considers himself poor on four hundred, even if he has the wireless, the cinema, free education, airplanes, electricity, and a motor car, all thrown in. The miracles of yesterday have become the necessities of today and are taken for granted as such.

"And I want them to take leisure for granted. Nature may abhor a vacuum, but man must work for it. Without leisure there is no hope. It is the one thing we can say for capitalism, that it has given a vast number of people time to play with. It is obvious that very few of these people know what to do with their leisure, but they will learn. It is something new that is coming into the world. The future is in the hands of the leisured worker. Many of us are for the moment very like a pedestrian converted to motoring, who, instead of using his machine to go twenty miles with less labor than he used to walk a mile, proceeds to do a hundred miles, with the result that the labor-saving contrivance acts as a means of working its user to exhaustion."

But he had not come to talk about tramps and poverty. Out of his pocket came a long document, beautifully typed.

"I have altered my will. I want you both to sign this one."

"But we have already signed one!"

"I shall probably write out another one when this is signed. It is good fun, having a lot of money to throw about, the only fun. Somebody came down the other day to plead with me to give it all to artists and authors. But if you are unaccustomed to money you only waste it. Shelley was a practical man because he knew the value of money, but Sir Walter Scott and Dostoievsky frittered fortunes away and only wrote because the creditors were waiting at the door. I will give my money to accredited organizations and not to individuals. My mother was embittered because she expected money to be left to her and it didn't happen, and we all suffered for it."

We signed the will, and he gathered it up with great satisfaction.

"Let this be your last will and don't worry about finances any more. Settle down to your new play. That would be your greatest gift."

"Even if I wrote another play it would deal with a Will. It is of no use. I want to make my Will foolproof and prevent a lot of litigation so that the cunning lawyers do not run away with it all. The two institutions that have meant most to me are the Dublin Art Gallery and the British Museum Reading Room. A man of leisure is made rich by the presence of such places.

I was a poor boy then, but I had all the knowledge of being rich because I could enjoy the treasures which only cultured people can enjoy if they want to. At the Dublin Art Gallery I met A. E., the greatest of all Irishmen, who combined poetry and art with a good knowledge of practical affairs, and at the British Museum I met William Archer, who set me writing plays. You should build a studio in your garden and do as I have done, leave your house and studio to the National Trust, so that the people who come here will have the benefit that I have had."

"You mean as Watts did at Compton?"

"Yes. Ayot should become a place of pilgrimage. One day the whole district may be built up, and a lot of prefabricated houses and Nissen huts will surround us. Let this place be an island of art, so that people have an anchorage. They will need it."

24

Again the unbolting and the drawing of heavy curtains, and because G.B.S. was dining I waited in the drawing room. I never liked this room. Though it had good pieces of furniture, books, sculpture, paintings, it had no character. The chairs all faced the fireplace, close together as if for a lecture by their host. I knew that this was the room for visitors, and the only occasion it was used was when visitors came. Though there was a tall writing desk, he never used it except to be photo-graphed writing, and it did not seem as though the books were much handled by him. He came in, apologizing for making me wait in this room. "I have never felt at home in this room," he said, "though there are things here that I like very much. This Balzac head by Rodin has always fascinated me, and the Troubetskoy of me in that full length in quite good, but he has made me look a prince like himself, a tailor's model. And I am not a tailor's paragon, because I button up generally all the three buttons, when I should do up only the center button of my jacket. And besides, I never have any lining or superfluous pockets. It is of no use."

He saw my eye wandering upward in the direction of Charlotte's portrait by Sartorius.

"That's a good painting, done of Charlotte before I knew her; when she permitted herself, almost against her will, to be done by the person she thought the greatest painter of the day. It's her green eyes that were so beautiful; even in Ireland I have never seen such eyes. She loathed being photographed even by myself, and those that I have were done by stealth. I have never known a person who so hated the limelight."

It was obvious that she thought highly of Sartorius, because there are quite a number of landscapes by him in the house, pale, misty effects.

"My legs are giving me a lot of trouble," he said. "I tripped over the steps today. I don't want you to make matters worse by giving me a thousand explanations. It is a fact, and that is all there is to it."

"Turgenev asserted that when his sufferings were unendurable he analyzed his sensations and his agony departed for a period. He insisted one should always do this even to make happiness endurable."

"I've been thinking," he said, "that the only moments of happiness I have ever known have been in dream, and it was horrible to wake."

"How different from the world conception of you."

"I suffer from these false assumptions. The world is wrong, as it always is. I have found, as you know, that all the postulates of science, medicine, politics, almost everything, in fact, are always wrong. I have done everything I should never have done and have left undone all the things that are essential to my survival, and I am still alive; and, what is more, advanced thinkers are coming round, after years and years of my teaching, to my outlook. It is good form now for Fellows of the Royal Society to quote me in support of their views, and the listeners forget the views and remember the quotation."

"You have trained generation after generation in your way of thinking. These Fellows imbibed your views while adolescents, and all the orthodox teaching in the world could not wipe out the first influences."

"I have been seventy years at it, and the interesting thing is that I am still the heretic. Even my earliest essays seem revolutionary compared to the poor stuff written now. There is no class of person I have not shaken to the foundations. But none the less I am tired. It is time I went. Show me the man who is fit to take up my sword and I go."

This was not the first time that he had spoken like this. And though it depressed us beyond measure, we had discovered that the only way of dispersing this mood was to say something which aroused fierce opposition and watch the mood burning itself out in the fire of his denunciation . . . even if it was at our expense. "A couple has just been to see us," I said. "They are violently in love and want to marry. He is an Oxford man and wants to give up studying and go in for writing, while she works."

He flung his head back. "Tell them not to. It is most unwise for people in love to marry. I have myself loved one or two women, but the thought of living with them and sharing the everyday life would have driven me crazy and most likely have made the women hate me. The two things don't go together, and as to making a living from writing while she works! Better become a bookmaker. Then at least he could become a patron of the arts and be a respected citizen."

"I cannot imagine people living together without the bond of love," I said.

"You're an uxorious monster. Marriage should be prohibited to people in love. Marriage is a partnership of equals if you like, but let love come between them and all is lost."

"How can you talk like that when you have known the Webbs?" I asked.

His voice changed; in his eyes entered a look of childish worship. "The Webbs," he said, "were different. There are a few such couples that occasionally come into the world, but the usual run of men and women can never achieve the same height in the art of living. If all marriages were as happy, then civilized life would be the consummation of all young people's dreams. When I lived with them, as I did a great deal before my own marriage, I used to see them at work. Beatrice would suddenly fling away her pen and hurl herself at her husband in a shower of caresses until she felt that she had had enough and could go back to her work. I would write plays while they played, but their life convinced me that life would one day culminate in brain work reaching the same kind of ecstasy now obtained through sexual orgasm."

"It is a pity that they had no children. Do you think it would have changed their life?"

"We would have had authoritative works on education, which we lack so much today. Both of them conscientiously refrained from forming conclusions until they had investigated all the evidence, and then they had to admit that after all I was right, though I got there as an artist gets there and not as a scientist. I always start from a single significant fact, and one is enough, and knowing all the time that I can go to documents if necessary to prove my conclusions. The Webbs would argue violently with me, so violently that often friends would think that we were the greatest of enemies and would never come together again. They would be amazed to see us talking together in the most friendly fashion as if nothing had happened. Of course, we really agreed about most things. I learned everything from them, but what they got from me I don't know."

He was gloriously happy now and laughing at the memory of those very happy days. "Did I ever tell you the story of our visit to Paris? Sidney Webb and I dined at a little café, and Sidney teased the waitress by telling her that I was on the way to Oberammergau to play Christ. She was most respectful after that, especially as she did not notice that my other profile showed Judas Iscariot. By the way, Sidney spent most of the day writing love letters to Beatrice, and I am told he read Rossetti's poetry to her."

"I think it is our ignorance of the art of living together and of the facts of marriage which are the main causes of disaster," I suggested.

"There you are, running into explanation again, as if explanation can help anybody. The facts may be right, but the explanations are nearly always wrong, because they have to be in terms of our limited intelligence. Think of the explanations that used to satisfy our ancestors. Even a child would see through them now. Ellen Terry thought that when Watts kissed her she was going to have a child, and she was no fool, for many a graduate of Oxford and Cambridge knew nothing about birth or sex, and many knew too much, which is equally bad. And as to dealing with servants, that's an art in itself, which I am learning late in life to my cost. Charlotte trusted her servants, even though she knew that they would take advantage of it. But they didn't, not to any great extent. I have had a long life, as far as present lives go, and when I look back I can't think of many occasions when I have been over-cheated. I always allow a wide margin of deceit, I expect it, and sometimes I am pleasantly surprised. You will find that whatever these people take in theft, they treat as honest gains. A friend of mine invented a contraption which would make it impossible for conductors of horse-buses to cheat in the collection of fares. But what was the result? The conductors went on strike because they could not live without the extras which they had allowed themselves. There are people who think that they are deceiving me, but I prefer to be innocent and treat them as such, poor people."

He walked with me to the gate, but it was so dark that I saw him back again into the house. As we stood, looking at the peaceful sky, I asked:

"Do you believe in the planetary law of distances in the relation of people to one another?"

"Most certainly. It is dangerous to get too close to people."

A world-famous philosopher came, sat down, and talked. He said: "The intellectual man cannot be satisfied with a world of perpetual change, defeat, and imperfection and must substitute the society of ideas for that of things, of permanent principles for transitional palliatives."

I assured the philosopher that G.B.S. was thoroughly at home in a world of perpetual change. A perfect world would be hell to him. There would be nothing to upset. What would a doctor do without patients, an economist without poverty, a dramatist without unhappy marriages? The world was in a mess and therefore was a paradise for world-betterers.

The philosopher, being a polite gentleman with a long experience of suffering fools gladly, told me that G.B.S. would be long remembered as the seer who played with ideas as a dog played with a bone and looked as if he enjoyed it. He made people see that they were missing something by not thinking. Why was it that Leonardo da Vinci had so little influence upon science while Galileo had so much? The answer is that Galileo was always discussing his heterodox ideas and results while Leonardo locked his up in notebooks. Though Shaw's methods are all wrong, they must be all wrong because he leaps and laughs and turns into air as soon as you think you've got him. His mind runs to maxims and principles, as a plain man runs to pills and salts."

"Young men who have proved brave beyond compare, who have endured pain and torture, have come all this way to catch a nervous glimpse of him and have fled at his approach."

"Because even the brave know," he answered, "that thinking is the bravest of all activities. People will do anything to avoid thought, even go to the very source of it to snatch a few epigrams so that they shouldn't have to think. Quotation is the homage paid by the ignorant to wisdom. He has gone on thinking all these years and has come out of it unscathed, with the will to live strong within him." He gazed long at the portrait of Bernard Shaw standing before him and for a long time made no remark about it.

"Art is a closed book to me," he said at last. "For me mathematics has always expressed the desire for aesthetic perfection. And yet, the longer I have lived in the realms of pure thought, the more ordinary has my life become. It is ages since I have picked up a book of poetry or looked lovingly at a painting or listened to a piece of music. My taste is probably shameful. Leonardo da Vinci must have been the last of the integrated lives, but now we are all specialists, and nothing leads anywhere except to momentary forgetfulness."

We sat in silence, for I would not interrupt the flow of his thoughts. He was still staring at the portrait, and I sat facing the windows from which I could see the tall elms. There they stood beside their shadows, a great clump of generous branches against a blue sky. In the shadows I could make out black cows grazing and intensifying the silence of the scene.

"Tell me," he turned to me suddenly, "how I can get to understand art?"

Here was a famous man of seventy-odd years, filled with a sudden desire to enter a world about which he realized that he knew nothing; standing with eyes wide open like a blind soldier for one with sight to lead him across the road. I could easily have provided him with the current verbology, but what satisfaction would that have given him?

"If I may venture on advice," I said, "there is no obligation to manifest a colorless respect for the choice of dealers, whose motives cannot always be aesthetic. Take a page out of Shaw's criticism and go all out for the things you like, and you may ultimately be led to the things you now dislike. Art, like all good things, is an acquired taste. That is why there are so few Christians, vegetarians, and country lovers. The thing is to come across a work which you like—it may be Watts's 'Hope' and it might be Holman Hunt's 'Light of the World'—two paintings that fill me with horror, and it may be Pissarro or Paul Klee. If I were asked the secret of Mr. Shaw's abundant curiosity, I would put it down to his aesthetic training."

There was the loud rat-tat-tat-tat which I knew to be G.B.S.'s knock. Through the glass door I saw him dressed in his Irish cape and large cowboy hat. He left the hat outside on a chair on the porch, leaned his stick in the corner, but came in with his cape on. After being introduced to our visitor, G.B.S. turned to his portrait and with twinkling eyes said:

"There is Bernard Shaw," and, pointing at himself, "and here is a weak imitation. People will remember me as the model who sat for that painting. Allen Lane asked me the other day to autograph a book for his child, and I wrote: 'When you grow up, you will ask, or rather your child will ask you, who is this Bernard Shaw?' "

My visitor seemed embarrassed. Out of his pocket came *The Political What's What,* with a shy request for an autograph.

"Why do all these people," G.B.S. said, "want me to spoil

the only clean unspoiled page in the book?" But he sat down beside the philosopher and wrote his name in the book.

I had a strange dream that I walked along the lane and before each cottage sat the householder, smoking a long pipe. All were strangely silent but very content that peace had come at last. The continuous droning of the airplanes had stopped, and the fear of bombs and blasts had gone. Even G.B.S. sat there in front of his gate on the very stool which always stood in front of his fire, staring dumbly before him. I passed all of them without thinking it necessary to greet them, and I became aware that though it was so still there were snowflakes falling. They fell fast and covered the ground. I bent down to pick up a handful, and as I looked at them I saw that they were not the usual snowflakes but pages and pages, innumerable, as though all the books that were ever written were falling fast and silently around us. Yet no one moved or seemed aware of the deluge of wisdom. A relief from all the tension at last.

"Now that peace has come," said G.B.S., "I fear more than anything a deluge of visitors. The war at least kept them at bay, but now they will all be wanting to cheer me in my lone-liness. They are all convinced that I must be lonely. If they take that away from me they take away all. They can take anything they like from me but not my loneliness. I have heard this morning that somebody is coming to tea, and at my invitation, too, so could you, Inca, come along and help me get rid of them?" Inca was the name I was called by intimate friends and in the family.

"Come along about half past five. That will be quite long enough for me. That's as much as I can stand of company nowadays," he added.

I did come and noticed that the more boring and common place he seemed the more the visitor worshipped him.

"I didn't know that you would be so nice," she gushed. "I have always had the impression that you were a real tiger and nothing but bones are left in the end."

G.B.S. had mistaken her for someone else and had agreed to receive her. Her name was identical.

You are a wonderful man," she said, "wonderful. I have known you in spirit for forty years, and when war stopped I said to myself, I shall give myself a treat. I'll go and see George Bernard Shaw, and here I am. My friends told me that it would be hopeless, but won't I have something to tell them!" She looked round with wide-open eyes, not curiously, but with a desire to take in everything for future conversation. She was a plump lady and very happy with life.

"I wish you would have a cup of tea, Mr. Shaw; I don't like having some on my own without you joining in."

G.B.S. cut a piece of cake for himself and ate it very slowly.

"It must have been horrid for you here in winter. You should spend your winter, now that war is over, in South Africa." G.B.S. yawned, and I realized that this was the first time I had ever seen him do it.

"Have you ever been to South Africa?" he asked.

"I'd be scared of the lions," she roared.

"They'd probably be scared of you," G.B.S. suggested.

"Me? I wouldn't hurt a fly. There's nothing scared of me.

And I know. If ever you're hard up for a subject for a play, I'll tell you tons of things about what's happening all round me. Men leaving their wives because these aren't up to standard, what they dreamed about, and wives keeping quiet about their love affairs. Women wanting to go on gallivanting just as they did while their men were abroad. Oh, yes!"

G.B.S. looked quizzically at her.

"Tell me, what made you write to me?"

"I write to anybody whose name's in the papers. It's my hobby. Some go to first nights of a play and howl themselves hoarse at any celebrity. I started it when I was in a nursing home, and I've gone on since. I get to know all sorts I'd never know. What's the harm?"

She looked at the Rodin bust. "Is that you?" she asked, but without waiting for an answer she said: "It's not much like you. You've got a lovely head. It reminds me of my father. He was the image of you—might have been a twin brother. Not so old, perhaps; he was seventy-eight when he died. Poor man."

Here then was the first messenger of peace.

"If we don't go for a walk," G.B.S. pleaded when the waiting taxi hurried her off at last, "I'll die on the spot."

"She went to a lot of expense to see you," I said. "She had a perm and a face lift and probably bought a new dress and wasted all her coupons."

"What on earth do they do it for? I suppose I should have made an effort to please her."

G.B.S. was thoughtful.

"She wasn't at all bad-looking," he said, "in fact, quite good-looking."

25

There was going to be a general election along the good old party lines, and the men who had worked so well together to save the world from disaster now rose to great heights in mutual recrimination. Churchill was convinced that Attlee wanted dearly to turn our country into a Gestapo-ridden terror, and Attlee assured us in tones of great sincerity that he did not want us to return to the good old times of poverty, disease, and dirt. Here in this village there were no meetings and no canvassing. It was taken for granted that all would vote one way.

Shaw said: "I once saw a real popular movement in London. People were running excitedly through the streets. Everyone who saw them doing it immediately joined in the rush. There could be no doubt that it was literally a popular movement. I ascertained afterward that it was started by a runaway cow. Most general elections are nothing but stampedes. The point to remember is that peace is not only better than war but infinitely more arduous."

As I walked along the lane one dark evening, a leaflet was slipped into my hand by a passing stranger. When I looked at it later in the light of a lamp I found a statement to the effect that "God is Love."

This election must have been staged for G.B.S.'s delight. He listened to these infants of sixty holding forth on the wireless, and he awarded marks for delivery, sense, and sincerity. Like all of us, he was particularly impressed by the quiet dignity of Attlee's address. "It's not the first time," G.B.S. said, "that I have seen an accompanist become the solo player. He will win because he sounds less of a politician than the others. The wireless is a good thing, because it discourages the spellbinder and brings out the quiet, homely, sincere person like myself. If there had been the wireless forty, fifty years back, politics would have taken a different turn. Nothing shows up more than sincerity on the wireless. I won't say there would have been no war, because Labor was not interested in foreign affairs in those days of misery. A foreigner like myself had to jog them out of false sentiment into common sense. Well, I've lived to see the paradox of yesterday become the platitude of today. There must have been some intrinsic merit in what I say because my sentences sound equally good on the lips of Attlee, Eden, Bevin, and Dalton. Years ago I went to a play of mine where no less than three eminent politicians appeared. As I entered, one of them turned to me trembling with anxiety and asked with the deepest earnestness: 'Has Oxford won?' "

On polling day we drove down with Shaw along the narrow

winding lanes to the village school, two miles away, where, after depositing our ballot paper, we spent some time inspecting the gravestones in the little church nearby. G.B.S. said: "I suppose they will plant hideous war memorials all over the place. Ours in the village isn't too bad. A sword carved on a cross sums it up nicely. We have very far to go before both sword and cross are forgotten symbols. Even I still talk about 'handing the sword to him that shall succeed me in my pilgrimage, and my courage to him that can get it.' "

"The cross stands for that courage."

"No," he answered, "it stands for the ignorance and bestiality of the mob. But now that I have trained the people to be in advance of their rulers, all the leaders need fear is the humiliation of power and not the terror of the cross." We drove back to the village when not a soul was to be seen. He came down to sit with us a while. Suddenly, as if continuing a line of thought, he exclaimed:

"To think that the Sistine Chapel was in danger! Better that the whole human race were exterminated than such a work of art. But from the sublime to the ridiculous, for clothes are ridiculous, you will agree—you have not remarked about my new suit." We had certainly noticed his new suit, and as it looked exactly like all the others it was unnecessary to make any comment. He continued:

"The others have lasted me over thirty years, and this is made to last fifty. You will notice that it is unlined, like all my other suits, and it is made to stand much sitting. I want to announce that I have found a local tailor, probably an ex-plumber, and that makes him all the more versatile. I myself find it easier to settle down to another *Back to Methuselah* than to stitch a button on my jacket."

As a matter of fact, the button on his left knickerbocker was already hanging loosely on a thread, and it only needed a light pull to dislodge it completely. He explained innocently that one of his legs was thinner than the other and therefore he had to shrink that part of the knickerbocker by dipping it into cold water to contract it. It was an ingenious idea and must have taken much time, first to conceive it and then to carry it out. It was a stealthy operation, but I know that he did not succeed in keeping it entirely secret.

"This tailor, of course, saves me a lot of money, because naturally he does not charge Bond Street prices. Were I to go into Savile Row, it would mean first a journey right down into London, then probably a wait of six months or longer before I could have the suit, and then he would charge the price of a work of art."

"Only munition workers who have been doing overtime go to Bond Street tailors nowadays. These pay in treasury notes. A police inspector told me the other day that he found a coat with seven hundred pounds in treasury notes and nobody claimed it. The man who lost it probably didn't miss the notes or didn't think it worth-while to claim them."

"Our rulers must learn to dress well. I'm all out for the democratic evening suit, and if I went to Ascot I would sport the Royal gray with the finicky pride of a Quaker. Let the discarded aristocrats and millionaires put on their boiler suits, but the workers can only maintain power by holding fast to fashion. Look how well the Bolsheviks look in their aristocratic garb; fashion and convention have already taken the place of liberty and fraternity."

"And you modeled your new suit on the one you had made thirty years ago?"

"My uniform hasn't changed a bit, except that my pockets are better lined. I hear that Wells is on the way to Golders Green. He thinks that humanity has missed the bus, but he does not know that I am keeping the bus waiting a bit by amusing the driver. How much longer I'll be able to do it I don't know. It's fun, great fun for the driver, but not for me. We've had long innings, both of us; the difference between those who have been influenced by us and those who have not is as the difference between two epochs. You know, Wells insisted on a martyr's crown by staying in London right through the war, but this was denied him. He will probably die of a gnat bite, like me. How do you cope with gnats? I went to the chemist yesterday and he gave me something which was to save me from perdition. I have asked him to send you the same. I found that the stuff I have been using only attracted them all the more, and they have determined to make my life miserable. Every morning I start from scratch, for they have learned from me how to get beneath the skin, and I suppose, like me, they are harmless enough. What they find in me I don't know, when there are so many juicy flesh-eaters of their own kind they could have for the asking."

I do not know how many works of art were destroyed in this devastating World War and how many potential creators of great works of art, but like the coming of the aconite, the snowdrop, and the crocus after a season of blizzards, the old masters showed again at the National Gallery. Michelangelo, Rubens, Rembrandt, El Greco, and Velazquez attracted great crowds, mostly young people. I recalled how I felt after the first World War, when, after years away from the things and people that mattered most to me, I did not come back a disillusioned man but sang:

> "I am the man who heedless of the crowd
> Stops long to watch a passing cloud;
> I am the man who in the traffic maze
> Feels he is held by warm sun rays;
> I am the man who carries through the street
> His child, that all may still seem sweet.
>
> I am the man who loves the wind and rain
> And laughs at the slow aeroplane;
> I am the man whose heart and mind can soar
> Beyond the stars through heaven's door;
> I am the man who meets God face to face
> In everything, in every place."

I do not know in what mood the young people came back from this war, and how they voted in the election, but I can only judge from the crowds that flood the concert halls and galleries and theaters that there is something of an aesthetic renaissance which may be stunned into impotency by the economic blizzards which follow wars. The newspapers, however, were filled with photographs of Buchenwald, with descriptions of the horrors of concentration camps and the

Saint Joan
  (Sculpture in bronze by Clare Winsten, in Bernard Shaw's garden)

Au revoir

remains of vast populations they had deliberately destroyed in their gas chambers.

"They might have taken a photograph of me," G.B.S. said, pointing to a particularly emaciated specimen. "When these things happen in other countries we get quite excited, but they hated me when I pointed out the sweated industries in this country, the back-to-back houses which still exist, and the Board Schools where children are concentrated in large numbers and have to learn a lot of rubbish, often undernourished and half awake. When I stumped the country pointing out honest facts they called me every conceivable name, but I had grown an elephant's hide impervious to vilification. In every factory, in every street, and in every school there is a dictator; the boss, the landlord, the schoolteacher are all incipient dictators, and I have always been on the side of the victim. They hated me because I proved to them that it isn't God that is at fault but they themselves, and that was an unpardonable reflection on them."

I mumbled unthinkingly that power always corrupts and was met with a ready answer: "If we are foolish enough to let the foolish get the power into their hands, what are we to expect?"

"Power," he said, "does not corrupt men; fools, however, if they get into a position of power, corrupt power. That is what happened with Hitler in Germany."

This jockeying for power. The cruelties inflicted on the quiet and the meek, the visionary and the sensitive by these tin gods were well known to me, but I also know those great souls who grow sweeter and simpler with power given to

them, who withstand calumny and persecution and still remain
incorruptible.

"When things look very black," G.B.S. said, "it is well to
remember that public evils are not millionfold evils. What
you yourself can suffer is the utmost that can be suffered on
earth. If you starve to death, you experience all the starvation
that has ever been or ever can be. If ten thousand others starve
with you, their suffering is not increased by a single pang;
their share in your fate does not make you ten thousand times
as hungry nor prolong your suffering ten thousand times. You
should not therefore be oppressed by the frightful sum of
human suffering. There is no sum. Two lean women are not
twice as lean as one nor two fat women twice as fat as one.
Poverty and pain are not cumulative, and you must not let
your spirit be crushed by the fancy that it is. If you can stand
the suffering of one person, you can fortify yourself with the
reflection that the suffering of millions is no worse. Do not let
your mind be disabled by excessive sympathy. At present
nobody can be healthy or happy or honorable; our standards
are low, so that when we call ourselves so, we mean only that
we are not sick, nor crying, nor lying, nor stealing.

"How can one," I asked, "be disabled by excessive sympathy? It seems to me that the condition of the defeated
country will demand all the sympathy we can muster."

"You will not go about it in the right way if you are thinking of philanthropy. What we need is the knowledge of the
fact and, above all, intellectual conscientiousness. People
with tendencies to insanity, instead of being given all the
power, should be prevented from entering politics, which

seems to draw them like a magnet. If the world is to survive, and it means to survive, it will have to take my advice sooner or later. We can despair of democracy and trade unionism, as we have despaired of capitalism, without despairing of human nature, but you must bear in mind that people who talk goodness are the very devil sometimes because when their goodness hits on the wrong way, as it generally does, they go much further along it, and because they fail they become more ruthless than the bad people."

The results of the general election came through, and even in this rural constituency of ours Labor was victorious. "Let Labor beware," G.B.S. said, "my advice to the new government is to adopt the Committee system which worked so well in local government when I was associated with it." We grew reminiscent, recalling days not so very long ago when a snatch victory at a Guardians election was a mark of the coming revolution and when a hundred votes polled at a Parliamentary election was nothing less than a moral victory. He said, "For my part I hate the poor and look forward eagerly to their extermination. I do not want any human child to be brought up as I was brought up, nor as any child I have known was brought up. Do you?"

"Judging by the ultimate result, I should say you were not brought up too badly," I suggested.

"I don't know. Without Lee I would have remained a barbarian instead of the almost-great man that I am now, almost-great because I am not the he-man of the popular imagination, the man of romance. I am the typical suburban who goes off to work every day, respectable, debt-paying, and secretly proud of the fact that my roses are the reddest in the road, only in my case it happens to be plays and not roses. Whenever I am attacked, it is suburbia that throws red roses at my feet." This new-found enthusiasm for suburbia amused me. He explained: "It is the suburban vote that tipped the balance, make no mistake about it. Respectability has triumphed over the gay irresponsibility of the Tories. We shall now get down to sinks and drains, the things that make up our existence."

26

He came in depressed and looking very aged. The news of the atom bomb startled the world, and we were all regaled with vivid accounts of mankind's new plaything. Japan was the privileged victim of the crowning glory of science. Even G.B.S. was bereft of words. I said to him:

"We are afraid of adopting the straightforward precepts of the Sermon on the Mount, but rush gaily into a world of horror." The answer came quickly:

"If a world government is not established by agreement, it will have to come in a more dangerous form, by one power dominating the rest of the world, and it won't be England. And now we will have to go on as if we are going to survive. I must go on living because the Life Force is in desperate need of an organ of intelligent consciousness, and my brain, with all its imperfections, is its most elaborate experiment in the evolution of such an organ."

As we walked along Ayot Saint Lawrence, it seemed only a suburb, a helpless suburb of Hiroshima.

At Cambridge there exists a famous lectureship called the Halsean Lectureship. The founder ordered by his will that the lecturer in any given year should discourse upon some one or another of the attributes of God and that when these were exhausted some other religious or moral subject should be selected. I do not know if the attributes of God have yet been exhausted, but it is a pity Bernard Shaw has not been invited to deliver such a lecture. I know that he has not the academic qualifications, but it is a subject on which he could throw some light and probably discover one or two further attributes not associated generally with the omnipotent power. He would insist that the human race can no longer be divided into sinners and righteous.

He would also prove that even God is amenable to argument and would have cited many a precedent.

"Tolstoy wouldn't hear of it," G.B.S. said, "when I suggested to him that the world might be one of God's jokes and we must try to make it a good joke instead of a bad one."

"So, in spite of the atom bomb, you still think the world one of God's jokes? You are endowing Him with the humor of a young boy."

"Yes, He has not grown up, this is only one of His experiments, and there is no doubt He will soon discard it and try His hand on something new. It will probably be some new demoniacal contraption. Why on earth did he create the toothache? I have only one tooth left, and it insists on possessing me body and soul."

"Why not try Faith Healing? Give the good angel a chance and not the demon."

"I am going to try the dentist first of all, otherwise I will have to resort to reading my own plays, because there is no better healer. It is all very well for the world to have me to go to, but what am I to do when I want a little fun?"

"Write another play. That is, if you still take us seriously."

"I write too slowly now. It will probably take me fifteen years to do a thing which once took me as many months."

"Why not? You have the time. Everything is at your feet."

"The truth is that I don't know what to write about. I get so preoccupied with little things. I am always worried by letters from people who want to ruin me, people who want to know how to be vegetarians and still go on eating meat, people who want me to advise them how to bring up their children, and there is one letter I received from a girl who is asking me to support her and her illegitimate child or some such request. I really have no time to relax."

"You should get someone to answer these letters."

"None of my people would know how to answer. No, I must do it all myself."

"Well, I suppose it is as amusing to read these letters as reading fiction."

"All the same, I would even write a play if I knew I could circumvent the dentist's visit. I really don't need any plot . . . and I never think out beforehand what I am going to write. You said everything is at my feet; well, let me tell you that my feet are getting the best of me. I find I can't walk at all. I can just manage to come here, and that is all. I must not let the village see me like this because they will think I am drunk."

Then he confessed that he had taken to drink in his old age. He was having a cup of tea in the morning for breakfast because he could not obtain the drink he had accustomed himself to take.

His first request when he came in was to see Clare's paintings. Someone had praised her work, and he felt he must follow it up. She was glad to show him her last study for a large painting she was working on. He looked at it studiously and then asked for the subject.

"Something you will not be interested in," Clare answered, "it is a study for the Last Supper."

"Oh! Then you must put me in as Christ. A bit too old perhaps, but I won't object if you alter it a little."

He criticized each figure and showed a knowledge of the disciples, and I have never seen him study a painting for so long, except perhaps his own portrait.

"What happens to such paintings when they are completed?" he asked.

Clare laughed. "I start another painting immediately."

"That's what I do. I never wait until the managers ask for my plays. The moment one is finished, I lose all interest in it and never wish to see it again. Morris always said that the artist should hide his paintings behind a curtain."

"That was because he was more interested in textiles," Clare said quietly.

"You are wrong there. Morris was interested in everything, from cathedrals to carpets. And when he saw a beautiful thing he bought it first and asked the price afterward and never bargained, you know! He knew the value of everything and didn't care a cuss for the price."

"That," I answered, "is just how art should be regarded. It proves him the true art lover. He refused to be commercial in his handling of beautiful things. How can you enjoy and respect things you have haggled about? Especially if the artist himself is the person you haggle with. Most artists would rather give their work away than be placed in that position."

"That's where you are wrong. An artist should know that life is like a coin. You can see only one side at a time. When the painting is finished he must become the businessman and sell his stuff where he can. It is of no use ignoring the commercial side. H. G. Wells always maintained that an artist should have a few thousand a year to live on, so that he can have a life worthy of his position, and also that he can himself become a patron of the arts. But that income has to be achieved as I have achieved a much greater one. An artist must sell; the moment a painting is completed it becomes merchandise, at the mercy of supply and demand. It is time that the artist priced his work so that the chauffeur and the cook can see their own portraits over the mantelshelf and instead of going to an expensive court photographer can go to a modest artist who would provide them with a work of art. The artist should charge, say, five pounds for a head and twenty-five guineas for a head and shoulders, including a smile." He had long worked out a whole price list to be placed outside each studio as a barber places his charges for all customers to see.

"Then there must be tips. . . ." I suggested.

"Tips? If the artist lives in Melbury Road or Fitzjohn's Avenue, then the prices can be trebled, because there is a certain life to keep up, and also the client can meet important people. The artists should get together like the gas workers and the transport workers and thrash out a policy which will give them at least security; I did this with the actors and actresses, and I did it with the authors and playwrights, and now someone will have to do it with the artists. It will probably fall on me, as everything else does." We were not too anxious to enter at this moment into the intricacies of finance, especially as the "Last Supper" was not for sale.

"It looks to me," I said, hoping to dismiss the subject, "that an artist would have to paint three or four hundred works a year all up to the standard worthy of your chauffeur and cook to gain a livelihood which they would not consider sufficient for themselves, and so the artist would fall even more in their estimation."

"Because an artist is born with a talent, there is no reason why he should be a snob. There is no snobbery more ridiculous than aesthetic snobbery. Do you remember the time when the mere mention of Botticelli was an open sesame to the most select, the most exclusive circles? Now it seems to be Pissarro. . . ."

I knew that he meant Picasso, because we had shown him a book on the moderns, and he had brushed them aside.

"Of course," he added, "I never buy works of art and so

can talk to the artist instead of the artist trying to get rid of his works on me. Charlotte liked beautiful things, and so she would lumber up the rooms with good pieces. I hope I am not shocking you. All the old can do for the young is to shock them and keep them up-to-date."

Shaw put away his country attire, picked up his blue writing pad, and drove off to London in his Rolls and for a few weeks made Whitehall Court the center of inactivity. We saw him only once in London, and when we told him that we were returning to Ayot he almost pleaded with us to take him with us. He recalled a visit to a Chinese temple and the soothing effect it had had on him.

"There is nothing like it in England," he complained. "When I was in Hong Kong I was entertained by Sir Robert Hotung, who, after lunch, took me into his drawing room, which was as different from this as Bunyan from Shakespeare. It was really a temple with an altar of Chinese vermilion and gold and cushioned divan seats. Everything was in such perfect taste that to sit there and look was to worship. I did not understand a word of the service, but I went out a new man, soothed and serene. That's how it is, I suppose, that the Chinese can go on fighting forever and still retain their sense of humor." We were standing on the balcony, where by turning in a certain direction one could feel oneself standing on Westminster Bridge.

"Wordsworth," I said, "found the same peace when looking over that very bridge:

'Never saw I, never felt, a calm so deep!
The river glideth at his own sweet will;
Dear God! The very houses seem asleep:
And all that mighty heart is lying still!' ''

G.B.S. dismissed Wordsworth as irrelevant. He said:
"The fault with our own service is that the people understand too much and so are mystified. In every good Chinese
work of art there is this same central calm because age and
not youth is the center of living."

"I agree, the Greeks are to blame for this youth worship;
Hitler tried it, and see where it has led his people."

"In the West we feel ashamed of growing old, instead of
feeling proud. An Easterner flatters you by saying that you
look older than your years, but you mustn't dream of saying
such a thing to any lady you know here. You would soon have
the roof over your head come down about your ears. This
adoration of the youth has put a blight on human development, and we think of the wise old man as a decrepit, dodder-
ing burden, and young people shrink from contacting him.
Young people don't like me. An Englishman thinks because
his country produces the best footballers in the world there
is no need to appreciate philosophy and wit. He thinks that
as he has beaten the world at football he need only to take to
things intellectual for want of doing something better and he
would beat the world at that. Yeats thought that he combined
both the West and the East, and so did Annie Besant, of
course. I got on very well with Yeats, because he shed all his
Eastern affectations when we two got together. Not having

any tricks myself, he soon saw, as everybody does in the end, that it is wiser to be natural with me; for example, I never heard Oscar Wilde utter a smutty joke in my presence, and Sir James Barrie never talked cricket scores with me, knowing that I was more at home with music scores. Unlike Wilde, Yeats could not spell and had no sense of number. That is why his poetry went wrong."

"Einstein," I said, "suffered from the same weakness. He had no sense of number. He got a very great violinist to help him in his playing. The violinist beat time, one two, one two. But Einstein did not play to his satisfaction. After trying many times, the violinist lost his patience: 'I'll tell you what is wrong with you, Mr. Einstein, you can't count. That's what it is!' and, having discovered the mathematician's weakness, he went on with the teaching."

"I always say," G.B.S. said, "if you have a weakness, turn it into a strength. You must never forget that people often rise by their very weaknesses and vices, which they have tried hard to hide. William Morris used to say: 'The Scots are all virtue, I can't stand them; the Irish are vicious, I love them.'"

"He was obviously playing up to you," I said.

"Playing down, certainly down. He was a great man if ever there was one. A great man is one whom you instinctively believe. Hyndman, educated at Trinity College, Cambridge, and not at Oxford, like Morris, was the better talker of the two, and it was a pleasure to listen to him because one instinctively disbelieved all he said."

"You were born in an age of giants. You were fortunate."

"I don't know," he answered. "It is true that some of them

reached very great heights. I have seen the Himalayas and I have seen Popocatepetl, and they have left me unmoved; in fact, the Irish hills still seem higher to me. Anyhow, it doesn't really matter what age one is born in: the description of a great man in the Greek days would apply equally to a great man of today. That is why my historic plays are so absorbing; they are easy to write because the facts are a gift: all that has to be done is to supply the ideas and the people personifying the ideas."

"A very modest ambition, I agree."

"I have never wanted to preach the worship of a great man as Carlyle did, nor achieve greatness at the expense of others; but I always did want, and still want, to put ideas into people's heads, so that they can conceive something better than themselves and strive to bring it into existence. You talked of the age into which I was born as a great age. I regard it as the most villainous page of recorded history, redeemed only by men like Morris and Tolstoy, Ibsen and Gorki, Zola and Dickens. And the twentieth century is no better. We need minds larger than those of villagers. I have been described as a man laughing in the wilderness. That is correct enough, if you accept me as preparing the way for better things."

The war noises which we had all learned to ignore for years now, the warnings and the all-clears, the flight of planes and the fall of bombs gave way at last to the sound of distant bells, chiming with the wind in the trees and bringing the neighboring villages into our homes. How near to the heart were those bells. They never drew me into church, but they converted the countryside into a holy place for me.

Even then we could not do without London. More and more young people appeared upon the scene, but whatever they had experienced they had little to say. Theirs was a stern look, determined not to look back even if there was nothing to look forward to. After all, the problems facing us were the old, old problems, of food, of clothing, of housing, and these were a matter of chance. A rumor would go round that certain things were to be obtained somewhere, and soon a queue, a weary, patient queue, would form to await the purchase of a simple necessity, and mostly a limited quantity, and therefore disappointment and frustration for many. In preventing the world becoming fit for Neros, we did not even expect it, this time, to prove fit for heroes. Perhaps the surest sign of peace was the fact that at the nearest station to this village, instead of six people scrambling for an only taxi, there were now six taxis scrambling for one passenger. Were we returning to cutthroat competition? No. Planning had become the slogan of the day, but it was planning to prevent economic disaster and not to build a new Jerusalem. Victory simply meant a change of focus: instead of concentrating on young men in the heavens, we listened to old men talking politics. G.B.S. came to report a village incident. There were petty wars nearer home, and he was asked to help. If he claimed that he was still too young to deal with the world situation, he certainly did not feel wise enough to tackle a little parochial problem nearer home. He explained: "I understand that the big house is now being used as a hostel for girls who work at an airplane factory. The airplane, in my humble opinion, may well prove a diabolical contraption, but that is not taking us any further. The point is that draftsmen refuse to mix with mechanics. They will not share rooms, nor even mix in games. I have been asked by the warden for advice, and as you are an expert in community matters I am prepared to pass on your advice as my own and get the credit for being a man of the world. You see, it is only a man of the world who can tackle village problems, but the village mind can't tackle world affairs. I remember the opening of the village Institute here, but there again, the classes wouldn't mix: the housekeeper would not sit down with the maid; there are subtle gradations. I can remember one of my earliest experiences in life was my father finding me playing with a certain little boy in the street and telling me I was not to play with that little boy, giving me to understand that he was a very inferior and objectionable kind of boy. I had not found him so. I asked the reason, and my father explained that his father kept a shop. I said to my father: 'Well, but you keep a mill.' Therefore my father pointed out to me that he sold things wholesale, and that this little boy's father sold things retail; and it was part of my duty and part of my honor to regard that boy as inferior, though he was a more vigorous and larger boy than myself. I have always maintained that equality is essential to good breeding, but unfortunately equality is incompatible with differences in income, as the people on the lower income level always tend to consider themselves superior to those above them. I could have given them each a copy of my *Intelligent Woman's Guide*, but I haven't enough to go round. I gave the Warden my *Political What's What* as a nerve restorer, because print has that effect on illiterate people. I went down to talk to these girls. It was a very trying half hour. They knew nothing about me, and I could see that all the time they were making a gallant effort to suppress their giggling. If they had laughed outright I would not have minded, because I am not unaccustomed to laughter. But to see them regarding me with those knowing, smiling eyes put me right out. I found myself giving them a little lecture on biology, saying: Killing men did not matter so much so long as women were left. We could keep the earth populated with one per cent of the men. I said: there was nothing meaner than to throw socially necessary work upon others and then disparage it as unworthy and indelicate. I begged of the mechanics not to look down on the draftsmen. I accepted the female as the superior sex and appealed to her practical sense, her love of orderliness in the home, to grapple with the world problems which face the inexperienced old and the village problems which face the experienced young. My reception was frigid. I don't think I increased the sale of my books by one. To see if I could write, two or three girls very politely asked me for my autograph, but I warned them that the most intelligent men I know cannot even count the number of noughts on their checks and always sign their names with a cross. These are the men you should be after; they are worth getting, conquering, and putting in their place. I advised these good girls not to behave like victors squabbling over their losses but as sensible women, living in brotherly love."

This story reminded me of a coeducational school built by the County Council in a neighboring town. The building was one, but the headmaster made the girls walk out of one door and the boys out of another; they were not allowed to play or to sit together, and they prayed to the same God in separate batches. How quickly we fall apart. G.B.S. said:

"One of the first things the new Government should do is to introduce the coupled vote. A good slogan would be: the coupled vote for all single-minded people. The next thing, of course, should be an alphabet of forty-two letters. I am probably the only single-minded person left. In the recent election I gave my coupon to an Independent, a Communist, and a Labor man, and I daresay if a suitable Conservative had asked me I would have given it to him as well."

"No, no, you wouldn't be the Vicar of Bray, though you live in the Rectory!"

"The Vicar of Bray has always been my favorite character." G.B.S. fell into singing the song. He knew every word of it and insisted on singing it to the last verse. His voice was fresh and buoyant, and his accompanying gestures were so full of fun that one had to join in. I said:

"You should have sung this at the hostel; mechanic and draftsman would have forgotten their differences in their new-found enthusiasm for the Vicar."

"I often get letters addressed to the Reverend George B. Shaw. You can deceive people some of the time, but they ultimately discover your true vocation. As a Quaker I would make an excellent archbishop. Though I am not unaccustomed to talking, my worship is always silent. Luckily the churches are empty, so I can slip in and commune with the Life Force. As a professional morality-monger I am always prepared to repair worn-out moralities. Remember, the objection to all progress is that it is immoral; the church is in need of more immorality."

"Your qualifications are beyond dispute. Many years ago you wrote: 'Who am I to be just?' and recently you wrote again: 'Men must learn to be kind and just to those whom they very properly hate' and now you are even prepared to rule out hate. You are coming on nicely."

"Yes," he said, "the first quality of capitalistic mankind is quarrelsomeness. For that reason life is made lonely and difficult in a thousand unnecessary ways. So few people are clever and tactful and self-controlled enough to pick their way through the world without giving or taking offense. The whole social atmosphere is so impregnated with false pretenses that the only man who is accused of falsehood and corruption is the truth seeker. I rule out hate, certainly, but I do not teach contentment. When older people preach contentment you may be sure they are either thoughtless or hypocritical."

27

An idea had come to him at last for a new play! He asked to see the "Last Supper" again and again. He studied the painting seriously and then he said: "What if the central figure is a man of wealth and very old? And all the other people gather round to advise him what to do with his money?"

We thought it a wonderful idea and would make an excellent play. We could already see that each suggestion in turn would be proved futile.

"There will, of course, be no love interest?" I said.

"Oh, I don't know so much. On the strength of favors to come there is many a man who can stand the presence of a woman and many a woman prepared to tolerate the occasional sight of a man. The joke will, of course, be, there is no such thing as a wealthy person nowadays with income tax at nineteen and six on the pound and fearful death duties."

"But they will know that, surely?"

"People know nothing. That is why plays are popular and the old, old story can be dished up again and again. It is original thought to which they all object."

"Haven't you outgrown the desire to be original?" I asked.

"I have never desired to be original," he answered, almost hurt. He wanted to walk. We had come to the decision that if he stopped walking he would be unable to walk at all. We deliberately chose a path where we would not meet any people. The lime trees were still humming with insect noises, heard only when we stood dead still in the grove. Two men came toward us, and though G.B.S. turned to avoid them, they came forward so eagerly that there was no escape. They were two German prisoners with great circles of blue cloth on their brown uniforms, and both carried sickle and slasher. They stopped in front of us, put down their tools, took off their caps, and the older one spoke:

"As a youth it was my great ambition to see you in the flesh, but how could that happen? A war came, I was taken prisoner after I had fought in many parts of the world, first in Holland, then in France, in Africa, in Russia. I was taken prisoner and sent first to America, then brought here to Scotland, to the north of England, and then I moved to Luton and here I am meeting you in this quiet place. When I saw you coming toward us, I remarked that our Goethe mockingly called himself the Child of the World, but you must be the Ancient of the World."

G.B.S. smiled childishly. "Your English is good, I can see, because like all continentals you have read our good literature. When an Englishman talks about German literature, he means \

Goethe and Heine, but when he talks about English books, he means the usual detective and murder stories which he takes to his bedside."

Both the Germans laughed and felt pleased, and we passed on.

"There is something I wanted to ask you, and I wanted you out of the house," he said, stopping and looking me in the eyes. "I have been looking at the 'Last Supper' of Clare's very closely and am convinced that she is the person to do the sculpture of Saint Joan which I want in my garden. Do you think that she would be willing to do it, say within a year, I don't even mind ten years? But I have no doubt that she is the person to do it, and I will not ask anybody else."

"I think you know by now that Clare would not refuse you anything you ask."

"Good! I have something to look forward to. It will give significance to my home at last. Really, when you think of it, there is nothing there to make people want to come and see it when I leave it to the National Trust."

28

Looking through my papers I came across a letter addressed to me by a distinguished author. It runs as follows:

If you were an actress, you would resent the assumption that you must also be a woman of easy virtue; and if you were a policeman you would feel annoyed when everybody meeting you instantly threw a measuring glance at your feet. Well, we all make absurd assumptions about each other, and it is my particular lot to suffer from the assumption that I share the typical tastes and opinions of our intellectuals. Among these tastes, for example, is a liking for the works of George Bernard Shaw, Bertrand Russell and Aldous Huxley and among these opinions is a bias in favor of democracy.

As a social reformer Bertrand Russell with his incapacity to recognize any good in Christianity appears to me as an overintellectualized man who has never realized the might of animal instincts. To me, in fact, he is like someone walking

313

into a jungle, who assures everyone that tigers, however hungry, will not attack men because they must know how deplorable it is to eat human bodies. And Aldous Huxley as I see him is an unimportant writer because he is quite unable to think outside the conditions of a disillusioned and necessarily ephemeral period.

Long before the war I used to declare that the best form of Government must be a benevolent dictatorship. I have watched with delight the career of the Duce. I do not believe in any form of democracy because I am sure that the Great Rejuvenator was right when he said: "People do not want to be free." In this country we cling to the doctrine that freedom is axiomatically desirable; but there were myriads of men who joining the army during the war, were thankful at last not to be free at all. They found that for the first time they could really enjoy themselves. . . .

I take down a book by Bertrand Russell and read:

"It is only a few rare and exceptional men who have that kind of love toward mankind at large that makes them unable to endure patiently the general mass of evil and suffering, regardless of what relation it may have to their own lives. These few, driven by sympathetic pain, will seek first in thought and then in action for some way of escape, some new system of society by which life may become richer, more full of joy and less full of preventable evils than it is at present. . . . A life lived in the spirit, the spirit that aims at creating rather than possessing, has a certain fundamental happiness of which it cannot be wholly robbed by adverse circumstances. This is the way of life recommended in the Gospels and by all the great teachers of the world. . . ."

This from a person "with an incapacity to see any good in Christianity."

And then I take down a book by Aldous Huxley:

"It is axiomatic that the end of human life is contemplation, or the direct and the intuitive awareness of God; that action is the means to that end; that a society is good to the extent that it renders contemplation possible for its members. . . ."

This from a man "who is quite unable to think outside the conditions of a disillusioned and necessarily ephemeral period."

And I take down another book, this time by G.B.S.:

"A man grows through the ages, he finds himself bolder by the growth of his spirit (if I may name the unknown) and dares more and more to love and trust instead of to fear and fight. But his courage has other effects: he also raises himself from mere consciousness to knowledge by daring more and more to face facts and tell himself the truth. . . ."

What would happen, say, if I asked the great men in science and literature, in music and art, in drama and in philosophy, in economics and in political work, in fact, in almost every branch of life, what they honestly thought of Bernard Shaw's contribution? It would be a worthy acknowledgment of Bernard Shaw's efforts to improve humanity. Of course, I was warned with a very emphatic finger that no one would be interested in such a book, nor would any person contribute to it. So *G.B.S.* 90 was conceived.

"I have become the father confessor of the whole world," he said, as I sat with him by his fireside. "Because I have managed to amuse one or two people they now insist on making this thin stick of a body into a Nelson column of Agony. They never try to amuse me. A reporter came the other day, and I was weak enough to grant him an interview, but he did all the talking and I didn't get a word in. I gave him permission to publish the interview as long as he kept all he said out of it. Generosity pays in the long run. There are many such people who talk to me for five boring minutes and spend the rest of their life condemning me. Nothing infuriates me more than being praised for attributes I despise, though I don't mind being despised for qualities it has taken me years and years to develop. In future I will demand that all journalists submit the full text of the interview before I agree to let them interview me. All this talk about my amazing vitality, my extraordinary wit, my terrific capacity for hard work, my radiant beauty must have been concocted in the village inn over a liquid meal before the person had even ventured on my doorstep."

He showed me a few letters which he had received and which he felt no desire to answer. When I looked through them I wondered why he, an old man, was selected for this burden. One of these read:

Dear Sir,

You may have written the words yourself at some time, certainly you will have come across them: a soul in torment, but have you ever been just that yourself?

I am a soul, not only in torment but so angry and desperate that it is using every ounce of energy in me to fight off the urge to kill my children and myself. The whole thing is beating me. I never did care for sloppy sentiment and useless pity. It is sense I want, wisdom. That is why I am writing to you. I do not think there is a saner man in the country than you. So I do not appeal to you as a kind softhearted and softheaded man, but as a fellow-human who is eminently sane, knowledgeable and clever. My appeal comes from the very depths of my soul. Advise me. Will you be the one man out of all the millions to help?

When I had finished reading this letter, G.B.S. said:

"I have also received an S O S from a poet whose suit had caught on fire and he was now left without any clothes whatsoever. No doubt consumed like myself by an inward fire! I could remind him that the happiest man according to fable is the man without a shirt to his back, especially in these days when laundries are so impossible. I've never worn a so-called shirt. I have helped a poet once before. I saw real merit in his work and, knowing that in this country of Shakespeare, Shelley, and Browning no poet can hope to make a livelihood, I gave him a useful sum so that he could devote himself completely to poetry and write the masterpiece I expected of him. Instead of writing a poem which might have placed him among the immortals, he settled down to writing a popular play so that he could pay me back tenfold. No one would touch the play, and in despair he committed suicide. As I don't want to kill off any others I can only save them by withholding all financial assistance. Now, about the business of soul torment. Don't you think it is better expressed in *Heartbreak House?* Surely killing himself is only a matter for his own judgment. Nobody can prevent him. If he is convinced that he is not worth his salt, and an intolerable nuisance to himself and everyone else, it is a solution to be considered. But I would always advise such people to put this off to the next day in case something interesting turns up in the evening. But as to killing children, it would be the act of a madman or a mur-derer. They may have the happiest disposition, they may be born to greatness: the children of good-for-nothings, Beethoven and Isaac Newton for instance, have grown up to be geniuses. My own father was a failure; only his latest years (he was long lived) could be called happy. I am conceited enough to believe that it is just as well that he did not kill me in a fit of low spirits. Instead, he did the more sensible thing; he relieved himself by drinking occasionally, though it only made him worse. You see this 'soul torment' is not a philosophy; it is a disease and usually cures itself after a time." He stopped speaking and poked the ashes of the fire, seeking out pieces of burning wood that were left, and then said:

"Life, happy or unhappy, successful or unsuccessful, is extraordinarily interesting."

320

Browning, Robert, 17, 42, 51, 70
Brownings, the, 42, 177
Bunyan, John, 37, 81, 261
Burne-Jones, Edward, 84, 95, 99, 203
Burns, John, 133, 137
Burns, Robert, 107
Butler, Samuel, 77, 90, 162, 163, 167, 177, 185, 233

Cambridge University, 296, 303
Cannan, Gilbert, 76, 77, 127
Carlyle, Thomas, 17, 37
Carpenter, Edward, 57, 117, 120, 130
Chekhov, Anton Pavlovich, 181
Cherry-Garrard, Apsley, 94, 152, 153
Chesterton, G. K., 86, 175, 237
Christ, paintings and statues of, 94, 95, 152-3, 190, 220, 221
Christ Church Priory, 196
Churchill, Winston, 89, 147, 285
Cimabue, Giovanni, 222
Civilization: Its Cause and Cure, 117
Codicote, 164
Coleridge, Stephen, 80
Collier, John, 52, 254
Confession, 129
Conrad, Joseph, 174
Constable, John, 185
Corelli, Marie, 137
Corno di Bassetto (pseudonym of G.B.S.), 131
Courbet, Gustave, 141

Court Theatre, 114, 149
Cowards Lane, 164
Crane, Walter, 119
Cymbeline, 176

Daily Herald, 253
Dalkey, *see* Torca Cottage, Dalkey Hill
Dalton, Hugh, 286
Darwin, Charles, 126, 128, 132, 237
Davies, W. H., 58-9, 70, 129
Dickens, Charles, 37, 192, 304
Dostoievsky, Feodor, 270, 271
Doughty, A., 108
Dublin, 61, 72
Dublin Art Gallery, 271, 272
Dumas, Alexandre, 37
Dumas, Alexandre, fils, 141

Eden, Anthony, 286
Edward VII, 137
Einstein, Albert, 303
Eliot, George, 19, 231
Ellis, Havelock, 117
Epstein, Jacob, 51, 94, 95
Erewhon Revisited, 163
Ervine, St. John Greer, 140

Fabians, 25, 34, 35, 80, 119
Fabian Society, 119
Ford, Henry, 232
Fougasse, *see* Bird, Cyril K.
France, Anatole, 142
Frost, Robert, 107
Fry, Roger, 224

324

the Germans, 28, 40, 173
visitor from India, 246-7
appearance of, 11
as genius, 21, 24, 87
   man of wealth, 20, 43, 53, 80, 108
   Mephistopheles, 104
   photographer, 101
   poet, 27, 59, 118
   prophet, 81
   Sunday School teacher, 17
   vegetarian, 61, 77, 89-90, 124, 135, 138, 195
at City Temple, 16
at Tower Hill, 17
books and plays, 38, 113, 145, 181, 223, 229, 231, 252, 304
   Admirable Bashville, The, 202
   Androcles and the Lion, 244
   Back to Methuselah, 43, 73, 108, 137
   Caesar and Cleopatra, 234
   Candida, 31
   Commonsense of the War, 91
   Doctor's Dilemma, The, 83, 187, 193
   Fabian Essays, The, 69
   Fanny's First Play, 127, 200
   Geneva, 173
   Gentle Swing to the Left, A, 69
   Heartbreak House, 222, 318
   Intelligent Woman's Guide to Socialism and Capital-ism, The, 69, 209, 306
   John Bull's Other Island, 172
   Misalliance, 231
   Mrs. Warren's Profession, 114
   Political What's What, The, 281, 307
   Prefaces to, 223
   Quintessence of Ibsenism, The, 57
   Saint Joan, 24, 116, 244
   Sanity of Art, The, 80, 238
   Shewing-up of Blanco Posnet, 32, 114
   Widowers' House, 117
comedic sense of, 43, 203, 231
desire to become artist, 35, 86
difficulties of early life, 72, 105
dislikes name George, 18
dislikes talk, 51, 115
education of, 37
German translator of, 111, 121-2
in China, 301
in pose of Rodin's "Thinker," 145
in Russia, 22
interest in theology, 16
leaves Ireland, 60
makes his will, 204, 271
modesty of, 28, 29, 68, 216, 312
on aesthetic sense, 25, 35, 195, 236, 237
   aestheticism, 141
   alcohol, 229